Constructing Collective Identity

Hal B. Levine

Constructing Collective Identity

A Comparative Analysis of New Zealand Jews,
Maori, and Urban Papua New Guineans

PETER LANG
Frankfurt am Main · Berlin · Bern · New York · Paris · Wien

Die Deutsche Bibliothek - CIP-Einheitsaufnahme

Levine, Hal B.:
Constructing collective identity : a comparative analysis of New Zealand Jews, Maori, and urban Papua New Guineans / Hal B. Levine. - Frankfurt am Main ; Berlin ; Bern ; New York ; Paris ; Wien : Lang, 1997
   ISBN 3-631-31944-4

ISBN 3-631-31944-4
US-ISBN 0-8204-3291-1
© Peter Lang GmbH
Europäischer Verlag der Wissenschaften
Frankfurt am Main 1997
All rights reserved.

All parts of this publication are protected by copyright. Any utilisation outside the strict limits of the copyright law, without the permission of the publisher, is forbidden and liable to prosecution. This applies in particular to reproductions, translations, microfilming, and storage and processing in electronic retrieval systems.

Printed in Germany 1 2 3 4 5   7

Acknowledgments

Constructing Collective Identity draws together data from three research projects that span 25 years. Numerous individuals, funding bodies and other institutions in the United States, Papua New Guinea and New Zealand provided invaluable assistance to me during this time. I have gratefully acknowledged their help in previous publications, and will confine my thanks here to people and organisations specifically involved with the production of this book.

David Pearson, Reader in Sociology at Victoria University, and Marlene Levine, Senior Analyst in the Department of Social Welfare, read the entire manuscript. Professor Niko Besnier, a fellow staff member in Victoria University's Anthropology Department, examined the first few chapters. Although I did not take all the resultant suggestions on board, their valuable comments and criticisms certainly improved the clarity, expression and framing of the finished product. Vanessa Byrnes and Johanne Benseman of the Waitangi Tribunal sent me the photograph reproduced in Chapter 5 and kindly identified the individuals who appear in it. I thank them for their efforts and the Tribunal for permission to use the picture in this book. Ute Winkelkötter of Peter Lang was most helpful and efficient throughout the publication process.

My employer, Victoria University of Wellington, New Zealand, provided the period of research and study leave during which most of the manuscript was completed. *Constructing Collective Identity* is published with the financial support of the University's Faculty of Humanities and Social Sciences Subvention Fund.

Table of Contents

1 Introduction 9
2 The Concept of Ethnicity 13
    Three General Approaches to Ethnicity 16
    Ethnicity and Cognition 22
    Data Gathering and Analysis 25
    Ethnicity, Identity Politics and the State 28
    Conclusion 32
3 Ethnic Formation in Urban Papua New Guinea 33
    The Colonial Origins of Urban Centres 34
    Towns in the Context of Their Hinterlands 37
    Building and Defining Social Networks 40
        Kepaka Clan Brothers 41
        Two Other Highlanders in Port Moresby 43
        The Personal Friendship Networks 45
    The Wantok System and Ethnic Stereotypes 45
    Kofena 50
        Lulu's Death 51
        Balau's Beating 54
    Rural Identity in Urban Places 56
    Three Examples of Higher Level Identities 57
        An Accident in Mount Hagen 57
        Rioting in Kokopo 61
        Papuan Separatism 62
    Social Action, Ethnicity and Cognitive Processes 64
    Conclusions: The Essential Ingredients of Ethnicity 69
4 Jewish Ethnicity in New Zealand 73
    Symbolic Ethnicity 74
    Assimilation versus Transformation 75
    A Meta-Ideology for Diaspora Jews? 77
    New Zealand Jewry – An Overview 79
    A Study of Being Jewish 80
    Orthodox and Progressive Congregations 82
    Friendship Networks 86

    Civil Themes in the New Zealand Interviews 88
      The Holocaust 88
      Israel 91
      Anti-Semitism 93
    Ignorance 95
    Some New Zealand Jewish Individuals 97
      Two Orthodox Youth 97
      Conventional Jews 98
      Crossing Boundaries 99
      Converts 103
      Disengaging 107
      Vaguely Jewish 108
      Leaving New Zealand 110
    Identification and Jewish Continuity in New Zealand 112
    Conclusion 114
5 Biculturalism 119
    Colonial History 120
    The Waitangi Tribunal 125
      Motonui 127
      Kaituna and Manukau 129
    Consolidating Biculturalism 130
    Muriwhenua 132
    The New Tribalism 137
    Inventing Traditions? 141
    Bicultural Identity and Counter Identity 147
6 Reconstructing Ethnicity 155
    The Fundamentals of Ethnicity 155
    Ethnicity in Contexts- Comparisons of the Cases 159
    Conclusion 167
References 171
Index 177

Figures

Map of Papua New Guinea 38
Kofena Diagram 50
Holocaust Memorial, Makara Cemetery 72
Ngati Awa Claimants Welcoming Members of the Waitangi Tribunal 118
Spectrum of Types of Ethnicity in the United States 160

1

Introduction

The literature on ethnicity is huge. It comes from a wide range of subjects and points of view. Far from being a sign of health and vitality, this diversity provides testimony to the deterioration of a potentially coherent concept into a series of vaguely connected discourses[1]. The problem is that, as the number of case studies grows authors try to shape the perception of what ethnicity is to suit their material. Academic notions of the phenomenon get pummelled, pushed, pulled and stretched out of shape. While this can result in better knowledge and advanced understanding, a lack of new syntheses stimulated by constructive theorising encourages nihilism. Current work focuses more on deconstructing ethnicity than anything else. A similar trend is apparent in the study of other key topics in anthropology like kinship and culture.

The major aim of this monograph is to demonstrate that, contrary to the laws of physics, this conceptual black hole can be made to emit light. The difficulty with ethnicity is, in fact, a particular manifestation of the central problem of cultural anthropology: understanding the genesis and reproduction of all cultural representations. So a useful approach here is likely to contain elements pertinent to other questions about how culture works. Anthropologists argue endlessly about the nature of culture. We disagree about precisely what it is and whether culture is epiphenomenal, something that merely responds to material conditions, or is a more fundamental ingredient of social formations. We do, however, agree about some basic things. Anthropologists take it for granted that culture has material and symbolic dimensions and that minds provide the essential medium for culture. Yet anthropology's conceptualisation of the contribution of mental processes to the actual construction of cultural representations is extremely impoverished. As Sperber (1985:73) says, "What I find naive is the belief that

---

[1] See Banks 1996.

human mental abilities make culture possible and yet do not in any way determine its content and organisation."

The case studies that make up the core of *Constructing Collective Identity* develop an explanatory synthesis that focuses on the role of cognition in accomplishing ethnic representations. I argue that a cognitive discursive approach (elaborated especially in Chapter 2) is capable of integrating the material, symbolic and "mental" dimensions of ethnicity in a way that can advance knowledge on a number of fronts. Inquiry into the social construction of categories of types of people allows us to see that ethnicity is fundamentally a phenomenon of descent classification. Understanding this basic aspect of ethnicity allows us to appreciate that cultural differences themselves, far from being a priori defining principles of the phenomenon, are secondary elaborations of, and accretions to, cognitive categories of common origin. Realising that ethnicity, although itself a cultural thing, is not primarily about cultural difference, enables us to see commonalities hiding behind surface differences and separate what is essential to ethnicity from related, coexisting (perhaps even parasitic) developments. The politicisation of religion here, of language there, sexual orientation or disability somewhere else, can be seen for what they are, either embellishments of more fundamental, ethnic or non-ethnic categories or examples of the ideological politics of identity. Identity politics often coexists with, and grows from a base provided by, ethnicity but the one should not be confused with the other.

Like most anthropologists, I write with a mix of theoretical and descriptive aims. Despite fundamental similarities in the way that ethnic construction works, the differing circumstances of Papua New Guineans, Maori and Jews, produce distinctive kinds of collective and individual identity. The case studies themselves (urban Papua New Guineans, and New Zealand Maori and Jews) will, I believe, prove intrinsically valuable as descriptive accounts of particular ethnic constructions. Following the second chapter, which serves as a theoretical introduction, I begin to explore the cases, each in its context, and progressively introduce analytical points to make sense of them.

The third chapter is about the construction of ethnicity in urban Papua New Guinea. My informants, mainly highlanders in Port Moresby, Mount Hagen and Rabaul, had recently come from rural areas to places where their tribal identities had only limited currency. I found people both adopting and creating ethnic identities in varying circumstances in the course of a number of individual and group encounters related in depth in this chapter. My earliest research experiences in Papua New Guinea's towns greatly influenced my subsequent work. This fieldwork led me to question some of the basic premises of the literature on ethnicity and, ultimately, stimulated me to develop the approach elaborated in this monograph.

Chapter 4 is about New Zealand Jews. Drawing, as it does, on an ancient tradition, one might expect Jewish ethnicity to be the antithesis of the newly developed identities of urban Papua New Guineans. In fact, Jewishness in New Zealand – despite vast and obvious differences on the ground, in the literature and in the disciplines that produce the literature – shares much with the uncertain and minimalistic ethnic identities I found in urban Papua New Guinea. If the main theme of Chapter 3 is ethnic construction, that of Chapter 4 is dissolution. In both situations a similar core seems to remain.

The fifth chapter, about biculturalism in New Zealand, examines the progressive development of a Maori ideology of grievance against the New Zealand state in the 1980s and 1990s. Unlike Jewish ethnicity in New Zealand, Maori ethnicity is hot, a focus of much attention, debate and cultural production. Although readers will find plenty of heat in the Papua New Guinea material, the Maori have developed formal institutions of their own and exploited those of the state more effectively than my Papua New Guinean informants to construct durable ethnic political movements. The material on biculturalism particularly shows how ethnicity interdigitates with identity politics for Maori and stimulates parallel developments among non-Maori New Zealanders.

The final section of the monograph considers the differences and similarities explored in the case study chapters. It provides a synthetic, inductive, theoretical statement about the nature of ethnicity and the politics of identity in contemporary society. Although I can sympathise with a recent textbook review that says ethnicity "stubbornly resists definition" and merely serves as a shorthand for a vaguely connected series of literatures (Banks 1996:10), my own experience of different methods and social science sources in the presentation and analysis of these three cases leads to the opposite conclusion. The juxtaposition of the studies that make up *Constructing Collective Identity* increases rather than undermines my confidence that, despite appearances to the contrary, ethnicity is an authentic phenomenon – one that exists outside, as well as within, the imagination of academics. Ethnicity, identity politics, and other cultural representations of identity, develop from specific combinations of certain fundamentals. If we pay closer attention to how cognition and discourse engage categorisation and social structure, scholars interested in collective identity can develop more sophisticated analyses of the genesis and dynamics of some of the most basic and potentially explosive aspects of human social life.

2

The Concept of Ethnicity

> Almost any cultural-social unit, indeed any term describing particular structures of continuing social relations, or sets of regularised events now can be referred to as an "ethnic" this or that. This can be seen in the proliferation of titles dealing with ethnic groups, ethnic identity, ethnic boundaries, ethnic conflict, ethnic cooperation or competition, ethnic politics, ethnic stratification, ethnic integration, ethnic consciousness, and so on. Name it and there is in all likelihood someone who has written on it using "ethnic" or "ethnicity" qualifiers to describe his or her special approach to the topic. (Ronald Cohen 1978:379-403)

"Ethnicity" then is one of those concepts, like "culture", "custom" and "community", that social scientists use frequently but vaguely and idiosyncratically. Perhaps ironically, one of the earliest discussions of ethnicity, Weber's, provides a clear, concise treatment that focuses on the fundamental attribute of the phenomenon, and then rejects ethnicity as an analytically useful concept (Weber 1968:385-398). Weber says that ethnic groups are, "Those human groups which entertain a subjective belief in their common descent". He recognises that people use a great variety of cultural traits, such as language, religion, etiquette and morality, to articulate ethnic descent and often magnify these to define social boundaries. Since notions of common descent get manipulated so readily in the pursuit of political, economic or other goals, and the ethnic dimension of social reality forms part of a wider social context, ethnicity "dissolves if we define our terms exactly" (1968:395).

Weber's comment that "the notion of 'ethnically' determined social action subsumes phenomena that a rigorous sociological analysis... would have to distinguish carefully" (1968:394) remains a useful caution to scholars who continue to reify what should be their fundamental object of analysis. However, even when such analysis shows ethnicity to be more a product than a producer of social action the phenomenon does not somehow disappear. The subjective belief in common descent (descent used to define non-kinship entities[2]) constitutes a fundamental idiom of human social and cultural life. When people perceive, discuss or organise themselves and/or others into categories defined in terms of extra-kin descent, the boundaries, politics, stratification, or any of the traits mentioned by Weber, take on ethnic dimensions that fundamentally influence the social construction of reality. However, if such constructions of peoplehood do not involve these notions of common descent, something else is going on, regardless of attempts by the spokespeople for causes such as gay, deaf or "little people's" rights to ethnicise their identities.

Conceptualising ethnicity in such a minimalistic way, without immediate reference to its highly variable cultural content, avoids the tendency of many authors to confuse elaborations with the phenomenon itself. Part of the problem of separating essential qualities from embellishments, at least in anthropology, comes from the fact that researchers quite naturally construct definitions out of their particular case studies. If Jews in New Zealand struggled to maintain a strictly insular orthodox community, and this book considered them alone, a definition of Jewishness that stressed religion, language (Hebrew), customs, traditions and symbols might seem most appropriate. Many scholars doing the same thing overburden us with the ethnic "this or that" that Ronald Cohen bemoans. However, by explicitly comparing different cases, uncovering a great range of commitments to and expressions of ethnic identity, we can better decide whether to abandon, deconstruct, or argue for a more basic and universalistic definition.

---

[2] Although ethnicity involves using a subjective notion of descent, we need to recognise that not all users of descent idioms construct ethnic entities. Members of kinship groups use descent idioms to define social aggregates of various kinds. Anthropologists define the term "clan" as a set of people who trace descent from a putative ancestor. This provides an example of the subjective use of a descent idiom, but clans are not ethnic groups. Kinship terms and concepts use descent to distinguish between groups and individuals within a wider system of descent. The Scottish clans, for example, differentiate among Scots; members of each clan remain Scottish. The ethnic term "Scot", on the other hand, ignores internal descent divisions and separates the Scottish people from other people on the same level of generality, like the English. Where kinship uses descent to distinguish between people who share an ancestor a bit further down the line, ethnicity uses descent to distinguish "us" from "them", the people we are not related to. I differ here from Ngata (1981), for example, who also stresses the self-sustaining nature of ethnic groups and categories. She feels that the ability of ethnic categories and groups to reproduce themselves provides the principle point of separation between ethnicity and kinship. Ngata states that incest taboos prevent kinship groups from reconstituting themselves without outside links. Although marriage is always allowed and often strongly preferred within ethnic boundaries, some kinship groups can also be endogamous and therefore reproduce themselves.

The Concept of Ethnicity

In choosing the latter course, of reconstructing a comprehensive concept of ethnicity in a climate of deconstruction, it is particularly important to focus on the scale, type and expression of ethnicity at play in each case. Some ethnic terms connote little more than labels, or what Ardener calls "hollow categories" (1989:69). Jews call non-Jews "gentiles" and Maori call non-Maori people "pakeha". These words refer to categorisations, conceptual divisions within the universal set of people. Obviously we all make many ethnic and non-ethnic categorisations of other humans. All such commonly used categories are part of the cultural worlds (cultural in the sense of widely shared understandings) of those individuals and collectivities that use them. In order for a cultural category to be ethnic of course, it must refer to some notion of common origin.

Gentiles do not believe they share a common ethnicity nor do Jews attribute a single ethnic identity to them. In fact, the gentiles of New Zealand have little awareness of local Jews and their views of social reality, so the way that Jews categorise them lacks meaning and "gentile ethnicity" does not exist in New Zealand at all.

Pakeha ethnicity, on the other hand, is more problematic. We will see in the chapter on biculturalism in New Zealand that some non-Maori New Zealanders use this Maori term, at least in certain situations, to describe themselves. Leaving the issue of descent aside until Chapter 5, pakeha certainly describes a meaningful social *category* of New Zealand culture. Pakeha would need more than awareness and a label to constitute a social *group* (Pearson 1990)[2]. Groups form when aggregates of individuals who interact develop some shared understandings. When members of the group acquire a sense of solidarity and purpose, and construct organisations, they form *communities*.

Ethnic *identification* refers to allocating ethnic labels to individuals. People can of course label others without communication or agreement about the terms they use. Before we can call an identification an *identity* we need some evidence that individuals accept that the term is a meaningful description of them. The salience of ethnic identifications and identities can, as we will see in all the cases, vary greatly. To Maori, pakeha appear to be a group with an ethnic identity. Some white New Zealanders may embrace Pakeha identity

---

[3] Pearson's discussion of pakeha ethnicity uses the concepts of category, group and community developed by Anthony Smith (1989). At this point I am avoiding the use of the term ethnic when refering to pakeha, and concentrating on distinguishing between categories, groups and communities.

either reluctantly or with gusto, while others ignore or vehemently deny the meaningfulness of the label.

To recapitulate, ethnic categories exist when people label themselves or other people in terms of common origin. If the people labelled in this way identify with the category and interact consistently with each other, they form ethnic groups. Organised ethnic groups with a sense of solidarity and organisation constitute ethnic communities. The boundaries between categories, identifications, identities, groups and communities may be fuzzy rather than sharp, but distinguishing between various aspects and levels of association, even crudely, is crucial to understanding how ethnicity works. The accretions, symbols, myths, customs, traditions etc., that some authors feel define ethnicity, become most important in regard to organised ethnic communities. They strengthen solidarity and play crucial roles in political struggles but, again, they develop on categorical foundations and are not defining principles of ethnicity per se.

A major focus of each of the case studies that make up the core of this monograph is to consider how expressions of ethnicity come to take the particular forms they exhibit. Looking at the main approaches social scientists take to ethnicity, and the issues these approaches raise, will help clarify the significance of points developed in the case study chapters, particularly points about how the constructions and elaborations that accrete to ethnic categorisations relate to each other and articulate with different aspects of social life.

Three General Approaches to Ethnicity

The close association between ethnicity and origin gives ethnic phenomena an affective quality. Some researchers stress the compelling nature of these affective ties, attributing an almost mystical ability for them to motivate the human psyche. Shils, for example, mentions "a certain ineffable significance" that "is attributed to the tie of blood" (quoted in Thompson 1989). Authors who make points like this treat ethnicity as a primordial and enduring attachment. Thompson (1989:34-35) notes that some primordialists, like Shils, claim that "there exists an unalterable biological need for deep-seated affective primordial relationships, a need that, under certain socio-historical circumstances can be satisfied by ethnic or racial identities". Other primordialists stress that social and historical factors create the need for, and affective force of, ethnicity.

The existence of organised and purposeful ethnic communities is completely unproblematical in this paradigm. If people feel so strongly about their origins for mysterious internal reasons, then all the paraphernalia of organised ethnicity that symbolise common descent would seem to be completely unproblematical. The biggest drawback of the primordial approach lies in its inability to account for the creation of new ethnic identities or the waxing and waning of established ethnicities. The Papua New Guinean identities discussed in Chapter 3 derive from colonial divisions that became important in the period leading up to independence. Although my key informants came from tribal societies with deep and enduring ties that might well sustain a primordial description, the ethnic action leading up to independence clearly derives from recent events. Yet, as we shall see, even new, relatively undeveloped, categorical ethnicity can evoke strong sentiments. The psychological force (primordiality) of ethnic identities may derive partly from the notion of origin itself, but the framing of origin requires explanation. Sentiments attach to ethnic entities but do not cause them to emerge in any simple way.

Despite its obvious deficiencies we cannot simply jettison the primordial approach. Its emphasis on sentiments provides an important addition to situational explanations that stress the role of common interests in creating ethnicity. Papua New Guinean informants tended to interpret circumstances, that might well have reflected their class and political positions in the emerging state, as instances of ethnic conflict. Class and political ties can unite people with common interests, but seem less effective than ethnicity in promoting sustained commitment to causes. Ethnic ties combine interests with sentiments and thus provide a stronger motivation for social action (Bell 1976).

When anthropologists study urban migrants they often notice that, in towns, the significance and expression of ethnic identity seems to vary situationally. Mitchell (cited in Okamura 1981) defines a social "situation" as the specific set of circumstances urban migrants find themselves in and distinguished these micro-level sociological contexts from macro-level sociological "settings". Structural conditions set in place by colonial policy, migration patterns, economic and political relations, etc. composed the settings within which situations and ethnic variation developed. While settings impose structural constraints to action, cognition – the individual's perception of the nature of the circumstances and the identities they apply to themselves and others – is an important aspect of the definition of situations.

The situational perspective seems more helpful than primordialism in understanding the case material. The various identities developed by urban Papua New Guineans, the different ways New Zealand Jews conceive of Jewishness, and changing conceptions of Maori and Pakeha, necessitate a fluid circumstantial approach to ethnicity. However, like primordialism, situationalism has some blind spots. People may develop new identities, and ethnic commitments can vary by situation, but even in the very fluid contexts of urban Papua New Guinea there are definite limits to the kinds of identity that will endure. Some of these limits seem to relate closely to how Papua New Guineans classify one another. But Abner Cohen feels that the emphasis on cognition and classification apparent in the writings of Mitchell, Epstein (1958) and Barth (1969) is logically, methodologically and sociologically problematic:

> What it says is that people act as the members of ethnic categories because they identify themselves, and are sometimes also identified by others, with these ethnic categories. How do we know this? The actors say so, or so they act. Such statements and arguments will not become more analytical if we attribute identification and categorisation to so-called cognition and begin to construct "cognitive maps" to "explain" them. (Abner Cohen 1969)

There are two ways to meet these criticisms. Firstly, observers need to avoid the tendency in the situationalist literature to conflate informants' statements about ethnicity with their own analytical perspectives. When people make ethnic identifications they do so in circumstances that reflect purposes and realities far removed from those of the researcher (Okamura 1981). This difficulty of cross purposes can be addressed by paying proper attention to the ways in which macro-level sociological "settings" enter into situations. Analysts need to attend carefully to the issue of the saliency of particular expressions and levels of ethnicity. As Ronald Cohen puts it, "much less attention has been given to understanding what conditions tend to evoke ethnic identities of particular scale and intensity than to describing what ethnicity is as a phenomenon" (1978). The major goal of this book is to account for the salience and expression of ethnicity within and across the three cases. Abner Cohen's dismissal and subsequent warnings about sliding down a slippery slope to psychology and history notwithstanding, social scientists cannot reconcile the primordial and situational approaches without understanding how aspects of social and cultural situations come to take on the role of primordial givens in ethnic constructions. Accounting for the creation of meaningful ethnic symbols requires careful attention to informants' categorisations and an understanding of the fact that macro-level sociological conditions enter into cognition as well as into specific social situations.

The literature on ethnicity, like most discussions of collective representations, has studiously avoided any involvement with psychological theories of cognition (Boyer 1994). This remains the case despite the primordialists' emphasis on ultimate sentiments and the situationalists' interest in their informants' mental models of the urban landscape. Before I begin to consider the usefulness of current social psychological approaches to cognition for explaining important aspects of ethnicity, the issue of deconstruction needs to be broached. If ethnicity has no reality and lacks any unifying elements injecting a cognitive dimension into the subject will not, so to speak, raise the dead.

Postmodernists take issue with the idea that observers should carefully avoid conflating their concepts with those of informants. This intellectual movement presents itself as a challenge to positivism. Postmodernists stress the contextual nature of every point of view in an increasingly fragmented world of contingent identities. The concepts social scientists hold have no greater claim to truth than those of their informants or anyone else. Writers should take account of multiple and discrepant points of view and "de-centre" their descriptions, to reflect the collapse of what Lyotard calls "grand narratives".

Situationalists also stress the fluid nature of constructed identities, but postmodernists go further by rejecting the explanatory authority of social and cultural analysts. They pay particular attention to the constructed nature of culture and tradition and its "objectification". When people "invent" traditions and identities they make implicit lived experience into something explicit and rhetorically useful to advance political agendas.

Linnekin notes that although anthropologists like Wagner feel that cultural invention takes place in all societies, "In Pacific anthropology cultural objectification has been explored particularly in discussions of colonial history and nationalism. Much of this literature makes the point that models of culture, *kastom* and tradition are politically instrumental in the construction of anti-colonial and national identities" (1992:253). She feels that deconstructing indigenous discourse presents problems for anthropologists who usually promote the causes of their informants. This issue certainly comes up in the Maori case below where biculturalism stimulates an interesting combination of inventions and counter inventions of Maori and pakeha identity and culture. Unlike Linnekin, I worry less about the ethics of deconstruction than the conceptualisation in these arguments of ethnicity as culture and the reduction of culture to discourse and text.

Anthony Cohen, for example, defines ethnicity as "a mode of action and of representation: it refers to a decision people make to depict themselves or others symbolically as bearers of a certain cultural identity... In effect ethnicity has become the politicisation of culture" (1994:19). Culture and ethnicity certainly go together, at least in the case of ethnic groups and communities. The symbols people adopt, in religion, language, custom and tradition, that give ethnicity a veneer of primordialism, commonly derive from cultural systems. Although ethnicity involves the use (mainly the objectification) of aspects of culture, reducing culture and ethnicity to each other gives an excessively idealist tone to the postmodern and other culturist approaches to ethnicity.

The ongoing debate about "race relations" in New Zealand provides a good example of the pitfalls of cultural reification. Many commentators (mentioned in the third case study, which is analysed in Chapter 5) assume that New Zealand has two cultures, Maori and pakeha, that define ethnic communities. The bicultural solution to the nation's problems involves giving Maori culture an equal place with pakeha culture in the New Zealand state. Once that is done, Maori will be able to assume a position in the wider society commensurate with their status as *tangata whenua*, people of the land. Pearson (1991), Miles and Spoonley (1985), Sissons (1992) and Nash (1990) have pointed out that this view of two peoples misrepresents social reality. It ignores the socioeconomic causes of Maori marginalisation and fact that people do not automatically live different lives if they have different ethnic identities. Some of the most articulate and powerful spokespeople for Maoridom seem to have ordinary upper-middle-class New Zealand backgrounds.

In the Papua New Guinean and Jewish cases, also, identification with the cultural symbols of an ethnic category bears no simple relationship to culture as a way of life. "If 'culture' is defined in idealist terms as 'symbols and meanings' and if ethnicity is defined as possessing a set of symbols and meanings that confer collective identity of an appropriate kind then 'ethnic culture' (indeed, the concept of culture itself) is hopelessly trivialised." Scottish culture and ethnicity, for example, becomes reduced to bagpipes, kilts and haggis (Nash 1990:109). Nash notes that culture is not a set of artefacts and performances it is something that gets reproduced in an organised fashion. Cultural production in New Zealand does not happen in separately bounded Maori and pakeha spheres. "It makes no sense, therefore, to say that these groups are distinct cultures or have distinct cultures. At most, we can say there are profound cultural differences between them." (Sissons 1992:24).

However analysts may delight in deconstructing such naive views and point out that they hide more than they elucidate, the fact remains that understanding and explaining people's conceptualisations of ethnicity is not the same as evaluating whether they actually live in ways concordant with how they objectify their lives. The truth status of cultural claims to a distinctive way of life matter little when people use cultural traits as symbols to construct a sense of primordial identity. This does not mean that culture itself is only a system of ideas, meanings and symbols, but rather that cultural symbols enter ethnic constructions in an ideological fashion to help articulate differences.

Nash's comments notwithstanding, the cases presented in this book show that ethnicity can become minimal indeed. In fact, an interesting approach to ethnicity (which is applied to the discussion of New Zealand Jews in Chapter 4) emphasises that ethnicity itself may become reduced to a symbolic attachment for certain groups who formerly constituted powerful communities in the United States. Perhaps the culturists have the right idea after all?

Looking at a recently culturalised identity can highlight some of the differences that remain. Homosexuality, feminism and deafness present three examples of a culturisation of identity accompanied by an ethnicisation of culture. Congenital deafness provides the most interesting case because the "deaf culture" movement only recently began to articulate its position. Most hearing people think of deafness as an unfortunate condition that requires intervention. Speakers for the "deaf community" reject this view most emphatically. Lane, for example, wants to "replace the normativeness of medicine with the curiosity of ethnography" because relativism gives the concept of "deaf culture" a value-neutral connotation (1992:19). Treating deafness as a disability makes "sufferers" subject to treatment programmes that rarely achieve results other than to humiliate and torture the "patient". Children born deaf rarely acquire normal spoken language or perform up to their potential in hearing schools. Cochlear implant operations to "cure" deafness have become extremely controversial. Held out as marvellous advances of medical science to the parents of deaf children, they represent the height of invasive medical manipulation to advocates of deafness as culture.

Lane stresses that the congenitally deaf marry endogamously[4], have their own language (signing) and that deaf schools provide a common background and avenue of cultural transmission. When you ask deaf people where they come from they will reply with the name of their residential school. They feel that deaf people who speak, instead of sign, have embraced alien values. "If we respect the right of people in other cultures to have their own constitutive rules... then we must recognise that... deafness is not a disability but rather a different way of being" (Lane 1992:19). These points – that the deaf have a unique and vital way of life and should be free to live without stigma – are convincingly made, but Lane's promotion of an ethnic status for deaf people provides a clear example of how ideological conceptualisations of ethnicity get used to facilitate the flow of resources, in this case into residential schools and

---

[4] Indeed, the 90% figure he cites represents a greater level of endogamy than one finds in many Jewish communities, where Jewish parentage is generally a pre-condition of Jewish identity.

programmes that promote signing. Regardless of admirable intentions, and leaving the issue of what is best for deaf children to their "community", they do not form an ethnic collectivity even if Lane's picture of them is substantially accurate.

The fact that deaf children have hearing parents and give birth to hearing children means that they, and groups like them, cannot use descent to form ethnic identities, although they obviously practice cultural (and identity) politics. As analysts of social situations we should resist the tendency to conflate ethnicity with culture, discourse and identity, even if (indeed, especially when) our informants do so.

Postmodernists may object strongly to this last statement. As Bauman says, "How quixotic to debunk the distortion in the representation of reality once no reality claims to be more real than its representation" (1992:viii). How can a book that focuses on representations make claims about their status if representations create realities? The answer to this question has two prongs, one theoretical and the other methodological. The theoretical issue brings me back to cognition.

Ethnicity and Cognition

I highlighted the descent criterion in Weber's definition of ethnicity. His definition also emphasised the subjective nature of conceptualisations of common origin. Accepting that notions of origin form the stuff of erecting boundaries between "us" and "them", analysts need to consider how ideas of extra-kin descent become objectified, more real than their representations. Bauman surely has a point, relevant to the more "symbolic" manifestations of ethnicity, when he says that, "Having no other (and above all no objectified, supra-individual) anchors except the affections of their 'members', imagined communities [and we'll see some true flights of imagination in this book] exist solely through their manifestations: through occasional spectacular outbursts of togetherness" (1992:xix). However, where the postmodernist deconstructs – "Demolition is the only job the postmodern mind seems to be good at. Destruction is the only construction it recognises" (1992:ix) – people themselves construct and analysts can understand how their constructions take on the appearance of genuine things.

When I reiterated the distinction in the literature between ethnic categories, groups and communities, the reader might have gotten the impression that because categories are not endowed with the permanence of groups or communities, categorisation itself is a relatively unimportant ingredient or manifestation of ethnicity. In my view, categorisation is the central phenomenon, the base upon which everything else rests.

Ethnicity is one way or method people use to classify social types. Hirschfeld (1994:224) claims that "children naturalize social identities... they adopt from the start an essentialist approach to some social categories." If this is true, ethnic classifications come, at least partially, from something innate, within the mind itself. This constitutes a distinct cognitive domain to Hirschfeld, but according to other authors social categories are an extension or transfer from the domain that organises the conceptualisations of all living things (see Hirschfeld and Gelman 1994.)

Defining the precise nature of the cognitive mechanism that produces ethnicity is beyond the scope of this book. The main point is to show that ethnicity does indeed rest on a foundation of cognitive components. This fundamental claim means that aspects of ethnicity, like aspects of religion in Boyer's account of Fang ghosts, "Use principles that are part of a set of cognitive systems that are not culturally transmitted and in fact are not transmitted at all" (1994:404)[5]. Boyer asserts that cultural inputs trigger inferences spontaneously and that similar inferences come from similarities of situation. Different inferences then come from different situations, and ethnicity will have both universal (from cognition) and unique (from circumstance) expressions. Robust explanations of ethnicity will need to take both cognition and circumstance, as well as their interactions, into account.

Regardless of where in the mind they bubble up from, once categories exist they engage other important aspects of human cognition. When people apply categories to themselves the categorised entity becomes real to them. Initially this reality may reside only in their heads, but categories can become the basis of groups with more objective characteristics when they get substantiated in organisations. Social categorisation itself provides a sufficient condition for generating group competition, and members view people of other contrasting categories as having uniform characteristics (Hogg and Abrams 1988).

> This outgroup homogeneity effect occurs regardless of whether the group is students at a neighbouring college, members of another profession, or people who prefer the modern painter Klee when one prefers Kandinsky... when people use relatively well established categories such as gender and ethnicity, the schema seems to dominate subsequent irrelevancies. However, when people use weak categories such as occupations, majors or novel groupings ("day people" versus

---

[5] I doubt that Boyer means this literally. Something in the make-up of cognitive systems must get transmitted, certainly biologically, for them to have any consistency.

"night people") the schema seems to be weakened by subsequent irrelevancies. (Fiske and Taylor 1991)

When individuals put groups in their heads, they perceive themselves and others in depersonalised terms. Cognitive and motivational effects occur that facilitate collective action (Wetherell and Potter 1992). A problem with applying social cognition research to instances of collective representation lies in its tendency to view the perceiver as a lone agent sampling a complex social environment. In this view cognitive factors create social representations, a perspective that constitutes the kind of psychologism that anthropologists and sociologists find unacceptable.

Abner Cohen's point, that the existence of ethnic categories tells us nothing that is sociologically useful, makes sense if we see the categories purely in terms of the mind's inner dynamics. More fruitful approaches stress the discursive construction of categories (Edwards 1991). People make categorisations in interaction with others and this interaction takes account of, incorporates and influences existing social categorisations.

> The social structures individual perception, identity, and action. In this sense society, understood as a system of group divisions, comes first, but it is the individual's psychological response to this social stimulus which allows the social to continue, which produces group action and which completes the circle... A sense of identity and subjectivity is constructed from the interpretative resources, stories and narratives of identity which are available, in circulation, in our culture.
> (Wetherell and Potter 1992:47,76)

Observing, recording and analysing the discursive construction of categories provides a way out of the dead ends of retreating into a mysterious realm of the individual mind and the equally unsatisfying dilettantism of decentring and deconstruction. Humans categorise everything – the natural as well as all aspects of the social world. When they categorise other human beings in reference to perceptions and beliefs about their origins they make ethnic categorisations. They make these kinds of categories discursively in the course of interactions with other people in particular social contexts, contexts that ethnicity in turn influences directly. Attending to the construction of ethnic categories is an attempt to understand how ethnicity becomes palpable, a part of social and cultural reality. People have ways of making things appear objective and social analysts have methods of apprehending their methods of sociocultural construction.

Data Gathering and Analysis

The data analysed in this book come from case studies of ethnicity grounded in fundamentally different circumstances. I used a variety of methodologies and sources of data; ethnographic and survey research in Papua New Guinea, interviewing with New Zealand Jews; and the analysis of transcripts and reports of Waitangi Tribunal cases to understand Maori demands for biculturalism. Since all these methods (except the survey research) involve collecting qualitative accounts of ethnicity, a similar strategy of analysis was applied to each case.

Generally speaking, the researcher starts with some general topical interests that derive from a knowledge of "the literature", asks informants questions, and makes observations about a subject. While the data comes in we look for patterns by examining and classifying the material into concepts. Some of these concepts come from the literature but others, the ones most likely to result in new insights, are derived from the data through a creative process of inductive analysis. The researcher segments data into conceptual codes and looks for connections between them. This leads initially to a fairly crude and preliminary understanding of the topic which is continually refined through an iterative and recursive process. To give a brief example, if I overhear an informant say to another in Port Moresby, "We highlanders built this town and now the Papuans want us to leave," this can be coded as an example of ethnic labelling and boundaries (highlanders and Papuans), and conflict ("they want us to leave"). When collecting more data the concepts become refined, subdivided and developed, by looking for configurations in the data to describe their content, and searching for linkages across the various concepts to understand their articulation both with each other and with various aspects of social reality. The terms "highlander" and "Papuan", for example, have many contextual divisions that help to better understand the nature of ethnic labels. The conflict attributed to these labels and boundaries derives from a large number of developmental sources like urban migration, job and housing patterns, so an understanding of the construction of urban ethnicity in Papua New Guinea needs to reflect these factors.

Qualitative analysis requires engagement in a cyclical process. The questions become more specific, the interpretations of observations more precise each time one goes around. The researcher knows a topic is finished when they can anticipate the answers to questions or descriptions of an event or observation compared with informants. Unlike researchers employing the more linear quantitative approaches, qualitative analysts continually evaluate their data and work on their concepts. Analysis is not left until the end of the collection phase of research.

My own commitment to qualitative methods of gathering and analysing data comes from a conviction that they are well suited to answering the questions about ethnic construction posed here, not that they have any intrinsic superiority over quantitative methods. Validity tends to be high in qualitative research, but reliability presents problems. My construction of concepts and manipulation of the data may seem accurate and reasonable but another person might use the same data to develop different ideas. Researchers should present their material in a way that encourages readers to think of alternative explanations, because critical evaluation by colleagues and students helps us to develop more reliable qualitative accounts.

Representativeness presents perhaps the biggest problem for qualitative researchers. When presenting case studies, accounts and observations of events in urban Papua New Guinea, for example, generalisability rests "on the validity of analysis rather than the representativeness of events" (Mitchell 1983:190), because of the unique nature of the events themselves. Interviewing, both in the context of participant observation where it supplements observation, and when used as the major method, requires attention to how researchers can apply statements from a non-random sample of interview transcripts to a wider group.

The Jewish study involved collaboration with a research group to conduct semi-structured interviews designed to generate information on family background, exposure to Jewish customs religion and organisations, and degree of religious and secular Jewish participation. We asked interviewees about the location of family members and frequency of contact with them, intermarriage, the place of Jews in their social networks, and their thoughts about the nature and future of the Jewish community. These prompts reflect the importance of religious and secular symbols and family life as themes in the literature on Jewish identity, and also the experience of interviewers that these were the topics that made interviews "take off". When encouraged to elaborate on themes respondents found meaningful, such semi-structured "long interviews" opened fruitful avenues of inquiry in line with the goals and framework of the study.

The Jewish Research Group taped all the interviews, transcribed them verbatim and stored the material on hard disk. I printed and coded the transcripts and looked for themes about Jewishness. Using search and retrieval software, coded passages could be de-contextualised, re-contextualised, and used to develop a structure of concepts to aid in this process of interpretation (see Richards and Richards 1990).

The group chose interviewees to reflect known variation in the local Jewish population. The informants comprised members of long-resident families, more recent migrants, youth, people affiliated to the main congregations, unaffiliated people and converts. We approached 46 people in Auckland, Wellington and Otago, who agreed to be interviewed. The six informants from Otago were selected so that people from outside the main centres of Jewish population would also be included in the study. A member of the group did 20 additional interviews with 26 Jewish New Zealanders who immigrated to Australia.

The main strength of such a variable sample is that common patterns which emerge from it are likely to indicate shared perspectives and experiences. (Patton 1990:172). To give a concrete example, I interviewed a woman in Auckland who said that during her childhood in Dunedin people asked her to what religious denomination she belonged. When she told them "Jewish" they asked if she was a Catholic Jew or a Protestant Jew. Another interviewer, working in Dunedin spoke to a woman and her adult daughter. When he asked the mother when she first told her daughter she was Jewish, the older woman reminisced that this caused confusion for the girl at school when her teacher asked her religion. "She said Jewish and the teacher said, "I know but are you a Catholic Jew or a Protestant Jew?"

We had only two women in this sample who talked about Dunedin thirty years ago. The fact that they independently said something so completely unexpected suggests that we can have some confidence in the implications we drew from these two interviews that people in Dunedin at that time had little knowledge of Jews. When other people in the sample discuss how invisible Jews are in New Zealand (Beaglehole and Levine 1995), confidence grows that the interviews tap into a theme of the local Jewish experience connected to other themes similarly derived.

New Zealand has developed a particular forum for the articulation of grievances by Maori. The Waitangi Tribunal hears cases brought by Maori individuals and groups who feel their rights under the Treaty of Waitangi have been violated. The head of the Tribunal allowed me freely to examine files of evidence. These files and submissions by council, and also the Tribunal reports contain a large corpus of statements about the place of Maori in New Zealand society and their desires for change. Tracking a number of fishing cases over the life of the Tribunal, treating them much like the interview data discussed above, showed consistent ideological themes that changed over time. They clearly built upon each other and related closely to wider developments in New Zealand society.

Although the primary method differed for each case, investigation never relied completely on a single technique for gathering data. Using a variety of methods gave important opportunities to check the validity and reliability of interpretations of the themes uncovered by this body of qualitatively oriented research.

Each study involved a combination of participant observation, interviewing, archival and textual research supplemented by quantification when appropriate. The Papua New Guinean project was most notable in this regard. I travelled widely, had access to a great number and variety of informants and situations, and had the funds to hire the personnel to carry out a major survey.

Despite having less ideal conditions to do multi-dimensional research on Jews and Maori people in New Zealand, real efforts were made after having uncovered themes using one method to follow them up by employing another method. For example, when Jewish informants talked about the state of the community, attendance at services and migration to Australia, I could go to services myself and see who was there; listen to the rabbi farewell congregants emigrating to Melbourne who had been especially active in local Jewish organisations; and also hear his own goodbyes when he left. Presenting findings a number of times to two congregations, and considering the observations and feedback from the audiences, greatly benefited the project.

Likewise, presenting a paper to the New Zealand Association of Social Anthropologists meeting at Waihi Marae in Huntly resulted in opportunities to meet some people who took prominent roles in articulating Maori demands and discuss their rhetorical strategies with them. Waitangi Tribunal hearings and interviews with other Maori spokespersons, and discussing issues with colleagues in Victoria University's School of Maori Studies, also gave a wider perspective to data contained in Tribunal evidence and reports.

Ethnicity, Identity Politics and the State

The fact that we can empirically observe, describe, analyse and account for expressions of ethnicity implies that ethnic phenomena constitute a realm of cognitive, social and cultural reality not fully reducible to something like class. People classify others in terms of their origins for contextual purposes, so ethnicity always constitutes an aspect of some more inclusive social action. Bell's previously mentioned point that ethnicity combines interests with affective ties in a uniquely effective way means that it can obviously become a part of class action, or even hide or distort opposing class interests. Some of the commentators cited above, who object to the simple view of New Zealand as a Maori/pakeha society, make this very point. Like a smokescreen that can blow away, ethnicity hides class antagonisms in New Zealand and has no real substance of its own. This view simplifies cognition, social and cultural forces as much as the idea that ethnicity explains everything. We will see in the case studies that ethnicity and other idioms of social action (like class, identity and culture) have mutual influences upon each other, and interact in particular ways in the specific contexts elucidated by the case studies.

Nationalism and the state constitute important factors in this book that interact with ethnicity, class, identity and culture. Smith (1984) emphasises the durability of national sentiments anchored in ethnic communities. Nationalist movements can call for the regeneration of a "decayed" ethnic community (e.g. Jewish nationalism) that suffered decline, exile and suppression. Alternatively, ethnic elites may stimulate new nationalist movements by mobilising groups that were not nationalistic before. A third possibility is that nationalism can invent ethnic communities where they did not exist previously. Smith emphasises that in all these scenarios some perception of difference forms the basis for ethnic nationalism.

For Smith, mobilisation does not depend on emotions. Factors like external threat, economic expansion, secularisation that challenges traditional authority, and rivalry between culturally different groups can all motivate group formation. What gives collective motivation an ethnic form is the development of myths. "The ethnic myths act, therefore, like Weber's 'switchmen', mediating and directing the economic, cultural and political conditions, and endowing otherwise random events and chaotic processes with a peculiarly 'historicist' form and 'ethnic' content." They promote and define the basis for solidarity, and provide a blueprint for future political action to realise the group's goals and ultimate destiny (1984:301). The modern bureaucratic interventionist state stimulates ethnic nationalism in its attempts to create loyal citizens. Groups that perceive the state as an alien "colonialist" institution often develop counter national agendas of their own.

In his recent comprehensive review of the anthropological literature and "deconstruction" of ethnicity as a scholarly concept, Banks (1996:142-143) notes the current tendency for analysts writing about intergroup relations to emphasise nationalism and identity more than ethnicity. He feels that this shows how ethnicity, "the parent concept... has failed to encompass satisfactorily the variety of inter-group interests that it has been applied to". Banks also mentions that "identity", itself a vague term, now gets treated as an analytical concept. Is this another example of "agenda hopping" in anthropology?

> What happens in agenda hopping is that a given agenda of research reaches a point at which nothing new or exciting is emerging from the work of even the best practitioners. It is not that the old agenda is completed... practitioners have come to understand that the phenomena being investigated are quite complex (D'Andrade 1995:4-5)

Scholars begin to "jump ship" and often attack the old programme of research and its associated concepts. This has become so prevalent in the humanities and social sciences that an entire tradition of tearing down concepts has emerged as a central tenet of the intellectual movement of postmodernism. Banks' deconstruction of ethnicity provides an obviously relevant instance to consider. Others are engaged in the context of the three case studies. What deserves emphasis at this point is that shifting agendas from ethnicity to nationalism, culture and identity, solves nothing. If Banks is correct that the "parent concept" lacks precision, we should try to inject some rigour into the study of ethnicity. Plenty of room exists for this endeavour since anthropologists and sociologists have neglected the important cognitive discursive side of the phenomenon. Social psychologists, who most often write about human classification, lack a strong intellectual tradition of sociological and cultural analysis.

Nevertheless, the rise of "identity movements" is extremely interesting because of their similarities to (and subtle differences with) ethnic movements. The chapters that follow highlight how, as a dynamic aspect of categorisation, ethnicity accretes meanings and agendas that do lead on to other things.

Each case study in this book reinforces the generalisation that ethnicity primarily manifests itself in discourse about issues that involve the distribution of political and economic power in society. The categorisation and discourse central to the production and fate of particular expressions of ethnicity may come to have great personal meaning, but ethnic formation rests on attempts to connect quintessentially public matters with an "essentialist" discourse about descent.

Identity activism seems to engage more private issues such as those based on sexual orientation or disability. Activists bring these private identities into public contestation, where they attempt to recast pre-existing notions about stigmatised lifestyles or conditions into primordial "essentialisms" (Darnovsky et al. 1995:xiii). Doing this gives identity ideologues and theorists rhetorical problems that their ethnic counterparts find more or less already solved. Ethnic activists do not have to bring identities out of the closet and reconfigure categories in order to make representations of them. Descent provides an apparently ready-made basis for fundamental, public, cultural categories.

Identity rhetoric often models itself on ethnicity (e.g. the stance that people are born gay, with different brain structures than heterosexuals, and naturally develop their own culture) and seeks to capitalise on the gains that ethnic groups have made in many western democracies. As the case of the deaf shows, these groups face difficulties with recruitment over time, because they cannot naturally reproduce themselves. Indeed, their reliance on imagery, demonstration and the media for their very existence and perpetuation gives identity groups a quintessentially postmodern flavour.

When ethnic movements themselves come to make identity demands imaginatively in public forums and the media, the distinctions between ethnicity and identity politics become blurred. However, the point made above about resisting the conflation of ethnicity with cultural politics applies here as well. Disentangling identity and ethnicity will prove more productive than hopping over to the agenda of identity politics.

I am arguing that ethnicity is more than a "parent concept" created by analysts that is now inadequate and ripe for us to deconstruct. It is a fundamental given to the people who construct ethnic categories, something they treat as essential. The case studies show how these categories come to accrete (and shed) other meanings as social situations develop and unfold. Particular relationships between ethnicity, identity, culture and nationalism become important in each chapter but are most contentious (and therefore most interesting and potentially productive for observers) in discussions about biculturalism in New Zealand. When the Waitangi Tribunal developed its blueprint for a bicultural state, one in which Maori and pakeha values are accorded equal force, rhetoric moved beyond ethnicity and into the realms of identity politicisation. Biculturalists may want an ultimate redistribution of resources in New Zealand (a common ethnic strategy) but, as both a prior condition and a specific aim, they also seek to reconfigure New Zealand's culture by changing individuals' perceptions of themselves as New Zealanders.

Identity demands of this kind rapidly become all encompassing. They require changes in "material rewards, services, patterns of deference, daily routines, traditions, cultural values, habits, and other aspects of the identities of dominant and subordinated groups" (Hunter 1995:330). We may wonder about the feasibility of these projects and just what will have to "be modified to erode the social logics that have reproduced racial, gender, and national hierarchies?" (ibid.). The contrast between urban Papua New Guineans, New Zealand Jews and Maori highlight the situationality of the cultural, identity and nationalistic elaborations of ethnicity.

Jewish interests in the New Zealand state, like those of other diaspora Jewish populations, lie in establishing a connection between being patriotic citizens and remaining Jews. The Jewish position obviously contrasts fundamentally with the view Maori increasingly articulate of an alien colonial entity stimulating their demands for "sovereignty" on a tribal basis. Zionism, the national movement of the Jewish people, does not lead to identity demands in New Zealand. If anything, it suppresses Jewish activism and identity politics by drawing Jews away from the country, making New Zealand a less fertile land for a vibrant Jewish community. Papua New Guineans, in the last days of colonialism seemed worried as the Australians started to depart. They attempted to mobilise in terms of defensive ethnic sentiments to share in the distribution of power in their new decolonised state.

Conclusion

This chapter stressed that people's use of subjective beliefs in common descent to differentiate between themselves and others provides the essence of ethnicity. Flexible and responsive to many factors, these descent idioms supply the bases for ideologies that combine interests with what look (to participants in social action) like primordially affective ties. An understanding of how macro-level sociological factors enter into the construction of these subjective social categories requires a socially situated analysis of cognition and discursive interaction.

In some circumstances ethnic ideologies seem to float freely, constrained only by the individual imagination, accreting cultural, symbolic and other expressions of identity as they get bandied about in various ways. Sometimes these "accretions" in turn attract more ideological flotsam and jetsam, and burgeon into nationalist and/or identity movements, while in others they remain more closely anchored to developments in the economy and expanding state systems. In all cases, ethnicity is something constructed in ways that researchers can witness and attempt to account for.

Incorporating recent developments in cognitive psychology, with an anthropological approach to social situations and cultural elaborations, the following chapters present three extremely different cases of ethnic and collective identity construction. A final section of the monograph uses the similarities and differences between the cases to advance an integrated universalistic statement about how ethnic constructions and their elaborations become accomplished in social situations.

3

Ethnic Formation in Urban Papua New Guinea

> There is nowhere to compare with the multilingual diversity of New Guinea – so many languages crammed into an area of only 300,000 square miles... (Crystal 1987)

When they move from their tribal villages to towns, Papua New Guineans experience one of modernity's greatest social and cultural transformations. Urbanisation exposes rural migrants throughout the developing world to new realities, ideas, behaviours and forms of social organisation. They must adjust; find jobs, money and housing; and interact with strangers. But urbanisation is not simply a force that acts upon people externally. Papua New Guineans act back in a creative sense and change the formerly alien administrative centres of Australian colonialism into something uniquely their own (Levine and Levine 1979).

The construction of new ethnic categories and identities constitutes the most fascinating and dynamic development in the creation of Papua New Guinean urban culture. During fieldwork in Port Moresby, Mount Hagen and Rabaul, between 1972 and 1975, I witnessed and recorded a series of events and processes that arguably underlie the emergence of ethnic categories everywhere. This chapter deals with these events and processes contextually, building an analytical account of the fundamentals of ethnic formation from ethnographic descriptions of emerging ethnicity in urban Papua New Guinea.

At the beginning of the fieldwork, 9.5% of the country's population (231,000) people, lived in the towns. The extraordinary migration rate, then 16.4% per annum, meant that a third to a half of the migrants (and up to 90% in Bougainvillean towns) arrived after 1966. Rural identities and concerns became incorporated into all aspects of urban life and greatly influenced ethnicity. Papua New Guineans did not, however, simply import or re-form rural groups in urban areas. The nature of each town, its own regional setting in the emerging nation, distance from the home area of migrants, etc., encouraged a greater or lesser degree of amalgamation of social categories of migrants from different areas.

I found that a hierarchical set of labels, encompassing everything from small, village-derived kinship units to wide regional categorisations, provided a cultural mechanism for each town's inhabitants to identify the urban population's social types. The major aim for this chapter is to show how urban Papua New Guineans discursively turned these identifications into new ethnic identities by reinterpreting rural social and cultural idioms in the new contexts provided by the structural realities of urban life. Insisting that cognition and discourse play crucial roles in creating urban Papua New Guinean social formations does not require acceptance of the postmodernist doctrine that talk itself constitutes the social world[6]. Rather, people define ethnic identities and alignments in discussions that present us with contexts in which we may observe how cognitive and discursive practices engage a wider world – a world initially created by the colonisation of the island of New Guinea.

The first part of this chapter gives a brief overview of the colonial encounter in Papua New Guinea. The structures (conceptual, administrative and physical) put in place by outsiders provided the settings for the social processes of urbanisation. Social action, cognition and discourse within various urban settings produced ethnicity. To describe how ethnicity works the chapter contains very specific, in situ, examples of the social networks, interactions and dialogue of individuals and small groups. It concludes with a summary of the essential aspects of ethnogenesis derived from this account of structure and agency.

The Colonial Origins of Urban Centres[7]

Numerous waves of prehistoric migrants peopled New Guinea's fragmented landscape, settling, dispersing and developing a great diversity of small autonomous sociocultural groups. At the time I did my fieldwork, the modern state of Papua New Guinea, situated on the 700,000 square miles of the eastern half of the island, had approximately three million inhabitants. Nearly all its citizens could trace their origins from among 12,000 previously independent

---

[6] I am at pains to avoid the naive idea that discourse alone produces identities because that exaggerated form of relativism gives a blatantly incomplete view of the nature of social reality (Levine 1991).

[7] See Levine and Levine 1979 for a fuller discussion of urbanisation in Papua New Guinea.

tribal village communities. Anthropologists have documented an extraordinary degree of cultural variation in a huge literature on "traditional" Papua New Guinean societies.

A substantial similarity in social organisation co-exists along with these cultural differences. Rural Papua New Guineans subsist on the produce of small gardens supplemented by pig husbandry, as well as fishing in coastal areas. Virtually all pre-contact groups organised themselves along kinship lines and all group members had access to land and other basic resources. Although some men attained considerable influence in local areas, very few groups had hereditary status-hierarchies. "Big-men" typically exercised authority through their personal qualities and by bringing prestige and material benefits to their followers. Success in warfare, frequent in pre-contact times, and increasing again as independence approached, provided an important avenue for establishing personal prestige.

A milestone in bringing the people of these culturally diverse, but uniformly small-scale, societies into the modern world system occurred in 1884 when Britain declared a Protectorate in southeast New Guinea. The Germans began claiming the northeast within a few days of the British proclamation.

The Colonial Office soon transferred Britain's claim to Australia. The Australians, anxious about a possible alien presence in the north, declared British New Guinea an Australian Territory in 1901 and later re-named it Papua (Biksup et al. 1968). Australian soldiers captured German New Guinea in World War I and administered that territory separately from Papua, under a League of Nations mandate, until the second World War.

Neither territory attracted much foreign settlement or development. Although miners opened significant areas, no great mineral strikes eventuated. Expatriates, never more than 1.5% of the total population, established no industrial infrastructure. They came mainly as administrators and imported all the industrial goods they required. Coconut and rubber plantations accounted for most of the colonies' exports. Because colonial administrations alienated very little land Papua New Guineans escaped many of the destabilising effects that settler colonialism brought to neighbouring Australia. Although some specific groups lost considerable land to plantations or administrative infrastructure, colonialism for most Papua New Guineans meant little more than lining up for the occasional census and digging pit latrines.

Although both Papua and New Guinea remained backwaters of imperialism, colonial administrative boundaries had interesting ramifications for ethnicity.

The heterogeneity of tribal societies, their small size and relative isolation, left little scope for traditional social group identifiers or cultural symbols to take on meaning in social interactions between people from different home areas. Papua New Guineans use their own group names in interactions with people from places they know intimately, but as they become participants in the new colonial and post-colonial society they employ the names of colonial (now national) divisions – provinces, districts, sub-districts and council areas – to designate both themselves and others in inter-ethnic encounters.

This situation recalls a statement Ardener (1989:66) made about Bantu classifications in Africa. Changing the place, and paraphrasing, we have a situation where some part of the question of the particular scale of Papua New Guinean ethnicities lies in the criteria of classification determined in armchairs in Australia. One may wonder whether names of districts and subdistricts form merely "hollow categories", e.g. "situations in which everyone can point to a Kole, but no one calls himself Kole" (1989:69).

Chapman characterises identifications like this as "balloons, puffed up with the hot air of academic discourse and given substance in the modern world of nationalisms and anti-nationalisms." Other students of Ardener also emphasise how ethnic categories "tend to be both defined and filled through the work of external agencies... in order to define (by opposition) state-level national identities" (Banks 1996:137-142).

I develop a different view from my study of urban Papua New Guinea, where the "hollow categories" and "taxonomic spaces" (Ardener op. cit.) provided by colonial bureaucrats were filled in by local people in real-life situations – situations where random events, cognition and discourse occurred in particular infrastructural contexts.

Schools, plantations and, of course, towns became places where people from a wide diversity of villages congregated. The towns grew up from regional administrative centres as they accreted facilities such as hospitals and schools, and attracted trade and migrants. They remained overwhelmingly centres of distribution, administration and services, devoid of manufacturing outside Panguna (the former mining centre in Bougainville). Expatriates monopolised skilled positions until the 1970s. Locals did menial work as labourers and domestic servants.

A rigid segregation of living space prevailed in urban Papua New Guinea right up to independence. Australians stayed in "high covenant" suburbs composed of Queensland-style houses, some with small servants' quarters. Labourers on contract lived in barracks; and, as a group of "educated natives" developed, companies and the government built "low covenant" housing (small fibro-cement dwellings) for them. People undergoing advanced training or education received places in institutional dormitories. But when urban migration increased dramatically from the mid-1960s, planned suburbs could not accommodate the many uncontracted people looking for work and unable to pay rent. Migrants increasingly built their own homes, often in clusters with relatives, on bare land with no amenities.

The urban landscape, itself, at that time provided a very clear picture of social divisions within the towns. These divisions extended past the obvious expatriate-indigene divide to separate Papua New Guineans from different regions, especially as the pace of modernisation quickened prior to independence. Squatter settlements tended to house recent, unskilled and unemployed migrants from newly contacted areas like the highlands. Skilled Papua New Guineans usually came from places explored in early colonial times, such as the coast or New Guinea Islands, and lived in planned housing. This general congruence between area of origin and place in the emerging socioeconomic hierarchy gave the system of regional social designations an element of socioeconomic rank that became stereotyped. Highlanders gained a reputation as violent and primitive compared to educated, civil, coastal (Papuan and New Guinea Islander) office workers.

Towns in the Context of Their Hinterlands

Although all urban areas in Papua New Guinea developed in much the same way, each existed in a particular regional milieu. Except for the capital, Port Moresby, a significant proportion of every town's population came from its immediate hinterland. Migrants from these near-by areas brought local group identities, conflicts and alliances along with them, so the ambience of a particular town reflected the encounter of a local population with colonialism. The various experiences of my informants, and the wider incidents discussed below, took place in three different urban centres: Port Moresby, Mount Hagen and Rabaul.

Port Moresby, the centre of colonial administration and now the national capital, contained about 75,000 people (26% of Papua New Guinea's urban population) in the mid-1970s. The unique physical geography of the Port Moresby area struck even the most casual visitor. The city seemed like an alien growth, placed in the driest and most barren part of the country, with no substantial road links to the outside world[8]. Hardly connected to its

---

[8] Since that time new roads were built to link Port Moresby to the highlands.

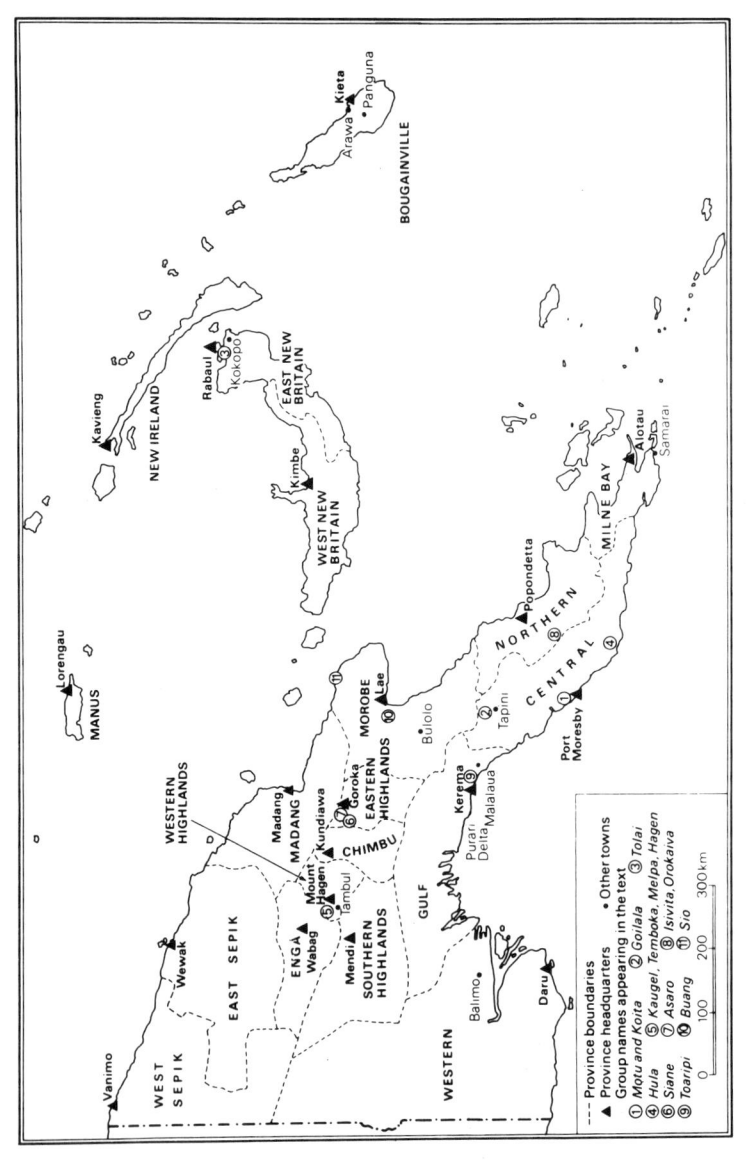

Papua New Guinea

hinterland, the capital imported most of its food from Queensland, including fruits and vegetables that grew well in other parts of the country.

The 7,000 members of the Motu and Koita groups indigenous to the Moresby region seemed swallowed up by the city. Local villagers had given up subsistence agriculture for wage labour long ago (Belshaw 1957) and their settlements looked little different from those of urban migrants. In fact, Motu and Koita groups lost control of much land formerly used for gardening either through alienation by the administration or through settlement by migrants from other parts of the country. Thus Port Moresby, too large for local groups to claim as their own, developed into a cosmopolitan Papuan centre – its inhabitants ever anxious about the increasing influx of migrants from New Guinea.

The experience of the head of a Koita land-owning group illustrates the predicament of the people local to the nation's capital. He lamented that he had allowed a man from outside Port Moresby to build a home on a piece of ground subject to dispute between his own group and some Motuan villagers. He felt that the presence of some allies from outside would keep his claim to the area strong. But the acquaintance, ostensibly looking after the Koita man's interests, proved a magnet for his own migrating relatives who covered the land with their houses. My informant felt powerless to act against the migrants and feared that he had lost control of the land.

The situation of autochthonous groups vis-à-vis the urban population of Mount Hagen seemed almost the reverse of that pertaining in Port Moresby. The problems the Koita man had with outsiders on his land could not happen to a Melpa land holder in Mount Hagen. The 10,000 residents of this highlands town were outnumbered ten to one by the people living in the surrounding villages. Mindful of the active "tribal" warfare occurring all around them, the townspeople of Mount Hagen could not help but feel besieged at times. Everyone knew the identity of local groups and where clan territory began. When tramping in the hills overlooking Mount Hagen, men cautioned me to stick scrupulously to the roads and have nothing to do with women, children or livestock. All migrants building their own houses settled on vacant government-owned land. Melpa clansmen seemed to consider the entire town to be their own, that it existed purely on sufferance, and occasionally they even threatened to burn it down.

Rabaul, like Mount Hagen, served a large indigenous population very sensitive to land alienation. The Tolai experience of colonisation and contact occurred well before the opening of the highlands. The earlier German and Australian colonists on New Britain's Gazelle Peninsula pursued more imperialistic policies than did later administrations. They took so much land for plantations and town projects that Tolai representatives complained to the League of Nations in the 1930s (Epstein 1969). In the 1960s Tolai protesters occupied an expatriate plantation and tried to evict workers from other parts of the country. They continued to object strenuously, and sometimes violently, to outsiders taking up jobs in their area.

For all the disadvantages of a long history of colonialism, the Tolai drew some benefits from their relatively intimate association with the modern world system. Many elite Papua New Guineans came from the Gazelle Peninsula and the area itself developed into a strong centre of indigenous enterprise. The Tolai resistance to colonial government and "foreign natives", and their desire for early independence, helped unite them into a potent political force.

Hageners, on the other hand, lacked confidence that they would benefit from the departure of Europeans. Despite the fact that government and plantation interests alienated more land around Mount Hagen than any other area of the highlands, people wanted more development. Notices, written by children at the request of their fathers, regularly appeared on the noticeboard of the Mount Hagen Post Office asking expatriates to establish plantations or trade stores in rural areas so Hageners could learn the ways of business.

Worried that the Australians would abandon them to domination by the coastals, tribal leaders accepted and even demanded the paternalism that characterised the colonisation of the highlands. While Tolai formed political associations, successfully contested elections and attacked outsiders, even assassinating an Australian official, local government councillors in the Mount Hagen area called their District Commissioner "God belong mipela". He often reminded people in church that God did in fact grant him his authority over the local population (Colebatch et al. 1971:219). Major conflict in the Mount Hagen area involved lower-level identities. The violence that so frequently pitted clan against clan made it difficult for the Melpa of Mount Hagen to form unified groups like the Tolai of Rabaul or Papuans of Port Moresby, even though they did oppose outsiders on occasion.

Building and Defining Social Networks in Urban Areas

When writing about urbanisation in Papua New Guinea in the 1970s Levine and Levine (1979) noted that as urban experiences changed the lives of the migrant tribesmen they, in turn, created new kinds of Melanesian places in the former colonial centres. Part of the process of social and cultural transformation involved the macro-level structural factors, classifications and conditions discussed above. However, structural factors, despite having real impacts do not in themselves create ethnic identity. Rather, they present people with issues, problems, resources, categories and understandings about the nature of things, that they use to construct notions of identity.

This does not mean that urban Papua New Guineans set out to construct ethnic identities and groups. They had rather more mundane and immediate aims. They needed housing, sources of income and companionship, and they built personal networks of social relations to help them adjust to urban life. It is when they looked back and defined their associations that urban Papua New Guineans began to talk about something we could call ethnicity. Perhaps the best way to appreciate how this happened is to consider the social adjustments and relationships that specific migrants made to life in Port Moresby and Mount Hagen.

The four informants with whom I interacted most frequently came from the highlands and lived in Port Moresby or Mount Hagen for considerable periods of time. Two, Anton and Tobeas, moved back and forth between the town and their home villages with shifting fortunes at work. The third, Matthew, received specialised training in Australia and obtained a good government post. The fourth, James, worked as a community officer after serving in the Pacific Islands Regiment. I got to know these men well enough to join them on social occasions and meet their friends in town. Three figure as participants in some of the wider examples of social action discussed later in this chapter.

Kepaka Clan Brothers from Tambul

Anton, a member of the Kepaka clan grew up in Tambul, in the Western Highlands. The second son of a prominent big-man, his elder brother received most of the benefits of his father's estate. Anton attended the local Catholic mission private primary school and left for Mount Hagen, 30 miles away, two months after graduation.

He found a job with Trans-Australia Airlines that lasted for four months. The position terminated when Anton overstayed his leave for his father's funeral. He found a new clerical job a few days later that he lost for mistakenly taking a day off on National Day. His further employment history consists of numerous experiences of this sort, with the job changes accompanied by shifts in residence.

Anton denigrated village life but, despite a desire to live in towns, his low pay meant that he depended upon kin, particularly for housing. Kepaka people supported each other for reasons of kinship, financial need and physical security. Tribal fighting in Tambul left them open to sneak attack by enemies. Anton and his clan brothers also feared Melpa and Enga people in the town and refused to walk around at night except in groups.

For example, one day when his two roommates returned late from work Anton started to make himself a meal. He lit a communal stove and went to his quarters to get some rice and a pot of water. Upon his return he noticed a Melpa man walking away after dousing the fire. He came to see me immediately in a state of agitation. He accused the "Hagen" man of wishing to harm him and said he would not return home until his clan mates got back. They would confront the Hageners and fight them if they meant to intimidate him. It turned out that the individual who put out the fire did not mean anything by it. He just turned off the unattended stove.

The proximity of Tambul to Mount Hagen also provided other reasons for these men to group together. They had interests and property at home and needed to know when anything affected these interests. Their pigs seemed to cause constant problems for the men, breaking into gardens and getting confiscated so they frequently returned home to sort these matters out. Since relatives could reach Mount Hagen so easily, each Kepaka played host to a seemingly never-ending stream of employment seekers and casual visitors. Many visits occasioned communal meals between Kepaka in town.

Anton was part of a large, active social network. Fifty-three of his 71 contacts either came from Tambul clans or married into these clans. Only one was from an unallied group. Anton met 18 other people through his kinsmen or at work. Almost all these newer acquaintances held positions like Anton's or worked in unskilled manual jobs. So, virtually all the skilled people Anton considered friends in Mount Hagen came from Tambul clans (Kepaka or the allied Sepaka). During my second research trip to Mount Hagen Anton lost his job and spent most of his time with kinsmen.

Matthew, a clan brother, moved in with Anton after he finished Form 3. He found a clerical job with the Public Works Department which later transferred him to Port Moresby. From there he went on to further training in Australia, married a girl from home and returned to Public Works in Port Moresby. Despite a considerably better career path than Anton's, Matthew envisaged a place for himself in his village and planned eventually to run a rural business when he retired from government service. He had fewer friends than Anton, 37, but they came from a much wider range of places. Five were Europeans, and seven from non-highland districts of Papua New Guinea. But Matthew also had friends from home. Interestingly, these included four Kukluminti-

Yap people. They were "enemy clansmen" from groups greatly feared by his clan brothers in Mount Hagen.

Matthew said that he purposefully sought enemies out because "we are all Tambuls and should forget our differences in Moresby". The distance from home freed Tambul people from the minutiae of tribal fighting, reports of casualties, strategy and tactics and the calls from their relatives to return home or watch out for sneak attacks. Tambul clanspeople felt isolated in Port Moresby and appreciated their similarities in a foreign environment. At weekends, they sometimes got together specifically to speak their language. The odd Enga or Melpa former schoolmate might also come along.

Matthew often stayed weekends at a local village with Papuan co-workers, and also spent time with a European couple he met at work who helped him prepare for his stay in Sydney. Most of Matthew's friends from outside the Western Highlands worked with him. He met the others at school or at the Catholic Mission Hostel. All, except for two, had the same promising jobs, qualifications, and level of education Matthew had. His contacts from Tambul, on the other hand, tended (like most highlanders) to have low-skilled manual jobs. They knew each other, but by and large did not know Matthew's friends from work, especially when they had different socioeconomic backgrounds.

Two Other Highlanders in Port Moresby

My key informant in Port Moresby, Tobeas, a man whose kin I came to know well, worked as a domestic in the University of Papua New Guinea's housing estate. He had no formal education and spent the first 16 years of his life in the village of Mondo, in the Asaro-Watabung council area of the Eastern Highlands. He signed on to the Highlands Labour Scheme and worked on a plantation in the New Guinea Islands for two and half years. He used some of the money he earned to buy a ticket to Port Moresby and moved in with relatives in the part of the settlement of Two Mile that forms the focal point for his clansmen in the city.

A fellow clansman who worked for a University professor brought Tobeas along to help in the garden, paying him out of his own wages. A neighbour of the professor hired him and got Tobeas a room in the University barracks. He stayed there for a few years and moved in with a relative in Morata, a settlement adjacent to the University housing area.

Tobeas seemed less urban oriented than Anton. He complained that his people found too much trouble in Port Moresby and that he had to spend money for things like food and housing that would have cost him nothing at home. Like many other urban Papua New Guineans, his attitude towards urban life seemed characterised by ambivalence. He liked the excitement and cosmopolitan aspects of town but also felt pressure to return home. His father often sent messages to him to give up his youthful infatuation with the bright lights and return to his village to advance himself and help his kin. The vast majority of his urban friends, 22 out of 27, belonged to his kinship group. He met the five others, from the New Guinea coast and highlands, when he lived at the University barracks. Like him, they had little schooling and worked as domestics or grass cutters when employed.

James, worked as a community development officer. He came from Kokup in the Nebilyer Valley outside of Mount Hagen and served with the Pacific Islands Regiment for four years after finishing primary school. His further training in the army allowed him access to clerical positions and he also completed a training programme with the Port Moresby Community Development Group. He expected to go back to Mount Hagen to work. His wife trained as a librarian and would run the Mount Hagen public library.

To a greater extent than the other three men mentioned above, James made an active effort to promote unity among the various rival groups in town and in his home area. He even shared a low-covenant house in the suburb of Tokarara with a fellow Community Development Group trainee from an enemy group. The government authorities recognised James' efforts to dampen enmity between groups in Port Moresby and chose him to join an official party going to the Western Highlands to promote negotiations to end tribal fighting in the Nebilyer valley.

James belonged to an informal group of elite people from Nebilyer who met regularly in Port Moresby for social reasons, and to discuss political issues and problems at home. Group members treated James as a person of importance. They admired him for his initiative, competence and vision in promoting peace. We first met at Rabaikini, the wider settlement area that includes Two Mile where Tobeas' kin live. Community development officers wanted to help the residents of the settlement to form a council to promote community spirit among the various ethnically labelled housing sections.

James had many friends from the highlands, all but two from Mount Hagen. He had 11 friends from elsewhere, overseas and various part of Papua New Guinea. Except for a Papuan neighbour, all individuals from outside Mount Hagen had jobs of similar standing to James. The unskilled workers he associated with came from "home".

The Personal Friendship Networks

Although the majority of people in all four of these friendship networks came from one specific area, both Matthew and James, relatively mobile in the urban system, had more ethnically heterogeneous sets of friends than did Tobeas and Anton. When the skilled men associated with unskilled people, they tended to come from the same home area. Conversely, Anton's friends with better positions than his in Mount Hagen town came from his home area of Tambul. Tobeas, who had no formal education, seemed more encapsulated socioeconomically than the other men.

These four networks (along with a much wider body of data described in Levine 1976, and Levine and Levine 1979) provided evidence that urban migrants remained involved with their kin and made friendly contacts with outsiders through work. Common work experiences led to social relationships across ethnic boundaries and ethnic commonality cut across differences in economic status. People tended not to mix their work and home-based friendships. Clusters of dense ties, where people who knew a person also knew each other, involved kin and other individuals from the home area. People were able to mobilise the dense area of their social networks more readily than the more individualistic ties made at work. Work-based friendships could end suddenly when a person was transferred or fired. Ties with people from home tended to endure.

The Wantok System and Ethnic Stereotypes

When speaking about individuals and their sets of friends, ethnicity seems rather peripheral. As mentioned previously, urban Papua New Guineans did not set out to create ethnic groups. They interacted with each other for much more down-to-earth reasons. However, in trying to say something general about the networks, the expression "ethnic boundary" is difficult to avoid.

It is important to emphasise that my use of the term "ethnic" here, an analyst's generalisation, is in fact very similar to my informants' way of talking about their own cliques. Urban Papua New Guineans developed a cultural system that they used to distinguish certain relationships from others, making an apparently ethnic distinction. They tended to call their friends "wantok", a Neo-Melanesian (New Guinea pidgin) term that means "one who speaks the same language, a compatriot" (Mihalic 1971:202). Urban migrants distinguished "real wantok", people who came from the same area and formed the dense part of one's social network, from others. A person could call work friends "wantok", too, but that involved an extension and dilution of the concept. If we conceive of a person's own place of origin as the centre of his or her social universe, "true" or automatic wantok came from that centre or from places near to it. People from other areas could be drawn in, but unless they were adopted into the group and became the wantok of everyone else, they remain the personal friends of only one particular person.

The process of delimiting the locales that made up a person's place of origin (and thus defined that person's wantok) varied. In general, the further away from their home village people were, the more inclusive their the definition of wantok became. Urban encounters themselves often blurred the distinctions between fellow tribesmen and people from other groups, especially when they both fell into the same general regional category. For example, in a study of Chimbu in Port Moresby Whiteman noted that small groups often showed up together at someone's house. "The hosts might not know all their names or what, if any, blood or affinal relationship they had to them. They only know that they were Chimbu, and that they came to visit them with someone whom they did know" (1973:93). Such aggregations of my own informants' wantok (friends, in-laws and acquaintances from different clans or tribes) had no traditional group name, but – because everyone came from a specific subdistrict or district – they, like the Chimbu, labelled themselves using these regional terms.

These clusters of renamed kin and affines left imprints on the urban environment more substantial than ethereal cliques of visiting friends. Rabiakini, where I met and spent time with Tobeas, consisted of clusters of houses built by urban migrants living there. Standing on a hill looking over the settlement my informants pointed to the Goroka people over there, the Kerema there, the Daru there, and so forth. A close analysis of the settlement clusters showed that the residents built their houses in the same way they built social networks. People came to the settlement and constructed their homes next to kin and affines already present. The clumps of houses were treated as ethnic settlements. When outsiders said "Gorokans" lived in a particular part of the settlement, the label stuck and became part of how the residents understood themselves and members of other groups whom they labelled in complementary terms: Kerema, Daru etc. Indeed, James and his colleagues had no problems convincing the residents of Rabiakini to organise their settlement committee along such lines.

This use of regional labels to characterise aggregations of urban wantok along ethnic lines appears at first glance to constitute little more than a categorising device for mapping urban heterogeneity. Anthropologists (e.g. Mitchell 1956, Epstein 1958) have discussed similar phenomena before with respect to towns in Africa's Copperbelt. Abner Cohen (1969) criticised them vociferously. He maintained that treating ethnicity as a cognitive map of this kind hardly explains anything. By itself, an elaboration of ethnic categories merely establishes their existence. Anthropologists need to explain more than that. Mitchell countered that, when he examined the housing choices of miners in Central Africa, he found that (like the inhabitants of Rabiakini) the miners' categories matched patterns "on the ground". This suggested to him that cognitive maps and housing patterns "have arisen from a common ethnic component of social life which was a reality in the daily lives of the people of Zambia" (1974:29). Although cognition is central to ethnicity, my fieldwork in urban Papua New Guinea leads to the conclusion that the categories here operated differently. The main point developed below is that ethnic categorisation was not simply inherent in social life. Rather it emerged when people reflected upon the mundane activities of themselves and others and translated these activities from merely random encounters to examples of behaviour generated by members' sociocultural groups named in accordance with the prevailing regional labels.

Urban Papua New Guineans seemed to make a conceptual shift when they talked of kin and affines as sets of wantok. They had no political or identity-group agendas or goals prompting them to describe people in this way. The instrumentality of the wantok system operated on the aforementioned personal level of wanting security in a new, potentially threatening environment. Informants' desires for help with housing, finding jobs, paying for food, and companionship, led them to seek out other individuals from "home". However, the existence of wider regional categories furnished a link between the idiosyncratic, discrete networks of individuals and more general, shared, urban cultural understandings about ethnic identification. By providing a label and boundaries for wantok identities, the cognitive map (based literally on an administrative map) channeled the development of wider group identities. These wider group identities were central to the more instrumental kind of political ethnicity of interest to critics, like Abner Cohen, who disparage focusing on categorical aspects of ethnicity.

The wider categorical labels did not denote a simple set of neutral place names. The labels came loaded with content because ethnic stereotypes attached to regional names and they constitute measurable boundaries of social interaction. The differentiation between Papuan and New Guinean, for example, did more than just distinguish between residents of two formerly separate territories. Papua's colonial administration did less to develop their colony than did New Guinea's and politicians from the two regions of the new state vied for resources as independence approached. Resentment over the relative underdevelopment of their area led Papuan members of the House of Assembly to articulate a series of separatist arguments that appealed to Papuan townspeople, alarmed at the influx of New Guineans to Port Moresby. They blamed these migrants for increasing violence in the town. New Guineans, for their part, characterised Papuans as lazy and reacted angrily to calls for their expulsion from Port Moresby.

The New Guineans most feared by Papuans came from the highlands, an ever-increasing source of urban migrants who worried people in other parts of the country too. Political figures in Madang, Rabaul and Bougainville also called for the removal of unemployed highlanders from their towns. Hardly contacted until the 1950s, people from highland areas seemed primitive to coastal Papua New Guineans. News of tribal fighting there frequently made headlines in the local media. These reports, and a number of riots in various centres that featured highlanders as prominent participants, strengthened the view that these people were violent primitives. "Coastals" living in highlands towns often feared for their safety. In Goroka, relatives of a child run over and killed by a car driven by a Bougainvillean beat the driver and passenger to death. These killings caused an outpouring of demonstrations, grief and anger. The political ramifications and calls for Bougainville (now involved in a war of secession) to separate from Papua New Guinea prompted the Chief Minister Michael Somare to travel to Bougainville in an effort to reassure people there that the government would act to protect them.

For their part highlanders had a rather ambivalent attitude to coastals. As members of a developing urban underclass, people from the highlands perceived similarities amongst themselves that they would have ignored at home (e.g. they tended towards short stature, cultivated sweet potato and raised pigs) but which became especially salient when they migrated to coastal towns. Also, closer to home, the fact that coastal people held the majority of well-paid and responsible urban positions did not escape the notice of even isolated villagers who came to town only on rare occasions. My informants felt that educated people deserved good jobs, but they wanted to see more opportunities for training available in their areas. They worried that with independence coming they might never advance because coastals monopolised positions of power and influence in the modern sector.

Many peri-urban people decided to set up cash crop and transport businesses to find wealth. Although this lessened their conflict with outsiders for urban jobs, rural tribesmen felt highland towns were on their land and they did not take kindly to outsiders interfering with clan property. Men fiercely protected local women, children, pigs, etc. and promptly demanded compensation for damages.

Position in the new state, then, provided the main theme of social stereotypes in Papua New Guinea. We have seen how the forces of development that distributed people from different regions into different sectors of the urban workforce fundamentally affected whom my four informants came into contact with on an everyday basis. If the urban networks of unskilled people – especially highlanders – generally lacked interethnic ties, whole stereotyped categories of urban dwellers were probably encapsulated socially as well as economically.

In order to test this hypothesis I carried out large-scale random-sample surveys of interethnic interaction in Port Moresby and Mount Hagen. Statistical analysis of the survey data (Levine 1976, 1991a) clearly showed that amount of formal education, level of employment, modernity of area of origin and time spent in town correlated positively with interethnic interaction. A path analysis of the various factors demonstrated that employment had the largest effect, roughly equal to the other variables combined. Origin and education influenced interaction indirectly: they worked through employment and residence. Well-educated, skilled, highlanders in heterogeneous neighbourhoods had interaction patterns like their coastal neighbours. The amount of time a person lived in a town had a small positive independent influence on interaction about one quarter as strong as the influence of employment.

Analysing the survey patterns in broader regional terms showed that people who interacted with acquaintances from outside their immediate area chose from within their own general region first. Papuans and New Guinea Islanders chose highlanders least often and people from New Guinea (the highlands, islands and New Guinea coast) chose Papuans next to last or last. These results fit well with what we know of the wantok system and indicate that relatively less social interaction took place across the broad stereotyped oppositions than within them.

The forces of modernity sorted people out in the towns and affected how individual Papua New Guineans categorised, stereotyped and interacted with one another. But these same forces also operated on a macro-level to structure particular urban environments in ways that greatly influenced ethnic constructions. Papua New Guineans created urban ethnicity within the contours of these macro-level and micro-level social conditions when they acted, thought and talked about each other in urban encounters. We can best appreciate how this happens by considering some concrete examples of this talk and action.

Kofena

The people who feature in the incidents related below came from Tobeas' part of the Asaro-Watabung area of the Eastern Highlands. Like other Papua New Guineans they belonged to a complex set of primary groups. The names of these groups appear here (with a summary diagram below) because they are relevant to the events that I will recount. The informants, Kofena from a primary division of the Kofena-Ka'nasa tribe described by Newman (1965:33), spoke a dialect of upper Asaro. The individual Kofena mentioned here belonged to two primary divisions of that group, Kombiangwe and Ongobayufa, which they further divided into three and four "men's house groups" respectively (see the diagram below). They said that their ancestors fled from their home area Lidima after a tribal war that took place around 1910. They settled in Mondo with the Lapopa, a group of Siane speakers who often fought against their Kapopa neighbours. Some Kofena returned to Lidima after the establishment of the colonial administration.

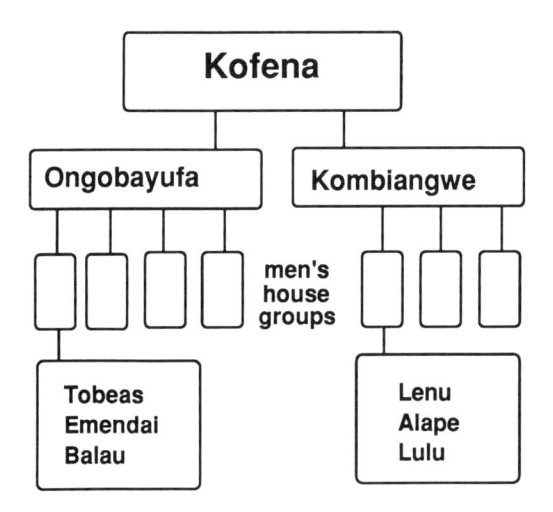

```
                    Kofena
                   /      \
           Ongobayufa    Kombiangwe
           / | | \        / | \
          [ ][][][]      [ ][ ][ ]   men's
                                     house
                                     groups
           Tobeas         Lenu
           Emendai        Alape
           Balau          Lulu
```

Members of all these groups, as well as a male Fikosa affine and several women of the groups that these men married with, lived in Two Mile settlement in Port Moresby. A Kapopa man named Barakwe first settled there. Lapopa and Kofena entered the settlement through affinal connections to him. Some Kofena moved on to a nearby company barracks, as well as the university workers quarters near their Fikosa affines, and to Morata resettlement area. The men, when employed, worked as domestics, gardeners and labourers.

Five Kofena men besides Tobeas became key informants during two years of research in Port Moresby. Tobeas, Emendai and Balau belonged to the same Ongobayufa men's house group, and Lenu, Alape and Lulu were similarly related in a Kombiangwe subgroup.

My first impression of these "Gorokas" (as I came to know them) at Two Mile was that they seemed very cohesive and cooperative. The following incidents show that this solidarity was more apparent at certain times than others. On many occasions traditional subgroup identities interacted with wider ones, sometimes taking precedence over them and at other times becoming submerged. This became most apparent to me when Lulu, a member of the aforementioned Kombiangwe men's house group, died.

Lulu's death

Lulu, aged 35, died in Port Moresby's main hospital after a short illness. People felt obligated to send his body back for burial on home ground. To bury him on foreign land would insult Lulu's kinsmen and demonstrate the poverty and indifference of the townsfolk. The Goroka people in Port Moresby wished to protect their interests and standing in their home communities, and set about raising money to honourably dispatch their obligation.

In addition to airfare for the body, Lulu's wife and three children needed tickets home. A coffin, hospital and morgue charges, and transport to the airport, added to the bill. Alape decided to accompany the family and present Lulu's kin back in the village with money for a mortuary feast. He would also take part in the divination to find out the cause of the death and the parties responsible.

When a relatively young man dies suddenly, kin assume enemies somehow poisoned the deceased. Eastern highlanders commonly marry women from enemy groups and Lulu's kin suspected his wife's brothers gave him a slow-acting poison when he visited them the year before. Lulu's father killed many members of the in-laws' group in past tribal wars, so they might have wanted revenge. Using this logic one could suspect anyone from an enemy group of murder, people living in town or at home. My informants felt that circumstances pointed to the perpetrator living in the village region. The time between the visit and death fit the slow-acting poison scenario and no other deaths like this had ever happened in Port Moresby. Lulu had lived in the town for a few years and only died after going back to visit his wife's place.

It seemed to me that the rural theory appealed to Lulu's kin in Port Moresby because of the mix of people from enemy groups in Two Mile. Fears of poisoning already prevented residents from eating with enemies. Parents warned children not to accept food from anyone other than close kin. Deaths needed to be paid back, but the social order of the settlement could not sustain vendettas.

Late in the week a formal death payment took place at Two Mile. The various participants grouped together on both traditional and ad hoc bases. The two Kofena subgroups, a Lapopa group, and a combination of other Lapopa and Kapopa, formed "lines". Each line pooled its money and a representative noted how much each person gave. Women prepared food and men sat on the side on a kind of dais. Every once in a while the man doing the accounting for Lulu's group would ask the others for their lists of contributors, but the others would refuse until they had committed everything to memory.

When the payments commenced, the spokesman for Lulu's group made a speech and the Kofena "lines" pooled their money. Then representatives of the other "lines" made speeches, cried and gave their money. A prominent old warrior, an enemy who still made my friends uncomfortable despite his advanced age, made a speech. Touching scenes of enemies putting aside their differences and stressing the ties that bound them were played out repeatedly. Each "line" clapped hands after presenting their money to signify that the cash represented a free gift, with no expectations of future return. This freeness represented an expression of the grief of those giving money. When the kinship groups had finished, various affines and maternal relations from the Asaro-Watabung area, who did not fit into the aforementioned groups, came one at a time, as did four former co-workers, who also made speeches and contributions.

The Kofena asked me to look at the counting and recounting of the money and to publicly verify the sum, A$609, and the trustworthy way the counting had been done. A man said to me "Tell them it's $609". I said to the assembly "It's $609." He then said to them "The white man says it's $609". Watching the money proved very interesting. When counted each smaller sum remained in a separate bundle corresponding to the groups that contributed. Repeated over and over (a mnemonic device, since no one wrote anything down except me) the counted bills stayed in piles not only equivalent in amount to that which each small group gave, but with the same bills in original order in each bundle. An audible sigh of reluctance greeted the physical pooling of the money. Each group's representative seemed upset as his "line's" contribution got merged into the whole, thus ending the need for "traditional" groupings in this context.

Over the following days Kofena people collected more money at Morata resettlement area, and also decided to send Lulu's father home with the body. They wanted to give $800 of the $1013 dollars finally raised to kinsmen at home. Despite the amity at the Two Mile collection some men later expressed bitter feelings and expected someone to kill members of Lulu's wife's group. But this would happen at home since "it's a village affair." I called the hospital just prior to the departure of the bereaved for Goroka. A doctor said that septicemia, the presence of a large amount of bacteria in the blood, caused the death. When I informed my Kofena friend, he replied that everyone knew that some sort of poison entered Lulu's blood and that Alape, on his return, would bring back precise news about it and how it got there.

Alape arrived back in Port Moresby about one week later. He informed me about the divination when I agreed not to tell the younger men the results for six months. We went behind a rock, out of sight and hearing of other people. Alape said that the divination procedure consisted of placing the body on a platform which four men carry. The deceased holds a piece of bamboo in his hand and the diviner asks questions about who killed him. The body gives a positive response by causing the bamboo to shake. If the body makes no response to a particular name the bamboo gets replaced before trying another name. "I asked (Lulu) 'The University?' Nothing! 'Boroko?' Nothing! 'Two Mile?' Nothing! 'Goroka?' Nothing! 'Watabung?' He shook!" As Alape got more and more specific the body revealed that the Onokifua, a group his sister had married into, poisoned Lulu because his father had killed many of them in the past.

The divination confirmed the rural origin of the act. "We know the group but not the individual man. This thing is finished." The elders felt that young Kofena might take revenge anyway, hence the secrecy. Since Bangen and one of his kinsmen were the only people from the Kapopa group responsible who lived in Port Moresby, and they resided only a few feet from a large concentration of Lulu's "brothers" in Two Mile, they needed protection. One man, a true brother of Lulu serving time in a prison outside the capital, did not even know Lulu died because his kinsmen feared his response.

However, the young men already knew the "secret". A grass cutter at the university received a letter identifying the group responsible before Alape had returned. Bangen also must have known, but by treating the outcome of the divination in the way they did, this amalgamation of rural enemies could continue to function as a community in the city.

Balau's Beating

A young child came by my home looking for Tobeas. He called to him from outside the house. Going to tell the boy that Tobeas was out, I noticed Balau, his face swathed in bandages. He wanted to tell Tobeas that four men had beaten him. When asked what led to the beating, Balau said Lenu resented that the $100 he had given to Tobeas came to nothing. Lenu advanced Tobeas $50 for brideprice over a year previously, but he remained unmarried. The other $50 went missing in a robbery. The beating occurred when a group of men from Two Mile went to a tavern. Balau bought a large bottle of beer which they finished. Lenu put the bottle in his bag to cash in later with others he collected. Because riots between Papuans and New Guineans in Port Moresby had occurred just a few days prior to this, Balau worried that the police might stop them on the way home and arrest these highlanders for carrying an offensive weapon. He asked for the bottle back so he could discard it on the roadside. Lenu became angry at being refused the bottle, fought Balau, and the others joined in. Balau wanted his fellow Ongobayufa to know what happened.

When Emendai and Tobeas heard about this they went to Morata to consult other kin and agreed that resentment about the money must have caused the attack. Although Balau had no serious wounds, the Ongobayufa felt angry. Tobeas planned to pay Lenu the $100 and let this sever the ties between their lines in Port Moresby, even though two Ongobayufa men had joined Lenu and Wauwe in hitting Balau. Emendai, more cool headed than Tobeas, led a delegation of men to Two Mile later in the day to claim $20 in compensation. By the time everyone collected together Tobeas had cooled down, too, and wanted to hear the other side of the story: surely Lenu knew that he could count on Tobeas' help when his children came to marry and would want to maintain the chain of reciprocity. Also, Balau often threw money away on beer, buying drinks for strangers and then asking his kin for money for food. Maybe drunkenness clouded his memory.

Our group left for Two Mile in a conciliatory mood. A little compensation would smooth things over. We arrived to scenes of obvious hostility. Wauwe shouted out in English, obviously for my benefit, "Bottles are very important. You make fun of it but they bring in money. Who can feed us unemployed? You can't make fun of collecting bottles." Then he said, in pidgin, that he heard this group wanted to fight and that his group would oblige. Emendai, calmly chewing betel nut said, "We are brothers, why are you making this rubbish talk about fighting?" Tobeas added, "I don't want to fight you, I call your father 'father' and he was always good to me when I was a child." I confirmed the peaceful intentions of the group and after some further exchange Wauwe went to get Lenu.

Lenu spoke in Kofena[9] with remarkable poise. He went directly to the centre of all those gathered and clearly displayed an offended dignity. Lenu told them Balau did give him a bottle of beer and warned them about getting arrested for carrying an offensive weapon when he put the empty bottle in his net bag. When a police car passed Balau said, "Now you've done it, they'll arrest us all." A policeman got out of the car and made a big show of searching the men and berated Lenu for having the bottle. Passers by often taunt unemployed men who collect empties on the roadside and call them "rubbish men," men of no consequence. Lenu, a big-man at home and important in Two Mile despite not having a job, could not stand this public slight to his dignity. Forced by Balau's foolishness to explain that he took the bottle to cash in he became angry and attacked Balau. The others joined in. They only used their fists and caused no serious injury. Brideprice had nothing to do with this. Didn't Tobeas remember that when his mother died Balau did nothing while he, Lenu, took a major role in the funeral preparations?

This speech quieted everyone, even Balau. Tobeas missed his mother's funeral because she died while he worked on the Highlands Labor Scheme which refused to give him time off. He and Emendai felt Lenu acted not unreasonably considering the provocation. They dropped any claim for compensation and declared that the trouble between the two groups was over. Mombia and Loimu, the two Ongobayufa involved, still deserved castigation but the group could not find them. On the way back we stopped at a labourers' compound to tell the other Ongobayufa not to go to Two Mile. From Wauwe's comments I expected at least 15 angry men to march on the Kombiangwe. However, it turned out that only two men had tried to go, but turned back because they missed a bus.

The next day I accompanied a group of men who set out to find Mombia and Loimu. Mombia had gotten arrested the night after the incident and Loimu still avoided everyone. When found a few days later he denied taking part and everyone became less and less interested in Balau's beating. Tobeas said he felt angry that Balau did not help at his mother's funeral and told him, "If you get drunk and find trouble I can't help you."

---

[9]The commentary was translated to me.

Rural Identity in Urban Places

Lulu's death and Balau's beating show that rural kinship-group identities remained important in towns, but they only continued to have meaning in small-scale social contexts. The urbanisation process sorted unskilled highlanders into informal housing and sporadic, low-paid jobs, where rural social idioms could be useful. However, the Asaro and Siane groups represented at Two Mile, and others like them, lacked material resources and "corporateness" in the city. Although they were surrounded by familiar people from familiar places, urbanisation created new social realities in Port Moresby. Lenu, an important Kombiangwe at home, was just an unemployed highlander, readily harassed by the police. The actions of the people involved in both these incidents demonstrated their acknowledgment that Kofena, Kapopa and Lapopa tribal units remain essentially rural entities and that life in Port Moresby had transmuted them into a new, urban, social formation.

The fact that some small-scale identities became amalgamated in Port Moresby does not mean that this is equally true for all such sets of people in all towns. The capital's distance from Goroka kept rural and urban concerns separate. Most other towns in Papua New Guinea existed in the midst of larger tribal areas, less cut off than Port Moresby from their hinterlands. In Mount Hagen, for example, people found it more difficult to distance themselves from events happening an easy bus ride (or long hike) from the town.

As independence approached, and the Australian administration began to disengage, the country experienced incidents of tribal fighting that recalled pre-contact times. My Mount Hagen informants belonged to groups currently involved in fighting. Whenever incidents occurred, someone from home would warn them against surprise attack by enemies either living in town or sneaking in looking for easy targets. Tambul friends, members of the Kepaka clan and enemies of the Kukluminti, insisted on my driving them home in the evenings and would not walk even a few blocks in the dark. Tambul people in Port Moresby, on the other hand, seemed much less wary of each other. They heard less about fights and felt that rural troubles, although upsetting, did not involve them directly.

"Tribal fighting" in Mount Hagen affected everyone in the town. Even Europeans took notice when warriors marched through the streets. Mount Hagen's expansion caused land alienation that exacerbated border disputes between the peri-urban Ndika and Yamka people.

In February 1974, some Ndika killed an important Yamka man working in a garden inside disputed territory. The entire atmosphere of Mount Hagen changed quickly when the news spread. The usual after-hours activities stopped, and tension grew as large groups of men congregated on the street. Members of the two tribes readied themselves to leave town and help their respective people. Men of other local groups needed to discuss their own positions vis-à-vis the combatants.

A few miles outside Mount Hagen large armed groups congregated. A Yamka named Hakai asked me and my wife to take him to the funeral of the man who was killed. Dressed in traditional garments, his body oiled, and carrying an axe, he crouched under some blankets in the back of our vehicle as we passed through Ndika territory. He said that Ndika and Yamka told their employers that they could not work for a while. Even well-educated men (including some university students home on summer break) prepared to fight. A student of mine said, "They (elders) ask us if we want to be European and let them all die. We have to join in if we want to remain a part of our villages."

In sum, a high degree of rural-urban continuity pertains in Papua New Guinea especially near migrants' areas of origin. At times, kinship group identities and their associated concerns overwhelmed participation in the urban system. But life in towns simultaneously brought all Papua New Guineans into contact with a wider social world. People, especially the well educated, work and interact with others from different parts of the country and overseas. More importantly, the culture of the towns influences all its residents. This urban culture provides definitions of ethnic identities that stimulate new animosities that cut across the oppositions and alliances of rural groups. These higher-level identities sit somewhat uneasily beside the more specific ones illustrated thus far.

Three Examples of Higher Level Identities

An Accident in Mount Hagen

One prominent and persistent high-level opposition in Mount Hagen pitted "Hageners" against people from the Enga[10] area commonly called "Wabag". Enga speakers migrated to Mount Hagen and the nearby agricultural settlement of Kindeng, and constituted 20% of the urban population in 1972. Like other highlanders the Enga took mainly unskilled jobs. My primary informants, members of the Melpa, Kaugel, and Temboka groups mentioned above, made negative statements about "the Wabag".

---

[10] During my fieldwork, but after the main events discussed here, the administration created a new Enga District from the western part of the Western Highlands.

Socioeconomic competition and the political changes leading up to self-government and independence seemed to fuel this animosity. Competition between locals and immigrants for scarce jobs and housing heightened the salience of ethnic boundaries in many places, and could ignite violence when the niches of two groups overlapped. Olzak (1992) notes that modernisation generally encourages a widening of ethnic solidarity because small-scale loyalties erode as people migrate, and more inclusive identities can mobilise larger segments of the population. However, my informants did not stress economic rivalry. In any case, such factors cannot explain the particular form new ethnic identities take. Furthermore, the solidarity of the wider categories remained highly situational given the continued strength of lower-level identities in Mount Hagen. Indeed, the term "Hagener" lumps Ndika, Yamka, Kepaka and Kukluminti together, hardly a promising basis for group mobilisation. Although labels like Hagener and Wabag have none of the supposed sociocultural givens of ethnicity discussed in the literature, they nevertheless accrete meaning and develop a most striking salience.

My informants told me that what annoyed them the most about people from Wabag was that one Wabag had killed four Moke, members of another peri-urban tribe, in an automobile accident. Incidents involving injury or death quickly become matters between groups in Papua New Guinea. Western highlands people had a long history of settling such matters by vengeance and/or exchange. Since everyone knew that the driver of the truck that collided with the Moke vehicle came from somewhere in the Wabag area, people held both the driver and his people, "the Wabag", responsible for the deaths.

No wider Wabag or Hagener corporate groups existed in Mount Hagen town so people could not use customary dispute settlement mechanisms to end tensions. My informants said Government attempts to organise an insurance payment and a contribution from some Wabag people that totalled $2500 would merely postpone Moke retaliation. Although Moke anger towards "Wabag" people is unremarkable, the incident stimulated ethnic formation in a way that merits explanation.

Further investigation of this matter made it apparent that talking about the crash stimulated the articulation of a rhetoric of grievance. Recounting the events served to shape my informants' ethnic consciousness, elaborating, reinforcing, and cementing the meaningfulness of the labels Hagener and Wabag, making them social and cultural identities. The accident became an exemplar of relationships, set in place by the forces of urbanisation and modernisation, between two very general categories of people.

Ethnic Formation in Urban Papua New Guinea

Hageners knew that divisions among Wabag groups paralleled their own. The news contained frequent references to Enga tribal fighting. I said to Anton and Hakai that they stretched things greatly holding such an amorphous category of people responsible for a random event. Surely finer distinctions should be made. Hakai explained:

> "It's this way. We speak the Hagen language all around this area. If you go by truck to Yalibu and come back to Hagen we are all called Hageners. And Wabag people from Baiyer River all the way to Wabag town are called Wabags. They speak one language and we speak Hagen. The Ndika, Moke, Yamka and whatever, from Yalibu to Mount Hagen are simply Hageners and the people who speak the language of the Wabag area are simply Wabag."

Anton, the Kepaka from Tambul whose network I described above, is an in-law of Hakai. He said, "I'm a Tambul so I'm also a Hagener". In fact Tambul lies just inside the southwestern boundary of the Hagen subdistrict but the local population resembles the Enga more closely than the Melpa (Bowers 1968). Did these men conflate administrative boundaries with cultural units? Why did they identify themselves as Hageners? Anton constantly complained about how Hageners intimidated him. He and his clan brothers insisted on rides for the shortest distances at night. Hakai soon armed himself against the Ndika, yet here included them with his clan and the aggrieved Moke as fellow ethnics. I asked Anton if the fact that he could speak Melpa made him a Hagener. Hakai answered for him:

> "It's because Hagen subdistrict administers Tambul. Because he has taken our language and not the language of the Wabag. He is from the border of Hagen and Wabag but he is on our side of it and follows us. In a fight or some other incident the Tambuls fight Wabags too. We think this way. 'You Wabag have killed some of our good men and now you work for money and are around in our area on our land, but you can't just go ahead and kill or chase a man and steal something from the Moke.' All from Hagen said this: 'Let's watch well. Four men have died, our brothers and wantok. We'll watch them and follow troublemakers and take care of them.' During times of trouble the Wabag gather together in one place and the Hagen people gather together in another place. Because the Wabag did not do enough to straighten out the matter of the four deaths, men from all the councils in Hagen... will join and fight the Wabag. They are just Engas, just Wabag, and that's all."

Hakai's comment, that people speak Melpa or Enga because they live in a particular administrative area, provides an illustration of how urban Papua New Guineans map social and cultural distinctions onto administrative boundaries. He clearly felt these divisions could promote cultural homogeneity. The hollow categories of colonial map-makers get filled with stereotypes when incidents like the crash become exemplars of group nature. They then influence further social action, becoming more sedimented and more like identities than mere orienting devices. When Moke attributed blame to "ol Wabag", all Enga-speaking people in Mount Hagen became potential targets for vengeance attacks. This, in turn, strengthened their solidarity vis-à-vis Hageners.

I also interviewed Tamoka, a man from a village near Tambul but on the Wabag side of the boundary. He recognised the existence of administratively derived social categories but did not think of himself as a Wabag just because he lived in that subdistrict. Tamoka thought that the enmity between Hageners and Wabag involved only people from the hearts of the two areas. However, over time continuing incidents increased the salience to him of Wabag identity in Mount Hagen. Bar brawls and a number of more critical confrontations occurred after the original automobile accident. Some Hageners ambushed a policeman from Wabag and severely injured him. A Hagener was attacked subsequently. The most serious incident since the collision occurred only a few days before our conversation, at Kindeng, a cash-crop resettlement area near town. Tamoka described it to me.

> "There was a party to celebrate the close of the school year at a school at Kindeng and the parents of all the children were invited. Some people brought liquor and, while drunk, some Hageners attacked a Wabag, a driver for the Public Works Department who owned a block at Kindeng, and hit him over the head breaking through his brain. They then removed one testicle and cut out his tongue. The killers were Moke. The Wabags have not paid back for this yet and whether they will or not is dependent upon the feelings of individuals."

The dead man had no connection with the original driver's group. He came from near Wapenamanda, close to Tamoka's village. Tamoka expected that the dead man's kin would consider vengeance. When asked if he thought they would specifically target the Moke he said, "They can kill a Moke. If they look for a Moke and one doesn't come along, they can kill a Yamka, Kindika or whatever, I'm not sure. It's Hagen, inside Hagen, and they will kill here."

The death at Kindeng, though gruesome, seemed to follow the logic of the social construction of the original accident. Olzak (1992:215) notes that one incident of ethnic violence often sets others in motion. "Immediately after an event has occurred, ordinary confrontations between members of different ethnic or racial populations take on a new and more threatening interpretation... race and ethnic membership become relevant where they were not before, and urban confrontations of all kinds increasingly come to be seen as racially motivated." Indeed, if a man from Wapenamanda could get killed, then all Wabags should take care. Non-Moke Hageners, in turn, should not expect that the Wabag will discriminate carefully between them either.

Tamoka felt drawn more closely to other Wabag people just as Anton did to the Melpa tribesmen who he nevertheless continued to fear and mistrust.

The bad feeling between locals and migrants in Mount Hagen mirrored problems in the rest of Papua New Guinea. In each area, ethnic amalgamations emerged in response to local experiences of urbanisation. While Papua New Guineans used essentially the same system of categories and cognitive and discursive practices everywhere in the country, the varying nature of the economic, social and cultural dynamics of particular areas presented them with different things to think and talk about. They ended up constructing wide ethnic identities that were qualitatively different in each area.

Rioting in Kokopo

The Tolai people dominated the Rabaul[11] region, like the Melpa tribes dominated Mount Hagen. New Guinean plantation workers, especially highlanders, first came to Kokopo, the plantation centre just outside the town, on contract work. When their contracts terminated many moved to Rabaul instead of returning home, and became part of the town's underclass. Tolai reactions to the migrants recall the Hagener reception of people from Wabag. Stereotypes of highlanders (called "Chimbu" after a particular highland district) emphasised their supposed primitive and violent nature.

Large-scale rioting between Chimbu workers and Tolai tribesmen broke out in Kokopo while I was in Port Moresby. A returning plantation worker in Mount Hagen told me about the fighting in detail. I later travelled to Rabaul to interview people about the riots. Although they gave different versions of specific events, all informants classified the protagonists in the same way.

A Papuan Welfare Officer working in Rabaul said that some men from the Southern Highlands, drinking in the Kokopo tavern, got into an argument about a remark one of them made to a Tolai woman. Her kin took offence and a brawl started that resulted in some injuries. The Welfare Officer said that many Southern Highlanders lived in one compound at Ulaveo Plantation and called each other "brother". Differences amongst them did not matter in this situation and a large group gathered to confront nearby Tolai. The police arrived and arrested some of these men. Escapees returned to Ulaveo and passed on the word that some of their fellows got arrested because Tolai had a fight with them. An armed group marched up the road and a highlander died

---

[11] A volcano recently devastated Rabaul.

in the ensuing fight. Some "Chimbu" killed a Tolai a few days later. Large scale unrest continued for the next ten days between Tolai and "Chimbu".

The Welfare Officers in Rabaul gave some structure to the system of urban ethnic categories by appointing representatives for each "community", Highlands, Sepik, etc. They introduced me to the Highlands representative, a Siane speaker from the Eastern Highlands who had lived in Rabaul for 17 years. He felt the Tolai had started things by assaulting the group in the tavern. The original disputants may have been kin, but when the fighting spread people from many areas of the highlands joined in. When asked if people differentiated more finely amongst these broad categories he said:

> "Some Tolai who have become teachers or medical orderlies or have been to our area, they know almost as well as we do. They know of Goroka, Chimbu, about Kundiawa or Hagen, Mendi and Tari. [Note that he names towns here.] But most Tolai, those who live in their villages, don't know what district we come from. They only know of one general name, highlands or Chimbu. They just call us Highlanders and we just call them Tolai."

Interviewing more informants made it clear that people recognised that plantation workers from the Sepik also took part in the fighting on the side of their co-workers from the highlands. Another man mentioned, "In Hagen we distinguish between the Southern Highlands and Western Highlands, in Rabaul we don't. We say we are from one place. Tolai call us 'Chimbu'. Sepik, Mendi, Tari or whatever place, they call us all 'Chimbu'." Here, a regionally based ethnic term gets applied to a heterogeneous group of migrant workers. This "ethnicisation" of emerging class distinctions, something we saw in Mount Hagen, also occurred in Port Moresby during another series of confrontations.

Papuan Separatism

The present conflict between secessionist forces on Bougainville and the central government of Papua New Guinea brings to mind the Papua Besena movement that Josephine Abaijah started for the separation of Papua from New Guinea on 3 June, 1973. Ms. Abaijah, then the member of the House of Assembly for the Central Regional District, stressed two themes in her attempt to gain grassroots support for her cause. Like the Bougainvilleans, Abaijah and her followers focused on dissatisfaction with the state of economic development in their region and the disruptive immigration of outsiders.

Papua Besena blamed Papua's poverty on a concentration of development projects in New Guinea. The presence of such a large number of New Guineans in Port Moresby created the same conflicts over resources that we saw in Rabaul and Mount Hagen. Capitalising on Papuan fear of violence and sexual attacks, Papua Besena articulated an ideology that these social problems represented the consequences of New Guinea's colonisation of their homeland. Frequent derogatory statements about New Guineans annoyed my informants in Port Moresby. Once, for example, when demanding official recognition of Hiri Motu, a Papuan trading pidgin used on the south coast, Abaijah derided Neo-Melanesian, the now-national lingua franca that originated in New Guinea, by calling it a *kanaka* (primitive and savage) language. My informants in Port Moresby told me of rumours that someone would kill her shortly.

Only a few weeks after Papua Besena started to articulate grievances, Papuan teams played soccer, rugby and Australian Rules football, against New Guinean teams in Port Moresby. After New Guinea lost the third straight contest, New Guinean fans rioted. They attacked Papuans in the streets, shops and cars, and stoned low-covenant housing areas. Although it seemed impossible to me to pick a Papuan from a New Guinean in a crowd or car, especially at night, New Guineans said that they could easily recognise Papuans by their hair styles. Men lined up along roadways, looked into passing cars and yelled further up the line the ethnic identity of the occupants. A Chinese shopkeeper related a fairly typical incident when a hostile crowd surrounded his store in the suburb of Waigani, demanding that he eject any Papuans inside. He denied having Papuan customers on the premises but when the people outside saw someone hiding under the counter they stoned the shop.

Port Moresby remained tense for three days as reports of continued fighting came in over the radio. Papuan women and children from the Sea Birds low-covenant housing area took refuge in the Administrative College. Canoe settlers anchored near Koki Market put out to sea. Many other Papuans left town or went to Hanuabada (a Motuan village inside Port Moresby) where guards could keep out New Guineans. The police blockaded the town and prevented an armed convoy of trucks from outlying villages from entering the town to help Papuans. A rumour spread that those turned back would break the blockade by sea. New Guineans expected highlanders working on nearby plantations to deal with any Papuans arriving from outside.

Considering the intense fear and disruption caused by the rioting, casualties proved light. However, it took a fortnight for the town to return to normality and Ms. Abaijah quickly made political capital of the disturbances. She said the violence proved that New Guineans, especially the unemployed, hated Papuans; most should be deported (something my informants feared all along). Papua Besena seemed to grow in strength as divisions between Papuans and New Guineans deepened in Port Moresby. The movement held an open-air rally in October attended by about 1,500 people. The good-humoured crowd followed Ms. Abaijah's lead singing songs on what she declared to be "a happy day for the Papuan people." She emphasised that Papua existed for 100 years and that her movement aimed to establish its independence. In an interesting allusion to the dormant nature of Papuan identity until recent events, she said that Papuans had been lulled into a long sleep.

> "We thought someone was looking after us but we were on our own. A wind come across the sea and opened our eyes. A wind from the mountains woke us up and we looked around and we were alone. Many people are still sleeping. We will not sleep again until we are free and equal. Any colonial tricks to give the country away will be denounced, we are part of Australia yet."

Matiabe Yuwe, the House of Assembly member for the Tari-Komo electorate of the Southern Highlands, also spoke. When this highlander stepped up a faint muttering rose from the crowd. Abaijah immediately stood up behind Yuwe and made hand and facial motions indicating that she wished the crowd to encourage him and the Southern Highlands into the movement. Welcomed with applause, he spoke in Motu, saying that he supported Papuan economic and social development but felt uncertain about Papua Besena. "Other highlanders say the Southern Highlands are too remote, coastals say we're remote. We don't know where to go. Europeans put us in Papua so we are Papuans." Abaijah closed the meeting by reinforcing this theme, saying that, "Boundaries and districts gave birth to a nation" that her generation would raise.

Although they expressed solidarity with each other, New Guineans in Port Moresby did not form a movement like Papua Besena. In any case, that organisation did not realise its dream. Papuans in Port Moresby, now the capital of Papua New Guinea, could not, like the inhabitants of far away Bougainville, oust government forces from their territory. But they did articulate another example of how individuals, reflecting upon and talking about administrative boundaries and the forces of modernity, construct urban ethnicity.

Social Action, Ethnicity and Cognitive Processes in Urban Papua New Guinea

Well prior to this research in Papua New Guinea, urban anthropologists (e.g. Gluckman 1958, Mitchell 1956, Abner Cohen 1969, 1974) had already mounted a sustained attack on the idea that urban ethnicity simply represents the maintenance of traditional social groups and cultures in new settings.

They clearly demonstrated that identities change, emerge or persist in response to urban social structure.

Sociologists like Yancy, Eriksen and Juliani (1976) elaborated similar views. They attacked the dominant theory in their discipline that ethnic groups in urban America either remained continuous with those from overseas (pluralism) or that the differences between Americans of varying origin would disappear as people acculturated and adopted more universalistic identities (assimilationism). Their "ecological" focus in the study of ethnicity reflected a wider trend in the social sciences as the situational determination of social knowledge developed into a major interdisciplinary theme. But according to Holmos (1976:26), practitioners in the various subjects, studying miscellaneous issues, generally neglected to consider "the way that social knowledge affects the social situation in which it appears". It seems that the study of ethnic phenomena has hardly changed in this respect during the intervening twenty years.

> Research speaks fairly clearly and articulately about how ethnic boundaries are erected and torn down... However, the literature is less articulate about the meaning of ethnicity to individuals and groups, about the forces that shape and influence the contents of that ethnicity, and about the purposes ethnic meanings serve. This requires a discussion of the construction of culture. (Nagel 1994:161)

The material in this chapter shows that urban Papua New Guineans created cultural categories when they interpreted new social groupings in the towns. Readers may wonder if only comparatively empty and provisional entities like "Hagener" and "Wabag" lend themselves to such an interpretation. Recent work into cognitive aspects of tradition suggests that what went on in urban Papua New Guinea is typical of the construction of collective representations. Boyer notes:

> There is a marked tendency in anthropology to ignore the fact that most representations about traditions are in fact episodic, occasion-bound... There is a systematic discrepancy between what anthropologists are seeking, namely some semantic memory data, and what conversations with informants provide in abundance: memories of singular situations. (1990:43)

Informants' familiarity with many cultural concepts comes from concrete experiences like those recounted here. Such cultural categories often have no core of pre-existing beliefs and values to tap into. As Boyer says, "this combination of extreme salience and apparent vacuity constitutes a challenge to the common anthropological ideas about traditional categories" (p.26). We can meet this challenge by carefully examining how collective representations become salient noting what circumstances are necessary for vacuity to give way to something more firm and polished. The material presented here shows how "empty" categories become part of the shared social understandings of urban migrants, and sediment from identifications into identities when conditions and emerging understandings encourage their repeated use.

People migrated to towns as individuals and initially constructed personal social networks with wantok from rural areas. Rural groups and their identities remained important in many urban situations, and the cultural ambience of most towns reflected the concerns of people in their hinterlands. But urban ethnicity in Papua New Guinea had little to do with extolling ties of blood or other "primordial" sentiments. The fact that so many small, socially and linguistically discrete, village communities contributed to the urban population meant that the usual cultural elements of ethnicity – a common language, religion, origin myth, etc. – had little meaning outside very particular social settings.

The complexities of the specific groups that did form from time to time, like the ones that Tobeas, Balau, Emendai and Lulu belonged to, had no meaning or relevance to the average resident of Port Moresby. Even in Mount Hagen, a mere thirty miles from Tambul, Kepaka problems did not interest Melpa, Enga or coastal residents of the town. So Lulu's death, Balau's beating, and Anton's worries about his tribal enemies and Melpa neighbours, situations in which rural group membership assumed importance, left no trace on the wider urban culture.

Tobeas, Michael, John and their kin in Port Moresby recognised this implicitly and made real attempts to transcend the schisms of the countryside. Unlike the Kepaka in Mount Hagen who remained personally involved in village affairs, the men who lived in Port Moresby, a city far removed from home, could not avoid participating in relationships that facilitated the assumption of new identities. Tobeas, the least cosmopolitan man of the four whose social networks were presented, interacted frequently at Two Mile with people from groups he would avoid at home. When events occurred that threatened the continuity of these relations (e.g. when Lulu died and Balau was beaten up), the urban migrants projected their schismatic potentials back to a rural source. They recognised their sets of urban relationships as something new and labelled them in terms of the colonially derived classifications they encountered and used in interactions with people from other areas of the country.

Although these categories appear at first glance merely conceptual or hollow, people fill them up. Something about the process of conceiving of themselves and others as members of stereotyped groups connects classifications with urban events and produces urban ethnicity in Papua New Guinea without the usual cultural paraphernalia of ethnicity in other places. This suggests that the basic ingredients and mechanisms of ethnic formation operate before culture and institutions enter the picture to elaborate the processes of descent-based categorisation.

The notion that people within categories have more in common than those outside them provides a consistent theme that runs through all these cases, from the most specific examples of network construction to the most generalised regional oppositions. Weber (1961) recognised long ago that ethnicity involves a "subjective belief" in common descent and the manipulation of cultural traits to produce social boundaries and communal relationships. My informants came from groups famous in the anthropological literature for conflating descent with locality. The tendency, especially of highlands groups, to assimilate the children or grandchildren of war refugees and other outsiders by incorporating them into local descent groups is especially well documented (Barnes 1962, Brown 1962). Urban dwellers do something analogous when they use district categories to describe wantok aggregations. People from one's district or region may belong to different groups, but in situations perceived in terms of opposing district or regional categories internal differences become irrelevant.

The tendency for individuals to use and adopt these labels so automatically, to describe themselves and others as Gorokan or Hageners with no apparent hesitation, struck me as the most interesting and problematical aspect of Papua New Guinean urban ethnicity. The comment by Matiabe Yuwe (the Southern Highlander who spoke at the Papua Besena rally) that "The Europeans put us in Papua so I am a Papuan" recalled numerous parallel statements by other people from all over the country. How can individuals identify with such categories and so readily pick up another set, like new clothing, in a different situation or when they move to another town? Something crucial happens to the way people see themselves during the course of social interaction. Cognition and discourse must constitute a realm of psycho-social reality where the construction of these categories is achieved. Anthropologists and sociologists preoccupied with the role of social boundaries, culture, urban ecology, etc., in the production of ethnicity have nothing to say about how categories become transmuted into identities. We need to scrutinise the insights of psychologists and cognitive scientists specialising in social cognition for some useful clues as to how this occurs.

According to Hogg and Abrams (1988:20,51) self-categorisation puts groups into individual consciousness and "transforms individuals into groups". The very existence of categories, even without any particular content "is sufficient to generate intergroup competition". When people used the system of origin categories to describe the automobile accident in Mount Hagen and the bar-room incident that triggered the riots in Kokopo, interpreting the subsequent confrontations in these same terms seemed to follow almost automatically. Papua New Guineans treat incidents of conflict between individuals as group concerns, so the widening of conflicts that such categorisation entails is virtually inevitable.

In any case, district labels provided a framework that channeled interpretations of random events, and gave them the appearance of concrete examples of conduct occurring between groups of people. When they applied these categories to themselves, Papua New Guineans put the groups into their heads and used them to make sense of the nature of urban social life. Other hostile events, interpreted as reactions to the car accident and bar-room brawl, accentuated the intensity and the salience of the group labels. The opposition between Hageners and people from the Enga subdistrict in Mount Hagen town, highlanders and Tolai in New Britain and New Guineans and Papuans in Port Moresby deepened from abstract to palpable. Even though the highlanders involved formed no groups in any of the towns, they developed a set of shared understandings about themselves as a kind of people with opposed interests to others that became a part of the urban culture.

Individuals who had no direct role in any of the events reacted to them personally. However, they did not merely assemble or apply "categorisations for making sense of experience", they involved themselves in the practice of accomplishing categorisation (Edwards 1991). Even though the administrative divisions were there for the taking, applying them to interpret urban interaction meant that talking became part of the process of constructing ethnicity (cf. Wetherell and Potter 1992).

We could see this in the accounts of the riots in Port Moresby and Rabaul, and the rise of Papua Besena. However, the most complete set of data that shows the specific contributions cognition and discussion make to urban ethnicity comes from the Mount Hagen incident. The experience of talking about the various revenge attacks, tagging them with these collective identities, clearly led my informants to magnify similarities within categorical boundaries and accentuate differences. It thus became easier to ignore inconsistencies and discriminate one group from another (Lakoff 1987:68, Barsalou 1992:171).

Hakai, Anton and Temoka all referred to Hagener and Wabag social identities when we discussed the crash but Hakai, a Melpa speaker, Yamka clansman, and a prototypical Hagener, pushed group solidarity the most. His perspective clearly differed from Anton and Temoka, who were not central members of their respective categories. These initially uninvolved individuals became more assimilated to the categories party to the dispute as further incidents, interpreted in terms of the first one, occurred. When a man from Temoka's part of Wabag was attacked in a payback for the crash he could see that the social construction of urban reality made him a Wabag too, someone with interests opposed to people whom he reciprocally labelled Hageners. If people called Anton or Temoka "Hagener" or "Wabag", then they would identify themselves as such when situations arose that demanded alignments of this kind.

Conclusions: The Essential Ingredients of Ethnicity

Fieldwork in urban Papua New Guinea showed that ethnic categories and groupings can develop without primordial sentiments, basic ties, ultimate loyalties or commonalities of language, culture, religion, etc. Ethnicity at its most fundamental became part of social reality when people divided themselves, and/or those around them, into contrasting categories based on flexible, subjective notions of common descent. The actual construction of specific categories (e.g. Hagener, Wabag, New Guinean, Papuan) involved the interaction of the following three aspects of social reality: cognition and discourse, administrative boundaries, and antagonism or grievance.

Firstly, I highlighted the realm of cognition and discursiveness. This was most important because the ethnicities of greatest interest in urban Papua New Guinea were almost entirely categorical. Hageners and Wabags in Mount Hagen, New Guineans and Papuans in Port Moresby, highlanders in Rabaul did not form groups more than sporadically or constitute communities in any more concrete sense. I also focused on the construction of categories because the literature treats ethnic groups as if they constituted already-formed entities. Even authors interested in ethnic construction almost totally ignore the role of cognition and discussion in creating ethnicity.

Postmodernists provide one exception, but they seem too wrapped up in discourse itself. Postmodernism treats all of culture and society as text (Sollars 1989:xi) and identities as inventions. One person's account or invention of identity is as good as another's and the observer has no privileged position to judge between them. This stance seems fundamentally at odds with social reality, something that postmodernists deny exists.

Ethnic categories become part of urban culture through intersubjective discourse. Individuals may not achieve absolute consensus about the nature and meaning of these categories, but they talk, not just out loud to produce text, but to each other to produce understandings. Social identity theory recognises this and provides resources better suited to the analysis of my data.

Wetherell and Potter, for example, note that discourse about identity depends on narratives that already exist and that this discourse "intertwines with other social practices" (1992:79). Although small, rurally derived identities and groups remained important to many situations in day-to-day life, the way they merged into the wider administrative categories my informants used to account for the urban social universe certainly bears Wetherell and Potter out. The regional categories also represented an acknowledgment of the townspeople's participation in a new social order. The perceived inequities of that new order provided much of the motivation and incentive for ethnic mobilisation.

We could see, especially in the Rabaul and Port Moresby riots, that ethnicity assimilated what looked like emerging class differences. In both situations, unemployed or marginally employed New Guineans, mainly highlanders, provoked defensive reactions from local people. But there was nothing of what Marx called "class for itself" – a subjective identification with class position, and a realisation that it "provided the crucial life experience which would determine, either now or eventually, the beliefs and actions of the individual" (Bendix and Lipsett 1967:8). Although rural origins, frequent moves back home, and the lack of a long history of proletarianisation, may help explain the dearth of class consciousness, it is unquestionably true that ethnic differences in Papua New Guinea tended to parallel class differences (Levine and Levine 1979:82-95).

Researchers examining labour markets in the United States have noted something very similar. "Informal job competition among different ethnic groups can heighten ethnic antagonism and conflict, strengthening ethnic boundaries as ethnicity comes to be viewed as crucial to employment and economic success" (Nagel 1994:159). In Papua New Guinea ethnic oppositions also incorporate elements of national politics and development in addition to job competition, and combine these in an idiom far more meaningful than class to Papua New Guineans.

Thus classifications, discussions and grievances provide the essential ingredients used to produce ethnicity in urban Papua New Guinea. People create "solid" ethnic categories by thinking and talking about each other in terms of administrative boundaries. Random urban encounters with others and emerging inequalities in the structures of the developing state provide urban dwellers with a great deal to think through and talk about.

However, other aspects of urbanisation and state development prevented these solid categories from evolving further. Individuals in towns remained, in the 1970s, committed to their tribal areas even when they lived far from home. Although this rural orientation did not prevent people from taking on wider identities, it undermined the potential for them to elaborate the organisation necessary for ethnic groups and communities to endure beyond sporadically occurring situations. In most of the developed world, modernisation causes low-level identities to erode as it simultaneously encourages the formation of more politically effective, wider identities (Olzak 1992). But things were very different in urban Papua New Guinea, and this allows us to see that – far from being essential to ethnicity – groups, culture and communities represent elaborations: secondary, not defining, properties of the phenomenon. These things that so muddle the concept of ethnicity constitute accretions to cognitive categories of grievance grounded in subjective notions of descent.

72   CONSTRUCTING COLLECTIVE IDENTITY

Holocaust Memorial, Makara Cemetery

The inscription in English reads:
"Lest We Forget"
This stone is dedicated to the memory of the six million Jewish men, women and children who perished in the Holocaust. 1938 - 1945

(Makara Cemetery is situated in a sheep-farming area 11 kilometers outside of Wellington.)

4

Jewish Ethnicity in New Zealand

From the time of Abraham up to the present covers the best part of four millennia. That is more than three-quarters of the entire history of civilized humanity...The Jews created a separate and specific identity earlier than almost any other people which still survives. They have maintained it, amid appalling adversities, right up to the present. Whence came this extraordinary endurance? What was the particular strength of the all-consuming ideal which made the Jews different and kept them homogenous? Did its continuing power lie in its essential immutability, or its capacity to adapt or both. (Johnson 1987)

"Mine is the last authentically Jewish generation."
"You mean in the sense of living every day in a Jewish culture?"
"Right. You know, when I read all these piles of studies on 'Why am I a Jew? How am I a Jew?... I realize that until I was seventeen I never asked myself the question. You were Jewish in the same way you breathed. Those were generations of real Jews, and there won't be any more... Not even in Israel." (Schnapper 1983:iv)

Who could have a form of ethnic identity more different from urban Papua New Guineans than Jews? As Johnson says, Jewish history goes back almost as far as history itself. Jews have a distinctive religion, origin myth, a complex set of internationally linked institutions, ideological ties through Zionism to a modern state, a basic, primordial, identity that survived many tests. How can the Frenchman quoted above say he belongs to the last generation of real Jews? What will come next?

According to Jacob Neusner we might witness the ultimate answer in New Zealand, the first voluntary disappearance of a national Jewish community. Perhaps in the end Jews in France and New Zealand will become members of a category, much like my informants in Port Moresby and Mount Hagen. Unlike Neusner I hesitate to make sweeping predictions about the future of the New Zealand Jewish community. Certainly, plenty of the New Zealand Jews interviewed knew about as much about Jewishness as Anton did about being a Hagener. Do the unformed or idiosyncratic ideas of these individuals mean anything to Jews as a group? Some recent literature on "symbolic ethnicity" in the United States suggests that it does. The persistence of certain ethnic groups, previously shapers of identity, now depends on the affiliation of those who choose to identify. In this chapter I attempt to show that although one finds a full kaleidoscope of Jewish expression in New Zealand, the notion of symbolic ethnicity seems to capture the essential nature of the contemporary situation of the country's Jewish population.

Symbolic Ethnicity

In the 1970s American sociologists noted the puzzling occurrence of a revitalisation of ethnicity among white ethnics, especially working-class Poles, Irish and Italians, people previously thought well on the way to assimilation. As they debated the significance of this phenomenon, some scholars realised that focusing explanation on nostalgia, yearnings for roots, and continuity with the past, missed the point of the revival. White ethnicity reflected uncertainties about the future of a changing American society and offered only the illusion of a direct connection with one's ancestors (Stein and Hill 1977).

Gans (1979:1-20) pointed to the essentially voluntary nature of this new ethnicity. One could choose between a variety of ways of identifying as a Jew – for example, affiliating with a synagogue, joining a consciousness-raising group, studying history, etc. People looked for easy ways to express identity that did not disrupt their day-to-day lives. "Symbolic ethnicity does not require functioning groups or networks, feelings of identity can be developed by allegiances to symbolic groups that never meet." Groups that never meet obviously lack coordination and cannot prevent individuals from developing increasingly idiosyncratic ways of expressing their ethnic selves.

Alba (1990) further elaborated the nature and consequences of symbolic ethnicity. He argues that ethnic identity for native-born white Americans has become a choice that gives a panache of distinctiveness to individuals. Fully compatible with the individualism so characteristic of American culture, this style of ethnic identification does not depend on ethnic social structures. In fact ethnic groups, associations, congregations and political organisations – once rooted in social networks, neighbourhoods, common occupations and face-to-face interaction – now depend on the voluntary affiliation of individuals to survive. Alba suggests that shorn of a social-structural base that transmits consistent cultural content this lifestyle ethnicity undermines the viability of ethnic groups.

What Gans and Alba say about the nature of symbolic ethnicity resonates well with recent, more general, accounts of the nature of self-identity in contemporary western society. We make and refashion ourselves reflexively as we move through lives increasingly unanchored to enduring social networks, stable institutions and communities (Giddens 1991). Individuals cobble together identities in the context of a culture that encourages them to choose what they like from a vast array of lifestyle choices that derive from interests, passions, abilities and descent. Jews, predominantly middle-class, white, native-born Americans, participate in American culture as fully as everyone else. Can the "extraordinary endurance" of Jewishness insulate them from becoming merely symbolic ethnics? In fact, Alba, whose study population included few Jews, speculated that Jewish ethnicity might prove exceptional because it contains an extra dimension. Jewishness combines notions of peoplehood with a religion that perpetuates exclusive institutions and group practices.

Assimilation versus Transformation

Jewish social scientists have developed a parallel discourse, a specific debate on modern American Jewry that develops themes very similar to those found in the literatures on both symbolic ethnicity and the effects of postmodernism on identity. Assimilationists look at increasing mobility, interaction with gentiles, and new secular forms of Jewish identity, as symptoms of decline. Like Schnapper's French informant, they see the imminent demise of "real Jews." Transformationalists look at the same changes and see vitality, resilience and Johnson's immutability through adaptation. Their argument centres on a disagreement about what constitutes authentically Jewish behaviour (Cohen 1988: 68-70).

Within this debate assimilationists are sometimes referred to as "traditionalist", because they see Jewish identity in terms of the Jewish religion. They worry less about quantity (the number of people who say they feel Jewish) than quality (whether people live meaningful Jewish lives in accordance with religious ideals). They in turn accuse the transformationalists, who focus on Jewish solidarity, of divorcing Jewishness from Judaism. "Eating in Chinese restaurants and going to services bring Jews together but do not have the same implications for Jewish life" (Silberman 1985:86).

While the traditionalists seem pessimistic, transformationalists appear happy with the present and confident about the future. Modernity may present Jews with less compulsion to remain Jewish, but it also removes pressures to become something else. Silberman recalls that in his youth Jewishness was an embarrassment and a burden. He quotes Heine who said, "Those who would say that Judaism is a religion would say being a hunchback is a religion. Judaism is not a religion but a misfortune." "It's hard now to recall how widespread that attitude was and how deeply rooted, for with the breaking open of American society... the old burden has been lifted" (1985:30).

Today's youth may not be the same kind of Jews their great-grandparents were, but they devise ways to express their Jewishness while remaining full participants in American life. New forms of Jewish expression, e.g. concerns for Israel, Soviet Jewry and other secular matters, show how cultural assimilation can take on a positive role in assuring Jewish survival. A "self-realized Copernican revolution" has occurred. Jews realise that the traditional view, that they were put on earth to serve God's will, needs to be reversed. Religion serves to promote solidarity and that is primary[12].

Many circumstances other than religion affect solidarity. In a wide-ranging study that compares historic and present-day centres of Jewish life, Goldschieder and Zukerman (1984) note that pre-modern Jewish communities in Europe constituted autonomous social and cultural orders with a separate religion, clergy, calendar and language. Jews living in these internally autonomous ghettos engaged in particular occupations and rarely interacted with gentiles. Modernity eroded this coincidence of structural factors and ethnicity to varying degrees in different places. Diversity in the cohesion of Jewish communities depends on "population size, economic concentration, residential distribution, religious denominations, strength of communal, social and political organisation" and the nature of the educational system. American Jews have acculturated, but areas of residential, economic, friendship and family concentration persist even in the most modern centres. These ties connect the least committed Jews to networks of family, friends and neighbours, and constitute important sources of communal vitality.

Goldschieder and Zukerman's comparative treatment of the cohesion of Jewish communities specifies and interrelates an important series of structural variables. But if social organisation determines solidarity, what about culture, the way of life of the people of these communities? Culture obviously depends on social interaction, but structural factors cannot account for cultural content. If Jews have acculturated to American life, communal continuity by itself will not ensure cultural continuity. Can Jews remain an ethnic group without having a distinct culture? Glazer (1989) feels that the simple refusal to become non-Jewish "has the effect of relating American Jews, let them be as ignorant of Judaism as a Hottentot, to a great religious tradition." Besides,

---

[12] Silberman cites Kaplan (1981) for this last point.

American society values religious pluralism and the Jewish religion provides a more legitimate American identity for middle-class native-born Jews than ethnicity, which would emphasise their foreign origin.

> The problem is the creating of a meaningful Jewish life...If Judaism is to become in America more than a set of religious institutions supported by a variety of social pressures, it will be by virtue of examples of Jewish lives that in some way are meaningful, that in some way permit one to be a Jew. (Glazer 1989:150)

Glazer raises an important problem, but his solution seems hopeful – to put it mildly. Jews have an ongoing problem with the relationship between culture and ethnic identity precisely because they have made such a successful adjustment to life in modern, western democracies. The Jewish religion contains the most potent symbols and practices of a distinctive culture, but to follow these practices faithfully demands a level of commitment that would interfere greatly with people's ability to participate in their wider communities. American Jews have found a quasi-religious solution of sorts, one that enables them to maintain a level of Jewish involvement beyond the merely symbolic and which does not encapsulate them culturally.

A Meta-Ideology for Diaspora Jews?

Support for Israel, remembering the Holocaust, opposing anti-Semitism, promoting the survival of the Jewish people, and a commitment to social justice, provide the ingredients of an ideology that substantially defines Jewishness for many American Jews today. Woocher (1986) calls this ideology the American Jewish "civil religion". Multifunctional, it serves as a basis for political mobilisation, unites an increasingly diverse category of people ranging from the unaffiliated to members of Reform, Conservative and Orthodox congregations, and provides the core of common belief and behaviour that generally obtains amongst American Jews.

Rousseau first used the term "civil religion" to describe an ideology that represents the state in transcendent terms. In a more recent sociological discussion, Bellah and Hammond (1980) define a civil religion as "a distinct set of religious symbols and practices...that address issues of political legitimacy and political ethics but...are not fused with either church or state." Civil religion differs from true religion in its generality and lack of depth. The sentiments promoted do not conflict with any specific religious creed, since their focus is integrative. The nation is seen to be a force for morality in the world, acting in accordance with God's will. This sacredness is reflected in, and attached to, its dominant symbols and ritual.

The State of Israel serves as a particularly multivocal, integrating symbol in civil Judaism. The "homeland" for all Jews, it is the spiritual centre of the Jewish world, a centre of independence and power, ensuring survival and a refuge in times of crisis. Israel can prevent another Holocaust and assist in the fight against anti-Semitism world wide, so a strong Jewish state is good for all Jews, even those who choose not to live there. The Zionist emphasis on actually participating in the building of Israel has been replaced by the idea of "partnership".

> It takes the combined strength of the Jews in the diaspora and the Jews of Israel to insure the destiny of the Jewish people. American Jews can serve as a living synthesis of these two traditions bringing both to fuller realisation and thereby serving both faithfully. (Woocher 1986:79,88)

Although one might wonder if civil Judaism actually constitutes a well-integrated "civil religion" for people "on the ground"[13] (outside organisations) Woocher's explication of the functions of the ideology is perceptive. The fact that these symbols can give the contemporary secular concerns of most Jews a transcendent, sacred ring has important implications for the nature of their ethnicity. By providing a link between all Jews it may blunt the disintegrative potentials of symbolic ethnicity for group formation and help counteract assimilation to some extent. However individuals feel Jewish, or express it, they can at least come together to support Israel and Holocaust memorials.

Although civil Judaism seems to provide an ideal solution for the problems of balancing Jewishness with secular life in America, will it continue to do so? Does it work as well for communities far from large centres of Jewish population, like the Jews of New Zealand?

The results of a recent, very large sample survey imply that the balancing act of American Jews will soon come to an end. An intergenerational analysis of the data shows indicators of observance and identification decreasing progressively. The inter-marriage rate for the recently married has climbed from 5% prior to 1965 to over 47% for post-1987 marriages outside New York. (The rate in New York is 25%). Optimistic opinion that mixed households augment the total American Jewish population by increasing the number of families exposed to Judaism appears plainly wrong. Only 28% of mixed households raise Jewish children. By 2021 the diaspora population should decrease by one million. Israeli demographer Della-Pergola interprets the survey results in a way that should give transformationalists pause. He predicts that the "core" members of diaspora communities will decline in

---

[13] Woocher surveyed individual Jews, but survey data cannot measure the extent to which individuals integrate and elaborate on themes provided by the researcher.

number and become more orthodox, while those in the "periphery" assimilate (Norden 1991, Horowitz 1994).

New Zealand Jewry – An Overview

If we look at American Jews from a New Zealand Jewish perspective, their communities – problems notwithstanding – seem positively brimming with possibilities to lead what my orthodox informants consider a full Jewish life. About 3,100 Jews live in New Zealand. This number, which makes up 0.1% of the population and represents a decline of 15% since 1976, could be contained in a handful of apartment buildings in New York. The country is not only far from the centres of Jewish life, but Jews and their concerns hardly impinge on the consciousness of other New Zealanders.

Most New Zealand Jews live in Auckland and Wellington. These cities have similar numbers of Jewish residents[14] and communal facilities. Each has one Orthodox and one Progressive congregation with Sunday schools, a day school, Zionist organisations, youth groups, etc. Christchurch and Dunedin also have small Jewish congregations.

A Wellington survey (Salinger et al. 1983) provides more data about local Jewry than is available from the national census. The community has an aging population, with few people in the 17-35 age group and is very diverse in its origins. A fifth of the respondents came from the USSR and eastern Europe, another fifth from western Europe. Only half are native born. The rest of the Jewish population comes from South Africa,[15] Israel, the USA and other countries.

There are no Jewish neighbourhoods in Wellington or anywhere else in New Zealand. The distribution of local Jews in the workforce differs from that of the general population. Professional and technical occupations, and sales, were more than twice as common among Jews than gentiles. Administrative and managerial jobs were four times more common. Relatively few Jews work in service, agriculture and production jobs. Jewish occupational specialisation in New Zealand looks very similar to that found in other diaspora countries, but it lacks some of the usual implications for Jewish solidarity in larger communities. The actual numbers of Jews in any

---

[14] Jaffe (1990: 38) notes that there were 1,451 Jews in Auckland in 1981. The Jewish Survey of Wellington, undertaken in 1982, received information from 763 affiliated individuals with a 65% response rate so there would have been 1,173 members of affiliated households in Wellington.
[15] The immigration of South African Jews to Auckland increased in the ten years since the survey.

occupation is so small that they remain essentially invisible. Professional networks of lawyers, doctors, university lecturers, etc.; do not bring Jews together as they do in large American cities.

This view from Wellington (which seems similar to Auckland in structural terms) suggests that New Zealand Jews form a small, heterogeneous, relatively dispersed ethnic community. The symbolic ethnicity literature, together with Goldschieder and Zukerman's account of structural factors and Jewish solidarity, would lead us to expect these conditions to encourage variable expressions of Jewish identity. However, the specific ways that individuals interpret their Jewishness and its various symbols in such "postmodern" environments cannot be predicted from structural factors alone. It is, after all, possible for such a small group of people to build and sustain solidarity through sheer commitment, supported by ideologies like civil Judaism and highly connected informal friendship networks.

Gans conceived symbolic ethnicity to be a form of consciousness. Yet qualitative analyses of the meaning of ethnic identity to individuals in contemporary society remain hard to find. Nor do the "identity scales" of the American literature (e.g. Cohen 1988, Sandberg 1986), created from ticked replies to highly structured questionnaire surveys, tell us much about the ways contemporary Jews conceive of Jewishness. Knowing how often people attend synagogue, read Jewish books, or light Sabbath candles may allow social scientists to discern some general trends, but an understanding of the relationship between such behaviours and identity requires that we know what being Jewish means to people. The research project, "Being Jewish in New Zealand", that I coordinated was specifically designed to provide a body of data from this missing, qualitative perspective.

A Study of Being Jewish

The data which formed the basis for my analysis of New Zealand Jewish identity[16] came from semi-structured interviews of 93 New Zealand Jews. Fifty-three people were interviewed in Auckland, Wellington and Otago, and 40 expatriates in Melbourne and Sydney Australia. The research group designed a quota sample to reflect the variation present in the Jewish community. Interviewees comprised members of long-resident families, more recent migrants, youth, people affiliated to the main congregations, unaffiliated individuals and converts. Interviewers asked respondents

---

[16] The Jewish Research Group (consisting of myself, Marlene Levine, Ann Beaglehole, Jonathan Besser, Allan and Vera Levitt) designed the study. The Foundation for Research Science and Technology and Victoria University provided me with the funding to carry it out. I am solely responsible for the analysis presented here.

background questions about their families' origins; exposure to Jewish customs, religion, and organisations; and their degree of present religious and secular Jewish participation. We also enquired about the location of family members, frequency of contact with them, intermarriage, and the place of Jews in the interviewees' social networks. Particularly important were the open-ended prompts in the interviews designed to encourage informants to expand upon their feelings about the Holocaust, Israel, and anti-Semitism. Interviewers also asked people to air their thoughts on being Jewish in New Zealand, as well as about the future of the New Zealand Jewish community. This approach led respondents to elaborate on themes they found meaningful and opened fruitful avenues of inquiry in line with the goals and framework of the study.

All the interviews were taped, transcribed verbatim and stored on hard disk. I printed and coded the transcripts and examined them for themes about Jewishness. Search and retrieval software helped the process of assembling the coded passages. Re-contextualising the material in this way made it easier to develop a structure of concepts to aid in this process of interpretation (see Richards and Richards 1990). Although the size and non-random nature of the sample preclude establishing statistical distributions, it did generate adequate data for developing logical inferences about links between elements of Jewish identity and secular ideology. Patton maintains that the major strength of such a variable sample is that common patterns which emerge are likely to indicate shared perspectives and experiences which the researcher can "extrapolate" to develop working hypotheses (1990:172,486-493).

Most of the rest of this chapter focuses on how New Zealand Jews construct some specific forms of identification in contexts provided by the community's place in New Zealand society and culture, and the particular religious and civil symbols of Judaism. The discussion begins with an account of informants' views of established groups: the different Jewish congregations, the formal organisations of New Zealand Judaism and the concerns of secular fraternal associations such as B'nai B'rith. It then considers friendship networks, a level of social organisation that stands between structure (groups) and expression, and then goes on to explore realms of symbols and elaborations of individual consciousness.

Orthodox and Progressive Congregations

About half of New Zealand's total Jewish population[17] appear on the rolls of the country's six synagogues. Of these, 1150 people (70%) belong to three Orthodox congregations; 479 in Wellington, 618 in Auckland and 60 in Christchurch. Progressive temples have a total membership of 495, comprising 200 in Wellington, 250 in Auckland and 45 in Dunedin. According to the B'nai B'rith survey, 22% of Wellington's affiliated Jews considered themselves observant and only 11% attended synagogue services more than once a month. The fact that Orthodox congregations have the most members, but relatively few practice Orthodox Judaism, suggests that affiliation is more of a symbolic act than an expression of religious commitment. As we shall see, the ways that informants spoke about the Progressive and Orthodox congregations illustrates some of the cultural contradictions of the Jewish religion in New Zealand.

One might expect Progressive Judaism to appeal to local Jews because this movement seeks to align religious practice with modern life. The orthodox and progressive varieties of Judaism differ in many ways. Their congregations recognise separate external authorities and conduct services differently. The order of prayer and conduct of ritual reflect the modern versus traditional ambience of the respective groups. Men and women do not sit together in Orthodox congregations as they do during Progressive services and only in Progressive congregations do women lead Sabbath and Bar Mitzvah prayers. The two movements define authentic Jewish ancestry in different ways and this led some Orthodox people to say that certain members of the Progressives were "not really Jewish".

Since Orthodoxy is mainly symbolic in New Zealand, religious themes did not dominate our informants' comments about the two varieties of Jewish religion. When mentioned, the Orthodox informants usually noted that they did not observe the Law more faithfully than Progressive Jews, and certain members of the Orthodox shuls looked at some Progressive practices, like mixed seating, with sympathy. However they tended to stress that personal practices aside, the authority of Halachic tradition needed to be publicly maintained. This difference between public and private expressions of Judaism had important consequences for communal life.

A concrete example was observance of Kashrut, the kosher laws. To a religious Orthodox Jew one is either kosher or not. To be kosher means to

---

[17] Since the census counts children, but synagogue figures do not, I cannot present an exact New Zealand affiliation rate.

follow all the food laws, all the time. But New Zealand Jews, like their counterparts in much of the rest of the world, tended to follow rules they felt to be most important. For example, almost 80% of the respondents to the Jewish Survey (which included people from both congregations) did not eat pork in their parents' homes. However only 7.4% used separate utensils for meat and milk products, or ate strictly kosher when dining out (Salinger et al. 1983:40). This latter figure could be taken to represent a maximum level of strict kosher observance.

The variation in kosher practice was such that some of the Orthodox rabbis we have known in Wellington would not eat in the homes of congregants. They feared that if they were to eat in the home of A but not B, this would imply that A was more pious than B and perhaps lead to communal tension. Food cooked at home cannot be brought into the Orthodox centres, so it must be cooked on the premises. Often this meant that a group of dedicated women would need to get together at the Centres to do the cooking for community events. They had to work in (at times) inadequate kitchens, using a small range of acceptable items under the rabbis' supervision. Casual "pot luck" events were not possible. People wanting fancy meals often held Bar and Bat Mitzvah and wedding celebrations outside the centres. In the words of one informant, this resulted in "less cohesion":

> "Fewer social events [are] going on around the synagogue... What used to happen in the old days when I was young, was that, if there was a social event on, all the women would bring something. No meat, but anything else, salad, fish and so forth, cakes – everything was brought in. Now, not so much as a salad can be brought in. And that makes a big difference to the ability to hold social functions."

The Orthodox are limited in their ability to change this, because to do so would be a public step away from tradition.

> "Listen, you must understand that this is a Jewish community. Jewish, and they have to go by the Jewish laws. And the Jewish laws, and the rabbi, cannot go conduct a shul where it's not kosher. The rabbi can't. So, if you mean, you could bring in something from your home what is not kosher... No, you are Orthodox Jewish. You are an Orthodox Jew. Yes, you have to keep to the Jewish laws, even if you don't keep at home the Jewish laws. We are not kosher, but the shul must be kosher."

This informant's husband said that watering down the religion is the first step towards assimilation. Their own lack of practice, presumably because it was less visible, apparently counted less.

Perhaps one informant, a very Orthodox person by local standards, best articulated the essence of the difference. She expressed ambivalence about Progressive Jews in these terms:

> "I really personally feel that they're dangerous, from one point of view only. While I feel that they're very good because people that are out on the fringes are brought in to the movement and are involved much more, their main point of danger to me is that they will accept as Jewish someone that's not Jewish according to Halakah. And that, in the future generation, can make it very difficult. It can create havoc and heartache... when these children grow up and want to marry. Basically that's my whole concern with them. Of course I personally don't like the fact that they've thrown overboard many of the traditions that I think are very valuable, that are a discipline as much as anything else. But it's each person's prerogative to do what they want, to do how they want, and I wouldn't gainsay that. But when they accept as Jewish young women who would not be accepted as Jewish without more intensive education, and then the children of those young women grow up believing that they're Jewish, they're going to find it very hard to accept, that's why I say they're dangerous."

When I replied that the actual practices and beliefs of Progressive and Orthodox may not differ, she concurred, but said:

> "The only thing is that many people who belong here [to the Orthodox congregation], and do very little in the way of observance, know that they're not doing the right thing. They're not trying to justify themselves. Well, they say, all right, I'm not supposed to ride [on the Sabbath], I'm not supposed to do this or that or the next thing, but certain things they like doing, they know they're not supposed to. With the Progressives, they have abolished all of that, and they say it's OK to do it. We can do it."

> "So the major difference is that one group feels guilty and the other..."

> "Yeah, that's the way it feels to me, really. Also, I've got a young relative, a distant relative, somewhere along the line, who said, you know, he does very little, but when he goes to shul, to go to the Progressive temple doesn't seem like shul at all. Feels almost like a church, and he doesn't appreciate that feeling. And yet that's one of the reasons why some of the people go there, because of its decorum and its dignity and its procedure from A to B, quite methodically. Not like here where everybody gabbles and does all sorts of other things in between."

The fact remains that theory and practice seem inconsistent for the New Zealand Orthodox. One reason for the persistence of this state of affairs may be, respect for the sensibilities of the older congregants. For example, the Dunedin Orthodox congregation became Progressive after its long-time leader died. Although this seems a most unlikely scenario in Wellington, at least in the short term, demographic differences between the congregations are striking. Specifically, a comparison of the age structures of the two congregations in Wellington shows that the Orthodox synagogue has a considerably higher concentration of older members (Salinger et al. 1983). The Auckland Orthodox congregation actually considered affiliating with the American Conservative movement (a sort of compromise position) but rejected this option when it became clear that this would only further divide the community. Some Orthodox congregants felt that if it was not for the Progressives the number of New Zealand Jews would be even lower than it currently is.

> "I don't know what the population of, Wellington alone, Jewish people would be, but without assimilation it could have been 10,000, between 10,000 and 20,000; and it's partially the fault of the congregations here because they made no effort once they married out. They let them slide you see, and they made no effort to bring them back to the fold, until the Progressives started and they are doing that particular work... and there's a need for it, I think you'll see. Although I myself am Orthodox [laughs], as such, but there is a great need for the Progressive synagogue here, but I'm not a member of it. I wish them well."

On occasions that emphasise cohesiveness and keeping people Jewish (as opposed to occasions of ritual and tradition) Progressive and Orthodox Jews mingled comfortably, particularly in the context of less religiously oriented organisations like the Zionist Society, B'nai B'rith, etc. Those who rejected the authentic Jewishness of various Progressive members would not raise this publicly. The differences become problematic only when questions of religious status arose, at marriage and certain commemorative occasions involving prayer, or as qualifications for membership of religious organisations.

However friendly their relationship, the very existence of the two congregations shows the relevance to New Zealand of the arguments between the assimilationists and transformationalists in the American Jewish sociological literature. Both movements favour Jewish continuity. Progressives seek to assure this by keeping Judaism in tune with the conditions of contemporary society. They accommodated conversion more easily, gave women free access to public roles, accepted the children of a Jewish parent of either sex as Jews, allowed people to bring prepared food to Temple, and conducted much of their services in English. While some Orthodox informants applauded their efforts and wished them success, others saw in all of this a process of "watering down" Judaism to the point where complete assimilation became inevitable. To them, Orthodoxy was acceptable to all Jews because it upheld the standards of the most religious. Ironically, at least in part because the most traditional Jews in New Zealand tend to leave, religious practice among the members of the two congregations appears convergent.

We have looked at the position of Jews in New Zealand society and the groups they have formed. The realities of social organisation seem to push Jews along a path toward symbolic ethnicity. Their position in New Zealand social structure presents substantial obstacles to Jewish solidarity. Jewish organisations themselves have a mixed impact on Jewish continuity. The congregations in New Zealand do assume central roles in providing a continuing Jewish presence in the country, but their source of strength seems to lie where the symbolic ethnicity literature would predict. People affiliate to express a commitment to a way of life that they do not necessarily follow. The Jewish groups thus depend on individual affiliation for their social and financial viability. The discordance between commitment and practice highlights some cultural problems that organised Judaism perpetuates in the New Zealand environment. It seems counterproductive to duplicate congregations, youth groups, etc. in such a small community. However, disagreements about legitimacy, authenticity, and public expressions of tradition seem impossible to overcome in the short term, and will probably prevent the amalgamation of religious organisations in Wellington and Auckland.

Friendship Networks

Retaining a strong Jewish identity requires solidarity, but solidarity does not wholly depend upon affiliation to formal groups. Many American Jews do not belong to any Jewish organisation, but retain a strong sense of identification through patterns of association. A survey taken in 1935, when most Jews lived in inner-city neighbourhoods, showed that three quarters did not attend services during the year. "One could live a completely Jewish life from a sociological point of view, and yet have no connection with any Jewish institution" (Glazer 1989:85,118). Families, friends and many workmates were (and for many Jews today, still are) mainly Jewish.

In the United States the proportion of affiliated people seems to decrease with increasing community size (Sandberg 1986). However, a combination of interaction and civil Judaism seems to considerably strengthen Jewish identity where numbers are large. Forty-five per cent of respondents in the 1990 National Jewish Population Survey agreed with an item that read, "Most of my close friends are Jewish". In New York, the strongest American metropolitan centre of Jewish identification, 63% chose this option. In Los Angeles, Jews have moved out of Jewish neighbourhoods and well under 50% affiliate, but 75% have Jewish "best friends" (Sandberg 1986:67).

The findings of our study and others indicate that in small New Zealand towns Jews are too scattered to make contact, civil Judaism is weak and identification tends to be marginal. In Wellington, the country's second largest city, 60% of people who responded to the Jewish Survey reported that at least half their close friends, and 70% of their friends made though business contacts, were non-Jews (Salinger et al. 1983). The Wellington Jewish Survey's respondents came from lists of Jewish organisations and no similar figures exist for the unaffiliated. Although our interview study does not permit statistical generalisation it provides qualitative data that suggests that New Zealand Jews have less dense Jewish friendship networks than Americans. Our informants tended to have few Jewish friends if they were vaguely identified, or mixed networks if they identified more strongly.

A woman descended from one of New Zealand's oldest and best known Jewish families provides an example of someone with vague identification who has few Jewish friends. "I had nothing to do with any Jewish children... during my whole upbringing. This was living in South Auckland, on a farm, so I never knew any Jewish kids to socialise with at all." A performer, she felt being Jewish affected her creative sense and liked the touch of the exotic that Jewish identity gave her.

Another woman, ambivalent about being labelled a Jew, has friends who were Jewish but only one "Jewish friend". She met this person while sitting outside during school prayers, perhaps the only non-Jewish context which would draw Jewish children together. The reason she calls this person a Jewish friend was because she was a New Zealander. The others were children she met in refugee circles and considered European.

Young informants involved in organisations, or who had gone to Hebrew school, were regularly exposed to Jews their own age. Interviewees in our study stressed the separateness of their Jewish friends from the rest of their social networks. One young participating woman said, "All of mine were non-Jewish. I can't really remember having any Jewish friends until oh, late, quite late, 14, 15. I mean I had Jewish friends who were at Hebrew School, but I never mixed with them during the week, or in the weekends". Her husband said, "Yeah, [I had] friends at school and Jewish friends pretty... much separate. There were no Jewish kids in my age when I went to school."

The split in the networks reflects the fact that Jewish friends were generally seen in the context of specifically organised activities, meetings, camps, Sunday school etc. Although some socialising occurred outside, the lack of concentrated Jewish settlement in particular areas, and the full participation by Jews in New Zealand society, tended to encapsulate Jewish friendships. They comprised social islands of closeness where, "we could talk about things like Israel and Judaism and things, and not have to explain and get into details..." But it was also possible for such contacts to be dismissed as a relatively minor part of one's life, a product of being forced by parents to go to Sunday School, camps and youth clubs.

A small group of highly religious and Zionist youth and adults may have made a special effort to have wider Jewish social networks. To these individuals, friendships with non-Jews had the potential to undermine Jewishness.

> "The non-Jewish friends go out on Friday night (the beginning of the Jewish Sabbath) or go to a restaurant or something, or do whatever. And they'll go with them. If you do something like that, you're not going to get struck down by lightening from God. So once you do it once, you can do it twice, and the third time and fourth time, and so on and so on and so on. It's all just normal."

Even these people had gentile friends and contacts, but they made special efforts to keep their Jewish friends most central to their social lives.

Civil Themes in the New Zealand Interviews

The Holocaust

New Zealand Jews clearly understood the connections civil Judaism makes between Israel, the Holocaust and anti-Semitism. Those affiliated to congregations and/or secular Jewish groups with their international linkages heard portions of the civil canon at very regular internals. The Jewish Chronicle discusses the Holocaust frequently, often focusing on the pernicious nature of historians who deny it occurred. A publication of the Zionist Federation, it carries columns and news from Israel in each issue. Despite this understanding the relevance of these themes of recent Jewish history appears less than central to New Zealand Jewry.

Our informants expressed a variety of views about the significance of the Holocaust. Those who had a personal link tended to be ambivalent about using their experiences even to influence their children's identities. As Beaglehole (1988: 61-62) says in her own study, "There was conflict between the parents' need to share their experiences, and their wish to spare the children knowledge of such horrors." The meaningfulness of the Holocaust to these individuals is obvious, but private, certainly not a political symbol.

However, one man in Auckland took a notably different point of view. A survivor of two concentration camps, he talked about his experiences regularly and felt a duty to inform people of what happened. He spoke to all kinds of groups and organisations, especially Lions Clubs and schools. Because he found people in the audience openly weeping when he talked about his encounter with genocide, he now glosses over specific horrors unless asked. He felt the Jewish community generally supported his stance of openness. Other individuals interviewed said that although they recognised the significance of the Holocaust for Jewry, it did not define their personal Jewish identity.

The fact that individuals differed in regard to how they personally felt about the Holocaust does not allow us to say much about the ideological importance of civil Judaism's construction of it. Public expressions of ethnicity are characteristically more uniform and symbolic than private ones (Weaver cited in Pearson 1990:221). It is possible that the Holocaust may serve as an important symbol of New Zealand Jewishness independently of its private impact.

I interviewed two people who held high office in different Jewish organisations and their comments support the view that the public significance of the Holocaust was slight. One person, the New Zealand-born head of a coalition of Jewish groups, said that the Holocaust service in the Auckland synagogue is poorly attended. She also noted that (at the time of the interview) no Holocaust memorial existed anywhere in the country. She worried about achieving a balance between underplaying and overplaying its significance.

A South African-born interviewee living in Auckland organised a memorial exhibition at the Orthodox Jewish centre. His account of the difficult time he had convincing his organisation's committee to host the exhibition shows the reluctance of local Jews to present Jewish concerns to the wider public. He also commented on some of the differences he saw between the ethos of Jewishness in New Zealand and in South Africa which has an active Jewish population.

He explained that he was an officer of an Auckland chapter of B'nai B'rith, an international Jewish fraternity. He had seen a video about a Holocaust exhibit circulating in Australia that impressed him very much. He felt his children should see it, and suggested to his organisation that they bring the display to New Zealand. He tried for four years before finally achieving approval.

> "Every meeting we had of B'nai B'rith it was put to the side and nothing happened... It was a very tense time and I had a hell of a lot of flak. I had people phoning me up, saying you shouldn't bring the Holocaust."

People told him it would cause divisions in the community and stir up anti-Semitism. He felt especially bad when a survivor castigated his efforts.

> "I re-thought. I spoke to other survivors who had different views, and I said, 'Fine. My kids need to know. The Jewish community needs to know. We will bring the Holocaust here'. We had it. It happened because of me. I won't take credit for the success, but it was unbelievably successful. It brought the community together."

The success of the exhibition demonstrated that the Holocaust could promote unity among, and sympathy for, New Zealand Jews. However, the stance of the locally born and long-term New Zealand residents of the community who voiced reservations about raising the issue publicly is reminiscent of Medding's (1968) characterisation of pre-War Melbourne Jewry, who worried that the pursuit of partisan Jewish causes constituted isolationism and would alienate other Australians. Melbourne Jewry's "group invisibility" only changed when the Holocaust, the creation of Israel and the arrival of post-War European Jewish migrants combined to change the composition and ideology of that community.

Although the Holocaust exhibition in Auckland went well, comments from other informants indicated that it was a unique event, the impact of which has dissipated. The interview material also suggests that New Zealand Jews tend not to make the strong connection between the Holocaust and Israel contained in secular Judaism. Only one young man, who planned to migrate to Israel so he can "live a full Jewish life" made comments which are notable both for their singularity and also because they seem virtually to come out of Woocher's book.

> "OK, I, we all feel very strongly about the Holocaust, as a piece of history. I see the State of Israel as the only answer. I think, if anything we learnt from the Holocaust it's that we have to be able to stick up for ourselves. It's very important, I mean, to remember and make sure it never happens again, to anybody... I feel that the State of Israel is the only answer to the Holocaust."

This individual was the child of a Holocaust survivor. Some other New Zealand children of Jewish war-time refugees (Beaglehole 1990), also saw Israel as a reply to the horrors of mass murder. The connection certainly had great personal significance for these individuals, but they made no reference to the wider New Zealand Jewish community. This lack of articulation between ideology and community can influence highly committed Jews to emigrate as the comments of another informant, born in Wellington and now living in Australia, illustrate.

> "It is my Jewish identity... My mother went through the camps and most of my family have died as a result of the war. It is something that is catastrophic and central to my sense of Jewish identity... It's central to my sense of understanding of Zionism... It is something that attracts me to the Melbourne Jewish community, because they are absorbed in that, and it's part and parcel with the way that ticks as well... And, I mean Melbourne just became the obvious choice."

Other expatriate New Zealanders made the same point about the public role of the Holocaust in Melbourne. One woman attempted to account for the contrast.

> "There weren't a lot of survivors living in Auckland. It wasn't enough to make you aware as a child of the depth of the situation. Now, being in Melbourne, you see so many Holocaust survivors. In Auckland the few who were living there, they didn't talk about what happened. You didn't know so much about it."

Israel

In the United States obligations to assist Israel financially and identify with the country emotionally seem more central to Jewish identity than religious practice is. "American Judaism recognises only one heresy which subjects the perpetrator to immediate excommunication, denial of support for Israel" Woocher (1986:77).

The New Zealand Jewish approach to Israel seems more restrained. Jaffe describes the situation that existed in the Auckland community before 1967 as "A benevolent quiet level of support". The Six Day War stimulated Auckland Zionism, but this "pride did not automatically spill over into other activities or community structures". Communal identification with Israel seems to have dissipated, "the loss of such a strong Zionist affiliation and identity became another factor bringing on the crisis of confidence in the community" (Jaffe 1990:37-38).

Our informants responses to interview prompts about Israel reflected a mixture of ideology and practical experience. The most committed people we interviewed either planned to "make *aliah*" (ascend, used in reference to migrating to Israel) or had migrated there and then returned. One middle-aged woman said, "Israel is important to me. It's the security of the Jewish race, and I feel very strongly about it. And I feel all Jews should fight like hell for it". The young man, previously quoted linking Israel with the Holocaust said,

> "There are people with strong Jewish identity who don't live in Israel or don't keep the religion, but I think that those are only temporary. I suppose technically you could say you could live outside Israel and keep up a Jewish identity but I think it's

a lesser Jewish identity. I think that those two things really make your identity, your Jewish identity."

Returned migrants, more ambivalent than the interviewees just quoted, still felt Israel was central to Jewishness. Their accounts of why they did not settle emphasised that the problematical realities of life there had overcome ideological motivations. A South African, now an active member of the Auckland Jewish community, had moved to Israel prior to coming to New Zealand.

"We never adjusted. We valued it and enjoyed it but the Israeli way was not the way we wanted... Being a pacifist, I didn't like carrying a gun on guard duty. We were struggling financially. Inflation was terrible... the pushing, the different type of etiquette rules. Johannesburgh was very ordered. People will stand on a queue. In New Zealand people will not push in... In Israel you start doing the same thing [as the Israelis] and I didn't enjoy that. So we went back to South Africa, where I met my friend who suggested New Zealand."

Another informant, also Orthodox and very active in community affairs, found the experience of living in Israel helped him define his feelings about being a New Zealander (although he later moved to Melbourne).

"I'd been incredibly influenced by the Six Day War. I was fifteen then, and all of this sort of razzmatazz that went with that. And so it was a very shattering thing to realise I just wasn't happy I just really couldn't cope there actually. I never realised how much I liked New Zealand and enjoyed being a New Zealand Jew... Still, whenever I start talking with people I'll often ask them the first question, 'Do you believe Israel should exist as a state'? And if the answer is 'no', then I usually don't carry on talking to them."

A few of our more liberal-minded informants, both affiliated and unaffiliated to local Jewish organisations, reacted to the "bad press" Israel often gets in the New Zealand media by distancing themselves from the Jewish state and Zionism. They felt that progressive political views were a part of Jewishness and that it was difficult to reconcile the notion of Israel as an answer to the Holocaust with news coverage of the war in Lebanon and the Intifada[18]. One man made a statement which seems to capture the essence of the relationship between New Zealand Jewish identity and Israel for these people.

"Israel has fallen into difficult times and people feel really in two minds about the extent of supporting Israel. And for the Jews who have become assimilated or

---

[18] The interviewing for this project took place as the television news was filled with images of the suppression of the Intifada (Palestinian uprising in the occupied territories). Had these ambivalent individuals been approached during the Gulf War when Iraqi SCUDs were landing in Tel Aviv, they might have made more supportive statements.

partly assimilated, that aspect of their Jewishness is under threat if they feel that Zionism is not as valid as it used to be. So, I think that the future of the New Zealand Jewish community has quite a lot to do with the future of political events in Israel. The community, unlike say the large communities in Sydney and Melbourne, doesn't seem to me to have a lot of self-sustaining Jewishness, outside the religious observances."

The most negative, condemnatory comments about Israel came from those least identified with being Jewish. For example, an informant who has a Jewish father but feels he has inherited only the Jewish trait of tolerance towards others said, "the modern Israeli state is a really poor... example of what it could be." Zionism was "quite distasteful."

Affiliated Jews quite naturally have the greatest commitment to Israel. It is not unusual for them to have spent a year there between the end of high school and the start of university and to send their children on Israel experience programmes through the youth groups Habonim and B'nei Akiva. Young people return highly motivated and assume leadership positions in the youth groups. But then as they readjust to life in New Zealand and face the apathy of local children they either lose their fervour or move away, often to Australia. For most local Jews, even those highly affiliated, the role of the Jewish state in defining personal concepts of Jewishness seems small in comparison with accounts contained in the literature about Jewish ethnicity in Australia and the United States. The fact that active, committed, Zionist Jews from New Zealand tend to emigrate dilutes the salience of Israel as a symbol in the communities they leave behind. But identification with Israel (and all other aspects of Jewish identity) also depends on influences from outside the Jewish community. For example, the perceived level of anti-Semitism in the wider society greatly influences how closely New Zealand Jews identify with Israel.

Anti-Semitism

Anti-Semitism strengthens Jewish identification and increases unity. To Jews the complementarity of Israel and the Holocaust seems particularly obvious when they experience hostility: since completely assimilated Jews died in the Holocaust, anyone, even the most vaguely Jewish, should want to combat anti-Semitism and support Israel. But anti-Semitism is a variable phenomenon, not a constant condition, so its functionality should also vary. When Jews feel accepted, civil Judaism can seem hardly relevant to daily life.

In his study of right-wing groups in New Zealand, Spoonley (1987:214) noted that anti-Semitic arguments did not engage much support "in a social context which does not differentiate Jews phenotypically and has never racialised them in the way other western societies have." Eighty-two percent of the respondents to the survey of Wellington Jewry cited above (Salinger et al. 1983) indicated that they saw little or no anti-Jewish prejudice in New Zealand. Our interviewees also did not seem very worried about anti-Semitism despite some individuals recalling unpleasant episodes. Although unsettling, these were generally minor and transitory incidents, like epithets yelled near the synagogue or insults at school.

Even petty incidents could have substantial effects because they instantly remind Jews that not everyone accepts them as ordinary New Zealanders after all. When I asked one woman from Auckland about anti-Semitism she recalled that,

> "When I was at intermediate school, there was a girl in our class who was most impressed with us because we had a ping pong table and she wanted desperately to come and play with me after school–I was in Form 2 at that stage. And one day I heard her say to her friend, as I was walking past, she said, 'My father hates Jews'. And from then on... I made sure she didn't ever come to the house. I felt quite hurt by that. I felt that was quite bigoted, and I didn't enjoy that particular class. Not solely for that reason, but because they seemed to be quite a bitchy lot of kids. And I made sure when I went to secondary school, that I didn't go to the school that they – those kids – were going to. I went to Takapuna Grammar which was quite a way out of the district, simply to avoid those people, and to make another start. I thought it couldn't be any worse than where I was."

Some informants commented about the New Testament and "traditional" Christian anti-Semitism, but this did not emerge as a strong theme in our interviews. Only one account, related second hand, featured any violence. A young man wearing a kipa (skull cap) was assaulted in McDonald's. A large fight broke out as his friends rushed to help him: "It was basically a bar-room brawl." The friends fighting on his side were not Jewish.

Interestingly, no interviewee mentioned the stabbing of four children at a Jewish school in Auckland in July 1990. This incident received a great deal of attention in the national and Jewish media. My parents called from New York only hours after. They heard on the Jewish radio station about an anti-Jewish outrage in New Zealand and worried because, "you are sitting ducks out there".

The editorial in the *New Zealand Jewish Chronicle* of August 1990 took quite a different tone, as did the national press.

> "The whole Jewish community was in a state of shock and sorrow... Nothing like this had ever happened before. That the children who were attacked as they arrived at school are not Jewish made no difference – it happened in one of our Jewish day

schools, where they were so welcome to share in an education based on Jewish values. This incident was not about anti-Semitism, except in the sense that there is a certain responsibility of people who allow anti-Semitic fabrications to circulate, which in this case became a focus for the violent delusions of someone suffering from a sad illness. This incident was about health care. It was about budget constraints, and about just one patient struggling to live with her illness away from medical care... It is also about another kind of prejudice, about the concern now being felt by many patients recovering from psychiatric illness".

The Jewish Council issued a statement in the same issue of the *Jewish Chronicle* that also noted the fact that the woman was deranged. They noted more strongly that her obsession with Jews and anti-Semitism could be accounted for by the ill-considered defamation sometimes heard on talk-back radio.

From the *Jewish Chronicle* editorial, two points about the local Jewish community seemed to stand out. One was that the Jewish school in the country's largest city had a large proportion of gentile students, which explained why Jewish children did not figure among the victims of the attack. The second point, the refusal by elements of the Jewish community and wider society to even consider this an example of anti-Semitism in New Zealand, let alone link it to any themes of civil Judaism, resonates with the tone of our interviews.

In the course of their interviews, people mentioned that New Zealanders admired Jews about as often as they recalled anti-Jewish incidents. Some said that Kiwis respect the intellectual achievements of Jews and the civic contributions prominent Jewish residents made in Dunedin and Auckland. A couple felt being Jewish had a certain chic and that other people wished they had an exotic ethnic background. The interviewees as whole seemed not greatly concerned with either anti-Semitism or philo-Semitism. The fact is that New Zealanders really do not know much about Jews, aside from what they glean from the news, Woody Allen films, or TV programmes like *Seinfeld* and *The Nanny*. The local Jewish community seems loathe to change this state of affairs by drawing attention to Jewish causes.

Ignorance

Informants from other countries found it surprising how little most New Zealanders knew about Jews. People with South African backgrounds noted that, given how little local Jews knew about their own culture, one could hardly expect other New Zealanders to have a high level of awareness about Jewish matters.

"[New Zealand Jews] haven't had the same Yiddishkeit [Jewish culture]. It's not a value judgement. The South African exposure is more prolific and intense. Non-Jews over there, in contact with Jews, would pick up so much Jewish culture. That's something that I noticed here, that people don't. They don't have the same background and understanding that the South African Jews developed around themselves. But they've been happy and kept things going, which is great."

"I don't think that [New Zealand non-Jews] really understand Jews or know Jews, whereas in South Africa they really do know Jews, they really do understand them. They'll understand Kashrut [kosher laws]. They'll understand the holidays, they'll understand all of that. I've had, and my husband's had, plenty of times at work [in New Zealand], 'I know you're Jewish,' and acknowledge all of that, and will literally say to him, 'by the way we're ordering a Christmas ham, would you like one?' There's really no knowledge."

Some New Zealand-born informants agreed. One man said,

"Most people do not understand very much about Jews or Judaism at all. Most Jewish people, and we're probably the same, don't proclaim themselves. Few people stand up and say I'm Jewish or readily identify themselves. It tends to come out quietly in conversation. Someone might ask what the mezuzah on the door means. Most people just associate [Judaism] with the dietary laws and very occasionally with the death of Christ business, [and] don't understand much more".

Another put it this way,

"I just doubt very much that the majority of New Zealanders are aware of who are the Jews in the New Zealand community, and that reflects on the Jewish community itself – the low profile that it has taken for many, many years".

Perhaps the most amazing comment of all on the theme of ignorance is from a woman who was brought up in Dunedin.

"I mean there's no anti-Semitism there because there's so few Jews. People weren't aware. My father was often asked if he was a Protestant Jew or a Catholic Jew."

My first reaction to this comment was that this was impossible. However another informant from Dunedin, when talking about her daughter, said,

"... and so she came home and she was very upset [addressing her daughter who was also present at the interview] oh, they asked you what church you went to, and you said you were Jewish. And they said, 'Yes, but what Jewish? Presbyterian Jewish or Anglican Jewish?' [laughs] This was Miss Smith – you don't remember."

These quotes provide further examples of the "group invisibility" of New Zealand Jews and also hint at some of the effects of taking such a low profile. We have seen how structurally dispersed and accepted Jews are in New Zealand society. With no structural and few social, religious or ideological barriers to assimilation, individuals can easily blend into the wider community. Without some ideology that positively relates Jewishness to being a citizen of New Zealand – and no elements of such an ideology came up in any interviews or other observations – Jewish identity can easily become relegated to a part-time, voluntary, symbolic ethnicity. Downplaying issues, like the allegations by the Wiesenthal Center that Nazi war criminals fled here, detracts from the cultural dynamism of the Jewish community and helps to encourage young, mobile, highly committed Jews who want to live a "Jewish life" to emigrate.

However, I do not mean to imply that personal Jewish identity rests completely on a base provided by religious and/or civil Judaism and their institutions. People do fashion interesting varieties of Jewish identification in New Zealand with or without involvement in organisations. A consideration of how specific individuals fit Jewishness into their lives can better help us to understand how expressions of Jewish identity relate to other aspects of life in New Zealand society. In the sections that follow, we will look at examples of some conventional and idiosyncratic interpretations of Jewishness.

Some New Zealand Jewish Individuals

Two Orthodox Youth

Although few New Zealand Jews actually practice Orthodox Judaism, most affiliated people (70%, as mentioned above) belong to Orthodox congregations. The rabbis, Sunday Schools, daily services, youth groups, visiting speakers and Israel experience programmes consistently urge young people to observe the Jewish religion properly and to migrate to Israel. When this is reinforced at home some children wind up taking Orthodoxy and religious Zionism very seriously. Comments from interviews with two of our twenty-year-old Orthodox interviewees show that being observant makes it hard for these young men to have normal social lives in New Zealand. Both, in fact, have emigrated to Israel.

> Stanley: "I'm an observant Jew. I think that the most important thing about being Jewish is following the Torah, keeping the religion, because that's really what makes us Jewish. I mean there's no cases of a family which has been four generations unobserving shabbat and have stayed Jewish. The other important thing about being Jewish is Israel, ideally living in Israel... I think that marrying out, assimilation is the worst. More people are dying – more Jews have died, this

generation because of intermarriage than anything else. I mean they're still alive but they're dying because they're not Jewish any more... I would bring my children up as religious Jews in Israel, I can't say more clearly than that."

Alan: "Yeah, I'll just be on kibbutz hopefully... I'll go to the army then. I want to do the army because it's part of my ideology to do so, but, of course, I'd rather not. I have been to Israel, I have seen the army there and I know it's not a joke. I know it's deadly serious. Deadly being the appropriate word... While people are out playing rugby or doing sport I'm at home or at the Centre or whatever. If it's sunny outside then, like Shabbat goes on for hours during summer and you begin to wonder, I'm bored senseless – what am I doing?... We talk about it and like we say it's not fair and we are genuinely depressed about it, I mean. We genuinely out of conscience don't want to go out with non-Jewish girls because it might lead to something we don't want. We genuinely make an effort not to go out with non-Jewish girls."

These comments need little elaboration except to say that they point out a problem for Jews in New Zealand not mentioned in the literature cited above. All diaspora Jewish communities worry about assimilation, erosion from the least observant end of the continuum of Jewish practice. In New Zealand erosion from the more committed end presents questions of its own. Some of these questions relate to the communal effects of such out-migration which I take up later in this chapter. However, continuing to consider individuals, can people fashion a stable type of Jewish identification somewhere in the middle, where they can stay Jewish and remain participants in both the Jewish community and wider society?

Conventional Jews

Keesing, Asher, Van Staveren – such important names in New Zealand Jewish history – have essentially disappeared from the community despite the fact that, for example, Rabbi Van Staveren of Wellington had 13 children. In 1986 many descendants of the Keesing and Asher families gathered from around the world to celebrate a family reunion in 1986. They asked the Grey Street congregation in Auckland to put on a Jewish service for them to add flavour to the occasion. Rabbi Genende was unimpressed. He noted that the joyfulness of the reunion for the family did not find a parallel in the feelings of Auckland Jews. For them "it was only tearful" because the Keesings and Ashers had left no Jewish descendants (quoted in Gluckman 1990:258-259).

However, there are sixth-generation New Zealanders who remain active in the Jewish community. The Levys of Wellington provide an example. Although some members of the family intermarried and migrated, they provide an instructive example of how a long-term Jewish presence in the country can be maintained. Benjamin Levy arrived in Wellington in 1853 and served as the second president of the Wellington Hebrew Congregation. He and his wife had 23 children. I interviewed Austin Levy (a great-grandson of Benjamin), his wife Naomi, their daughter and a granddaughter.

Austin spent seven years on the board of the Wellington Hebrew Congregation and was a foundation member and president of the local B'nai B'rith lodge. Yet he and Naomi sent their children to an Anglican school. They felt that this institution provided the best educational opportunities for their children and that the children should participate fully in all school activities. Austin recalled that sitting outside of prayers at Wellington College did nothing for him, so the young Levys took Scripture classes and even won prizes in the subject. The family remains observant but by no means Orthodox in their practice. They participate in community groups, both Jewish and secular, in business, sport, and service activities.

In Auckland, too, there are families who have adopted a similar strategy. They remain active Jews who also participate fully in the cultural, sporting and professional lives of their wider communities. They do not maintain all the standards of Orthodox Judaism, but Jewishness is important to them. They belong to congregations, marry Jews and raise Jewish children. Unlike the two uncompromisingly Orthodox young men, or the unconnected people who drift away, these individuals seem to constitute a somewhat fragile "core" of New Zealand Jews, one with rather different characteristics than Della-Pergola's predictions for America might lead us to expect.

Crossing Boundaries

The difference between Orthodox and conventional Jews is that the latter individuals manage to maintain a dual participation in religious and secular life. They choose to relax their religious observance enough so that it does not interfere with their secular activities, but not to the point where they risk assimilating. There are other possible choices of course. The people who best show some of the more fluid qualities of New Zealand Jewish identity are those who come closest to the boundaries between being Jewish and gentile. The first two people, discussed next show something of the permeability of such boundaries. One, Avram, actually crossed the boundary by converting from a "standard kiwi" to an ultra-Orthodox Jew. The other, Trevor, from an urban Jewish family, has become a stereotypical rural "kiwi bloke". Our sample included a number of other people who have converted to Judaism, but Avram is a rather extreme example. Trevor comes close to crossing the boundary in the other direction and his case involves a mixture of assimilation and acculturation.

Avram has become a Lubavitcher Rabbi. The Lubavitchers are an extremely Orthodox sect of Jews. They follow all 613 of the injunctions found in the bible and live their lives in a totally religious way. They dress in distinctive clothing, live in their own neighbourhoods and wear side curls. There are no such communities in New Zealand. Avram moved from Wellington to Melbourne and then to an inner-city Hasidic neighbourhood in Brooklyn, New York from Wellington. He was ordained there, married, and recently returned to give life in New Zealand another try. He eventually gave up and returned to the United States.

Trevor is the son of an academic, and came from an observant home. The great-grandson of a Wellington rabbi, his family belonged to an Orthodox congregation in Auckland. He is now a sheep farmer in a small North Island town, heavily involved in the local farming community. An avid rugby player, he reminded me greatly of the enthusiastically rural men I met in Southland, while doing research on Stewart Island. He has become that distinctive type of rural "kiwi joker", rarely seen in the urban circles inhabited by most local Jews.

Avram also seemed to epitomise a particular type of individual, in a forceful way. The point is not that he has converted and that he is more observant than many people who are born Jewish. He has gone far beyond all that, and actually dresses, eats, speaks and lives as a Hasid. Yet his ancestors came from England four generations ago. His family belonged to an Anglican church. He went to a Christian Sunday School, and attended a Presbyterian College. How did he become a Jew?

Avram answers this question in two ways. Firstly, he points out that he always had an interest in Jewish topics, and specifically mentions that James Michener's book, *The Source,* had an impact on him. His father also had a Jewish friend whom he knew. But these mundane factors do not mean as much to Avram as the fact that his very interest in things Jewish is evidence that he may always have had a Jewish soul.

My understanding of the concept of the Jewish soul comes from a study session which Avram chaired at the home of Wellington's Orthodox Rabbi. Each Jew has a soul connected to other Jewish souls, all present at the great events in Jewish history, such as the giving of the Law to Moses on Mount Sinai. Having this soul defines a Jew, so one can be Jewish without practicing Judaism. It is also possible to have a Jewish soul and not know it. As Avram said:

"Basically in Jewish law, when a non-Jew converts it is like a child is being born. A Jewish child is being born. In other words he sort of gains the soul, the Jewish soul which he didn't have before. Another opinion is that, really it was there before, but later it was sort of brought out and revealed. So by me, all I can say, is that from a very young age I always had this awareness, even from the first time I heard about a chosen people, let's say in Sunday School. It pricked my interest very much to know what it was all about, although I didn't have any means to follow it up. And then, when I first came to university, I got involved over here with the Friends of Israel group."

As he became more active, Avram approached the local Rabbi with a request to convert. As he learned more about the religion he decided, "Well I can't do so much in New Zealand. You can't really become Jewish in New Zealand in the true sense of the word, in the Orthodox sense of the word". The rabbi encouraged him to go to Melbourne where more Orthodox facilities existed. He converted there, studied further, and went to New York to become a rabbi himself.

He visited Wellington regularly during his years of study, and expressed his appreciation of his family's understanding that he had made a serious decision, one which they respect. But being ultra-Orthodox does distance Avram from his origins. "I don't think they ever will understand what I've done, in reality. I mean, even now they don't understand exactly. You know how big a step it is because, really, the truth of the matter is when a non-Jew becomes Jewish, he now becomes a new person entirely." Judaism, for him, is not just a religion but a way of life. He goes on to explain that in the "ultimate sense, in the spiritual sense" he cannot relate to his family. But he follows the biblical injunction to honour his parents.

Avram's definition of Jewishness is a religious one. An ethnic or cultural definition would exclude a convert, although the idea of a nascent Jewish soul opens the possibility for assuming an ultimately Jewish origin.

Trevor has also made himself a new person, but sees a less radical break with his past. He always liked rugby, which clashed with Saturday morning services, so he did not attend synagogue much after his Bar Mitzvah. (At 13 a Jewish boy becomes a man and thus responsible for his own religious participation.) After high school he did agricultural training and worked as a shearer to finance himself onto a farm. He settled in a small town and married a local girl. He got married in a church.

"Yeah, for her I did that, because it's always the lady's big day. The stag do's the guy's big day. Once he's through that it's all right. So, yeah, I did, and I suppose that's what she's always wanted as a girl. You get a choice of a church service, so I picked and she didn't have any objections. So there was a mention of God, but there was nothing mentioned of Christ or that in it. It was a good compromise, so that was fair enough, and the guy marrying us knew I was Jewish so he didn't – there was no trying to convert me or make me any different."

Trevor feels Jewish. "I definitely wouldn't be anything else". But as the only Jew in his town he has no scope for involvement with other Jewish people. He avoids eating pork and shellfish however, and this led to an interesting incident at a community function. Somehow it got around that he was Jewish.

"I told someone. I might have been talking about it, or might have been talking about something about Israel, and I've mentioned the fact. And being a small community, I can remember I was amazed at how fast it got round and... somebody all of a sudden put chops in front of me and everyone was having bacon and I realised well they must have found out, and known enough about it to know that I didn't eat bacon."

(Interviewer) "So it's not something you had requested, people hadn't seen you, say at home, not eating it or – "

"No, they did it off their own bat. The odd person asked me if it was true, what they heard, and I said 'yes', and we just carried on about something else, or asked me a bit about it. And then went on to what the conversation of the day was – test match or wool prices or whatever."

Unlike Avram, who sees himself cut off from his roots by an essential gulf of spirituality, Trevor sees the distance as more social and geographical. He said he would belong to a congregation if he lived in Wellington. He cannot really raise Jewish children in his town, but this is because he is far away from other Jews. He is accepted, and his Jewishness makes no difference to other people.

"I think in a farming community you tend to get joked on what you are, rather than who you are. It's like my father being a professor. It means nothing, it makes me no better than the next man. No one really expects me to be brighter than anyone else. I'm just another person, more judged on my own performances, which I think is good. And it's the same being Jewish, or Christian, or we've got a very good friend who's a Hindu, and he plays football in the same football club. His wife was chosen for him. He had to go away to India, and they had a big stag party before he went to India, 'cos even though he didn't announce he was getting married over there, everyone knew it was the tradition, that they get shipped back to India to get a wife and come back married. And so, no one thinks any differently."

You can be a good kiwi bloke by joining in with the rest of the locals. Playing rugby, drinking beer, going to social events, being a farmer and an all-around "regular joker" make your reputation. What you do at home, in your spare time, is your own affair. But Trevor has made adjustments that would be unacceptable to Orthodox Jews. He eats non-kosher food, as do most New Zealand Jews. He said in our interview that he would have eaten the bacon if he had no other choice, out of courtesy. He got married in a church, something that, to many, would constitute a break with the Jewish people. The fact that he can interpret all this in a way compatible with a continuing identification for himself, provides an example of the shift of identification, from a multifaceted, communal, "traditional" basis, to an almost purely symbolic and individualistic one.

Avram represents what a more "traditional" and "authentic" Jewish identity would have been like a few generations ago. He does not feel free to interpret Jewishness for himself. He says:

> "Judaism is not just a religion in the sense of other religions as you're probably aware. If you get into it more, you realise it even more so. Judaism encompasses every aspect of a person's living, from the way you tie your shoes to which hand you wipe yourself with, to which way you dress, all that sort of thing, every detail of a person's living. And to me that makes an awful amount of sense, because I mean that's what a religion is supposed to be. It's supposed to be a way of life, how you live, it's supposed to affect every purpose, everything you do in life."

To live this way, without compromise, requires residence in a kind of Jewish community not available in New Zealand.

Although both these men have moved across social boundaries, moving one way is obviously much easier than the other. Being a New Zealander was compatible with being a Jew for most of our interviewees. Trevor, however, has developed a more specifically kiwi lifestyle than most people who still identify as Jews. His case shows that it is possible to fashion an identification with Jewishness even while adopting the values and behaviours of the least Jewish sector of a country whose culture has virtually no Jewish content. Adopting a specifically Hasidic Jewish lifestyle, on the other hand, led Avram to leave New Zealand and created a fundamental gap between himself and his family.

Converts

Avram's conversion and subsequent Jewish identification made a radical break with his former life. We interviewed four other converts for whom becoming Jewish was less of a transformation, but who nevertheless crossed a social and cultural boundary. Their accounts show how the event of conversion elicits reactions from both Jews and gentiles who are directly involved. Jews are confronted by people who now claim to share some part of their identity, while friends and relations may now see the convert very differently than before.

Conversions done by Orthodox authorities tend to be accepted by everyone. Strictly Orthodox people (such as the informant quoted above who talked about problems when people from the two congregations want to marry) will not recognise Liberal converts or their children as Jews. These differences can create problems of identity within the community. Here is one example of an uncompromising reaction:

> "It's like if you decide to be a Christian you can go and get baptised the next day. Like if you want to be Jewish – a liberal Jew – you go and get converted the next day. Not quite the next day, but... Orthodox Jews, you know, we have to learn for a year or so, and then have to pass tests."

This characterisation of Liberal conversion practice, especially its purported similarity with Christianity, can be offensive to converts. However, our converted Progressive informants did not seem especially troubled as they are fully accepted in their own Jewish circles. For example, one man who married a Jewish woman felt extremely comfortable around her relations and said that being Jewish "just fit". He had come from a broken home and lost touch with his father. He liked the Jewish emphasis on the family and wanted to make his own as strong as possible. He felt totally accepted by the wife's family, and his mother had no opposition to his becoming Jewish. His friends knew nothing about Jews and held no particular opinions of them. When they saw that his personality did not change and that he still acted the same with them, "there wasn't a problem".

He did not convert in the Orthodox shul because his job requires working on the Jewish Sabbath. He occasionally attends services at the Orthodox congregation to be with his in-laws and understands that he cannot be called to read the Law there (that is, to participate publicly in the service). Religious politics can be unpleasant, but he avoids them. He accepts that he is not ethnically Jewish. But, as he and his wife both mentioned, he looks more Jewish than she does. They believe that this makes life easier for them than it would be if he was the blond one, as people seem not to be aware, or just forget, that he was not born Jewish.

This couple's story was echoed by a woman a generation senior to them. A New Zealander of Scottish background, she met and married a religious Jewish man from Dunedin. They wed first, and then she went to Australia to undergo an Orthodox conversion. Although both of their parental families expressed displeasure at the time, they got over their difficulties quickly.

She felt the community totally accepted her. "It was all really rather wonderful. And from then on, I haven't really given very much thought to not being Jewish actually." She participates fully in Jewish activities and, with her husband, has had a notable role in Auckland's civic affairs. Her children are active in Orthodox Judaism.

A Maori man married a Jewish woman whose parents opposed the relationship and essentially cut them off. They married in the registry office, and were blessed in the church of his community. A member of her family sent them a bereavement card. But after a while "things started to come right", and they began to visit and have dinner with her family. Meanwhile, the wife carried on with some Jewish practices in the home and our interviewee became interested in finding out more about Jews and Judaism. He felt there was not much chance of getting the knowledge he wanted in New Zealand, so he suggested that they move to Israel.

They migrated and went through the entire Israeli immigrant-absorption process. He attended classes at a religious centre for immigrants and eventually went through an Orthodox conversion. The couple bought a small farm and raised tomatoes. They had a Jewish wedding in Israel. Like virtually all Israeli men his age, our informant underwent military training and joined an army reserve unit. It was in the army that he really began to feel Jewish, because the other soldiers, whom he admired, accepted him as one of them.

> "They were actually commandos... Israeli commandos, but they had been too old. They got to around about 25, and so they were put out back into us... we were actually an attack unit. So these guys were sitting around, and it was the first time they'd ever spoken of their experiences and the things that they did in the name of Israel, or in the name of Jewish people. Not nice things, I'll say that, and they were actually sitting around there, huddled around there, just looking at the flame, and I could actually see the tears dropping from their eyes. These grown men, hard as nails, you know... and here they were, telling me their stories, and just letting it all out, like on a psychologist's couch or something... one after one they were telling me their story. And I felt so privileged of having these men, and being part of this group relaying all their inner feelings to me. Because the whole thing about being a Jew then was all, all related back to that, of them being Jewish, and them being, doing the best for their children, for their right to be on this earth, because it was not as if they wanted to do these things. But you know, these men were so hurt. You know, and they were just hard men. To me, they'd made me straight away, that they accepted me as one of them, no one else had sort of came out to me and said that. But they have since then, a lot of people, I'm now a member of Temple Sinai [the Progressive Wellington congregation]."

His experiences in Israel deeply influenced this informant. He thinks of himself as more Jewish than Maori, although he has lived back in his home town, keeps in touch with his family of birth and has since divorced. Both his sons have been Bar Mitzvah, and the elder spent a year in Israel. His wife acknowledges and promotes their identification with their Maori heritage, while bringing them up Jewish.

Our last convert is a woman who did not come to Judaism through a romantic attachment. An active Presbyterian, she became alienated from the church. Having read about Judaism, she decided to go through a Liberal conversion, and became active in the Wellington congregation. Most of her family expressed neither disapproval nor encouragement. Her brother was unhappy, however. "I said I was changing my religion, and he said, 'Oh you're not going to become a Catholic are you?' And, I said, 'No', and they said to me, 'A Catholic would have been better'." Her brother's attitude has softened since then, but she describes some awkwardness. The family does much of its socialising through Christian ritual, and this makes it difficult for her to participate. For example:

> "Three years ago I had a niece who was killed in a car accident, and when I went down there they wanted me to take the funeral. And they said to me 'Oh, you may not want to', but the minister down there, the Presbyterian minister, was someone who was just relieving, and they didn't know him and he didn't know their daughter. They wanted someone taking the service who knew them and they asked me to do it. So I thought, well they must respect me enough that they could do that. So I did it. They said 'You might not want to', but I mean I wouldn't turn anything like that down. Well it wasn't a particularly religious service, it was mostly about her. So I just felt that if they didn't mind, they were so lost at the time, that they wanted someone just to help them anyway, because it was just so terrible for them."

Christmas presented problems for her for some years. But now that her brother's feelings have relaxed, she is invited to spend Christmas with the family, and they accept that she will not go to church. Easter presents problems however. It conflicts with Passover, and the woman feels that there is some animosity towards Jews over the death of Christ.

The four converts discussed in this section have all experienced a certain amount of distancing from their relatives, but this was not always due to their becoming Jewish. The first man came from a broken home and saw Judaism as a way to build a solid family of his own. The other converts had some difficulties with their relatives when they became Jewish, but these were not insurmountable.

Acceptance by the other Jews with whom they came into contact seems high. The two Progressive converts were a childless woman and a man, so none of the four informants faced the difficulties of having their children's Jewishness called into question in any context. The fact that they were accepted in non-Jewish circles indicates that crossing the boundary between Jew and gentile in New Zealand does not create social difficulties. One needs to make some considerable effort to become Jewish, but the doors are relatively open to people willing to make that commitment. To move in the opposite direction seems to require no effort at all. As we shall see, one can quite simply cease to be Jewish.

Disengaging

Two of our interviewees, who came from solid, observant, Jewish backgrounds, provide examples of how an individual can let Jewishness lapse. I just assumed that one of them was Jewish because her parents belonged to the Orthodox congregation in Wellington, and she attended Hebrew school and a Jewish youth organisation as a child. She cautioned me not to jump to conclusions regarding her identity. We were discussing Israel at the time and whether she felt any tie to that country. Her reply was surprising:

> "Well, like when you say is it an important aspect of being Jewish you know, [pause] that just sounds much more a resolved kind of statement than I would make about myself. I would have some difficulty just saying terribly loudly, or strongly, that I am Jewish, for a start. So I don't think you should."

The phrase "loudly or strongly", seems significant because she went on to mention that she does not "look Jewish" or have a Jewish-sounding last name. Despite her earlier participation in the congregation, she did not have "Jewish friends" in New Zealand, although she did have "friends who are Jewish." Her ability to put Jewishness at arm's length seems to her predicated on the fact that people do not identify her as a Jew – which is hardly unusual since Jews are so invisible in New Zealand. The elaborate anti-Semitic stereotypes that exist in Europe, though known and occasionally broadcast here, seem absent from New Zealand culture.

If a person wants to assimilate, they can because there is little resistance from the wider society to their blending in, and the Jewish community cannot force individuals to be or stay Jewish. This woman correctly represented Jewish identity as a matter of choice, and upbraided me for assuming that she chose to be Jewish. Where I grew up, New York City, voluntary self-identification is important but the options to assimilate are more limited by civil Judaism, densely Jewish social networks and the high-profile nature of Jewish ethnicity.

Imran gives us a somewhat different kind of example. He says he feels Jewish, but it becomes apparent that he has his own, idiosyncratic way of defining this. Born in India to a Jewish family that came there from Persia some hundreds of years ago, Imran moved to New Zealand from Britain. Some of his siblings and other relations reside in Israel. He lives with a non-Jewish woman. Here is how he talks about being Jewish in New Zealand:

> "I've sort of changed it [being Jewish] and that's good... all this stuff about the moral perspective on the world. Where does that come from? Why have I got it? Why am I this sort of person? Why aren't I an amoral bastard, you know? Why can't I just go around destroying trees and jumping up and down on kiwis? I mean, I can't, I wouldn't, I mean, why am I like that? And I think for me personally, I'm like that, because I have a Jewish past that said, that gave me all these stories, that gave me all those things. So I think there's more there that would just emerge. I don't honestly see myself as becoming religious. I might actually get more involved in a cultural thing. I might actually celebrate the festivals in my own way. I mean, I've found myself trying to do that in New Zealand. I've gone out and bought some matzo and occasionally eaten it, you know, around about the right time. So, I might actually do little things like that, and I think it's a personal thing.
>
> "I've met, in the last year and a half, I've met elements of Jewish people that I didn't know existed here. Like I thought there was Webb Street and that was it. Now I've met some people who are connected to the Liberal Jewish synagogue down here. I went to a couple of dos, you know, but I didn't really feel very strongly connected. I've met a couple, some people I painted a house for in Mount Vic, a Jewish family. I must admit, it took quite a few months to paint this house because I kept coming back and going back. I must admit I felt 100% at ease around them, even though their Judaism and their whole background is really different to mine. Their kids meant something a bit more to me. I'm not sure what, but they did, and I found it very easy to relate to these little kids."

Imran feels Jewish but does not to want to affiliate to local organisations. He discusses the possibility of maintaining some religious observance but says this is not possible because his partner and her children are not Jewish. Jewish identification has become a purely internalised matter of "feelings". This itself is similar to the previous informant, and other people discussed above. They define what they like as Jewish, and come up with vague, idiosyncratic statements, because they do not participate in standard communal institutions and they live in a society where being labelled Jewish is unlikely. In other words, there is a lack of standardisation of symbols for these informants, and a minimal overlap in the ways they conceive Jewishness.

Vaguely Jewish

A woman introduced herself to me at a social event run by the school my son attends. She told me how happy she was that her son and mine had become friends. She said she wanted her son to interact with Jews because they were Jewish and it was so important to them. As I tried to place her in the local community she said that her mother's mother came from Germany and married a gentile New Zealander. The woman herself was married to a Catholic and her "Jewish" son had been baptised in the Catholic church! No one in the family belonged to any Jewish organisations, her son was not Bar Mitzvah, and they did not interact with other Jewish people. Jewishness may have meant a lot to this woman, but I'm not sure she had firm ideas about what precisely it did mean.

The conversation reminded me strongly of some of our interviewees' statements. Three people in our sample, all the children of mixed marriages where the Jewish parent made no special attempt to bring the children into the community, identified in ways similar to the woman described above. Two of the men became interested in their roots. One, Kevin, went to Israel and worked on a kibbutz and remembers feeling "very Jewish" at the time. He married a Catholic woman, who finds his Jewish background appealing, and they decided their children needed to have exposure to religious values. They have not decided between Catholicism and Judaism, so they planned to attend both kinds of services with the children and let them make a choice. Kevin felt comfortable with other Jews and thought his appreciation of culture and intellectual pursuits derived from his Jewish background. His friends envy the cachet it brings him.

Barry grew up thinking his immigrant parents fled from Germany for political reasons. He did not find out about his mother's Jewish origins until he was a teenager. He became close friends with a highly identified Jewish man of similar background while studying overseas and this stimulated him to find out more about his family. He seemed very unsure about labelling himself Jewish, but like Kevin has a philo-Semitic partner. She considers him Jewish and it rubs off. Her family even worries about whether he can eat what they serve him at meals. But Barry does not feel Jewish around other Jews. He has no intention of doing anything at all about being Jewish. However, it is still a meaningful part of his background.

Kate, the third individual, grew up in a small town where her father arrived as a refugee and married into a local family. She still finds it puzzling that her mother's provincial family accepted this Polish Jew so fully. Her Anglican mother had her confirmed in the church but wanted Kate to know about her Jewish background. Kate felt that her other Jewish relatives (the father helped his brother migrate to New Zealand) and the Orthodox community kept her from becoming Jewish. She understood that having a gentile mother made her non-Jewish by Orthodox law and with no Liberal congregations established until the 1960s she never could make satisfactory contact with formal Jewish life. She visited her Jewish cousins but knew that her uncle's family felt her father did wrong to marry out. She never felt like a typical kiwi, though, and convinced herself to go to Israel where she would find her people. The experience proved something of a shock and she returned a confirmed New Zealander. Her "lapsed Catholic" husband liked Israel and the Jewish people, and she enjoyed emphasising her Jewishness to her in-laws just "to be perverse". Their son feels he has a Jewish background but has no interest in Judaism. Kate feels most Jewish when her friends make anti-Israel remarks.

Leaving New Zealand

A number of our informants spent time in Israel and came back to New Zealand. Their experiences of the realities of immigrant life, problems with language and employment, cultural differences and loneliness overwhelmed their ideological commitments. When they came back they found it easier to fit Jewishness into their New Zealand lifestyle. Some, like Kate, relaxed their Jewish commitments, others remained conventional New Zealand Jews. Perhaps a selection process is operating here. The more fully committed, uncompromisingly Jewish individuals stay away and the more flexible come back or never leave in the first place. This issue came up before in the discussion of the two Orthodox Jews who went to Israel. However, another, easier option presents itself to people who find New Zealand Jewishness does not live up to their demands: migration to Australia.

According to Rubinstein (1991:42) Jewish commitment "is markedly stronger in Australia than elsewhere, conceivably with less assimilation than anywhere else in the diaspora." In Melbourne and Sydney three quarters of primary school age Jewish children attend Jewish day schools and more than half go to Jewish high schools. Although not everyone feels as positive as Rubinstein does about Australian Jewry, Melbourne and Sydney looked like very attractive destinations to a significant number of kiwi Jews. New Zealanders can freely move to Australia, a country socially and culturally very similar to their own. They can improve their Jewish lives and stay relatively close to home.

The New Zealand Jewish population decrease of 657, between 1976 and 1991, almost exactly matches the 647 New Zealand Jews living in Australia (Bureau of Immigration and Population Research 1994). As a member of the Wellington Hebrew Congregation it seemed to me that the people we saw departing were the ones most involved in the religious and secular activities of the community. The 31 expatriate New Zealand Jews interviewed for our project in Melbourne and Sydney reinforced this impression. They talked about the Jewish atmosphere of certain suburbs, the choice of synagogues and schools, and the Jewish neighbourhoods and shops that seemed so wonderful compared to New Zealand. The expatriates knew that people tried hard back home and they appreciated their efforts, but feared New Zealand Jews laboured under possibly overwhelming constraints.

> "I pleaded with the parents of people in Habonim (a youth group), 'For God's sake take your kids to Australia. You don't have the resources or the critical mass to be able to provide your kids with the full sort of Jewish life that is required."

Figures from this informant's New Zealand synagogue bear him out. The Wellington Orthodox congregation averaged about seven marriages and 14 births per year in the 1960s. There were only three marriages and 17 births recorded for the entire five-year period from 1986 to 1990. Deaths have outnumbered births for every year since 1970.

Although interview data and observation support the idea that migration to Australia involves mostly committed Jews, this is really a quantitative question. The non-random sample of interviews provides a good source of data for uncovering styles of New Zealand Jewish identity, but cannot form the basis for any generalisations about the distribution of the identity types discussed here. In order to find out if the people who left could be described as highly committed, I constructed a short postal questionnaire which I sent to a random sample of 140 people selected from the lists of New Zealand Jews in Sydney and Melbourne kept by two expatriate New Zealanders for their social clubs[19]. One hundred and ten forms (80%) came back, a very good rate of return for a mailed survey.

About two thirds of respondents agreed or strongly agreed (on a five-point scale from "strongly agree" to "strongly disagree") that they came to Australia in order to live in a more Jewish environment and had increased their levels of Jewish participation after the move. Virtually the same number indicated that their desire to find a Jewish spouse constituted an important reason for the move. Furthermore, there was a high correlation (.79) between answers to these two questions on Jewish reasons for migrating and Jewish marriage. Approximately 80% of the respondents indicated that they belonged to Orthodox congregations in Australia and were observant Jews. These survey results clearly supported the interview and observation data. Thus, strong observance and total Jewish identification may present as serious a threat to New Zealand Jewish continuity as does assimilation.

---

[19] Combined, the lists had a total of 280 different addresses.

Identification and Jewish Continuity in New Zealand

According to Silberman (1985) Jews remained Jewish in the past for three reasons: because it was demanded by God, they were born into a functioning community of Jews, or anti-Semites would not accept them. In New Zealand Jews worried more about assimilation than anti-Semitism and realised that being born Jewish does not automatically make a person part of a community. The viability of the Jewish organisations that function in New Zealand, like those of the "white ethnics" Alba studied in the United States, depended completely on the voluntary affiliation of individuals. Only the very observant said anything about religion, but even they did not mention the need to follow the Lord's commandments, emphasising instead that observance expresses and guarantees continuity.

Everyone who was formally interviewed, as well as everyone who was spoken to on the topic casually in the course of observation, agreed that Jewish identity in New Zealand was largely voluntary in nature. This idea, that one can choose a suitable degree of Jewishness, provides an example of the tendency for "thematicity" to pervade cultural knowledge. Holland and Quinn 1987:10-11) note that "a small number of very general-purpose cultural models... are repeatedly incorporated into other cultural models developed for special purposes". The general-purpose model that people work with is the idea that in contemporary society we consciously make and remake ourselves.

For the special purpose of constructing a Jewish identity, our informants' range of choice is circumscribed by the fact that Jewishness has content that defines specific authenticity. As Avram said, the Jewish religion has something to say about "every detail of a person's living". A few individuals, like him, completely accepted the authority of the Jewish religion and rabbinical direction (as well as the main tenets of secular Judaism), adhered to this religious, cultural and ideological corpus very closely, and constructed a "traditional" way of life. "Conventional" Jews joined and participated in congregations and secular Jewish activities, and they also recognised the public content of Jewishness and felt committed to it. However, they made compromises in order to maintain a lifestyle that was both comfortably Jewish and acceptably kiwi.

Other individuals lost touch with the public sphere and completely privatised their Jewishness. The individualism of the wider society defined the legitimacy of the privateness of their Jewish identification, and generated much of the diversity of commitment we saw in the interviews. Some felt that their serious intellectuality set them apart, while others emphasised morality. Like certain postmodernist theorists we will meet later in this book, authority, authenticity and public symbols mattered little to them. These people who I label "idiosyncratic" Jews not only created the Jewishness they wanted for themselves, they kept it to themselves and had no commitment to passing anything Jewish onto their children. They differed from "vague" identifiers because they made definite statements about being Jewish. Vaguely identified individuals sometimes considered themselves Jews, but only when their partners and in-laws so defined them.

Traditional and conventional Jews may express derisory opinions about the content of idiosyncratic and vague Jewishness, but the very private (and therefore culturally valid) nature of these forms of identification made rule-based evaluations besides the point. Since everyone, even the very traditional, acknowledges the private and voluntary nature of Jewish identification, the ability of traditional communal authority in New Zealand to establish even an appearance of conformity in individual identity is weak. When we shift focus from considering how individuals identify to asking how these types of identity relate to Jewish continuity, conventionally valid expressions of Jewishness seem to take on greater significance.

Unlike the situation in the United States where religiously orthodox Jews seem destined to form the core of succeeding generations, "traditional" New Zealand Jews augment the populations of Sydney and Melbourne. "Vague" Jews intermarry and do not have Jewish children. Erosion from "above" and "below" seems obvious enough, but will the middle hold? My data certainly does not permit any firm predictions, but it is apparent that conventional and idiosyncratic types of Jewish identity are not inherently stable.

Although the distinction between idiosyncratic and conventional Jews is conceptually clear, people can easily move between these two styles of identity. For example, if Imran met other Jewish people and joined Temple Sinai he would become "conventional". This might not make his children Jewish. Some "conventional" informants have children who do not identify as Jews because their partners promoted competing identities. Conventional Jews can also easily become idiosyncratic by ceasing to associate with Jewish people or organisations and then have children who are only vaguely Jewish. They can also end up with "traditional" children who become religious through contact with rabbis, Hebrew School teachers, youth group leaders and other highly motivated children. Stanley's intense commitment to the Jewish religion and decision to move to Israel surprised his parents. Conventional Jews show that individuals can build a kiwi style of Jewishness, but the intergenerational stability of conventional Jewish identification is variable.

Conclusion

Looking at individual accounts of Jewish identity in their own terms shows a little bit of everything: the immutability of a primordial identity, its adaptability and also its decline. Assimilation, transformation, continuity, change and symbolic ethnicity are echoed in various parts of different interviews. At this level the narratives look very "postmodern". People seem to "invent" Jewishness for themselves from a variety of resources and construct styles that range from close adherence to a venerable religious tradition to the eclectic use of images from popular culture. This fluidity of individual styles seems to support the idea of postmodern theorists that "there is no longer an unchallenged foundation, meta-narrative or reference point for understanding" that flows from established (in this case, Jewish) institutions. Instead we have "multiple worlds which are constituted by the historically situated imaginations of persons and groups spread around the globe" (Appadurai quoted in Smart 1993:146-147). On the other hand, the material as a corpus of data provides excellent evidence of how structural conditions lead to cultural transformation; in this case an overall symbolicisation of Jewish ethnicity. New Zealand Jews and people who talk about New Zealand Jewry sometimes fail to appreciate the limits social structure places on the types of identity people can produce.

When Jacob Neusner visited New Zealand in 1994 he commented on the "pathetic and dying community" in Canterbury and also predicted that New Zealand Jewry would be the first national community to voluntarily cease to exist. Clive Lawton, the head of Jewish Continuity in Great Britain, also visited New Zealand in that same year, offering us a very different view of the future. The keynote speaker at the "Beyond 2000, Jewish Continuity in New Zealand" conference held in Auckland, Lawton said that small communities have advantages. He regaled the audience with tales of Gibraltar (his mother's place of origin), a place of few Jews, but a real Jewish community. The secret to success lies in a return to observance. In essence Neusner and Lawton agreed that New Zealand Jews could use a good dose of Yiddishkeit, Jewish culture. Neusner scolded them for letting things slip, as if they had a choice, while Lawton called on the conferees to get started. Learn Hebrew word lists! Invite a friend to synagogue! Get the ball rolling! If Gibraltar can have a vibrant Jewish community, why not New Zealand?

The answer seems apparent when we consider that Gibraltar's land area is 6.5 square kilometres and the territory has a total population of 30,000. In those circumstances a tiny ethnic group (who seem from Lawton's account to be heavily concentrated in retail trade) can indeed persevere with individual determination and commitment. The Jewish population of New Zealand, dispersed residentially and occupationally, heterogeneous in origin and socially disconnected, contends with a set of conditions that present very different possibilities. People can choose to live observant lives, but strict Jewish observance requires functioning Jewish communities and a large measure of detachment from the wider society. In order to keep kosher in New Zealand a person cannot eat outside a very few homes. To properly observe the Jewish Sabbath (from sundown Friday to sundown Saturday) means missing out on sport and cultural activities. One should not use motorised transport, so even exercising the self-control to avoid secular activities and attend religious services (unless one lives within walking distance) results in "breaking" the Sabbath. The kind of observance that Neusner and Lawton promote requires individual fortitude. Difficult as it may be, individuals can make such a choice. However, when they do, it often means that the possibility of a more orthodox community diminishes because the strongly committed leave and thereby lessen the overall level of orthodoxy.

The overall picture of New Zealand Jewish identification that emerges from the material presented here seems to resonate well with the structural dispersion of the Jewish population. Participation in community life is limited, ideology muted, and Jewishness becomes privatised and individualised. The wider social and cultural context of New Zealand society interacts with and reinforces the dissipation of Jewish solidarity.

New Zealand has been characterised as a highly secular, individualistic and aggressively egalitarian society. Vowles says that, "It may be on the dimension of equality of regard that New Zealand egalitarianism had its soundest basis: in other words, in a relative lack of status barriers to social mixing, a relative lack of social snobbery" (1987:227). Jews participate enthusiastically and easily in New Zealand life, but in order to do so they forbear to raise particularistic Jewish issues. Particularism raises the spectre of difference and barriers to participation in society which are anathema to local Jews. The quietness about Nazi war criminals, expressions of sympathy towards members of Baltic families who may be wrongly labelled fascists and the woman who stabbed the children at Kadimah college, the low-key civil Judaism, all provide concrete evidence that acceptance is contingent upon privatised identity. Privatised identity helps create interesting varieties of individualism for our informants but undermines the forms of Jewishness that produce and maintain authentic public expressions of Jewish culture which can be passed on to the next generation.

Although the privatised nature of New Zealand Jewish ethnicity fits the structural conditions of New Zealand society and its Jewish population, these conditions do not necessarily constitute "causes". We cannot discount the possibility that the Jews who came here differed from their brethren overseas before they left. Sowell points out that Scots have fared well in America, but people of Scottish ancestry in Appalachia have constituted one of the most persistent pockets of poor whites in the United States.

> (I)t may be plausible to believe, that "objective conditions" in Appalachia, or the way people were "treated" there, accounts for the anomaly. Indeed, prevailing social doctrines all but require that approach. Yet, if the history of the Scots is viewed internationally, then it becomes clear that the subgroup which settled in Appalachia differed culturally from other Scots before either boarded the ships to cross the Atlantic. (1994)

Japanese migrants in the United States and Brazil present a parallel picture. American Japanese, interned in camps during the second world war, nevertheless remained loyal Americans while their much less discriminated-against Brazilian counterparts fanatically supported Japan. Conditions in either country do not explain these differences, rather the two groups had differing backgrounds in Japan.

The example of the returnees from Israel and the migration of Jews overseas provides evidence that something similar happens for New Zealand's Jews. People leave this country for Jewish reasons, but nobody immigrates or returns here to "live Jewish lives". New Zealand's isolation and distance from centres of conflict draw immigrants and tourists. Although Jewish refugees may not have had a choice of where to go when they came here (Beaglehole 1988) those who remained in the country or arrived under harrowing circumstances found something else attractive. A former orthodox Rabbi in Wellington put it this way:

> "In South Africa I worked in a smaller community, less than one-quarter the size of this one but every day we had a minyan [a quorum of 10 Jewish men need to hold a service]. Ninety percent celebrated every holiday, while here 20% are active, 80% you don't see... The Jews who came to New Zealand, I think Judaism is at the bottom of their list of priorities because if it were higher they would not come... People who decided to make the move wanted to be far away from Jewishness."

If that is the case, they certainly found themselves in a country with a Jewish community that did not pressure them to increase their level of commitment.

In a recent article about Greek Jews, Lewkowicz (1994:225-240) says that they worry little about anti-Semitism. The Jewish community centre in Thessaloniki sits in the middle of town, but is so inconspicuous that most people do not know it is there. The local university contains building material taken from Jewish cemetery headstones, but the Jews never complained. When Lewkowicz asked people about their Jewish identity their answers seemed vague. She feels that privatising Jewishness prevents confrontation with other Greeks, "who remain absent from the private spheres in which Jewishness becomes expressed."

The type of answers Lewkowicz got to her questions about Jewish identity in Thessaloniki are familiar. The synagogue in Wellington is reasonably close to the centre of town and difficult to pick out as a Jewish building. Perhaps another reason Greek Jews privatise their identity is that Greekness is closely associated with Greek Orthodoxy, just as Judaism is the religion of the Jewish people. Although one can be a Greek national and a Jew, can one be ethnically Greek and a Jew at the same time? Perhaps privatised Jewishness helps people to avoid this conundrum. It certainly does in New Zealand, where Jews do not seem to be recognised as an ethnic group. The ignorance that our informants stressed provides one manifestation of this. The current emphasis on biculturalism provides another. Implementing the principles of the Treaty of Waitangi, and working out the interrelationship between Maori and pakeha occupies almost the entire landscape of contemporary ethnic politics in New Zealand. As we shall see in the next chapter, this strengthens and stimulates public expressions of Maori ethnicity. Thus Jews become part of an amalgamated pakeha category by default, and find their (not undesired) invisibility reinforced by yet another condition of New Zealand social and cultural life.

Ngati Awa Claimants Welcoming Members of the Waitangi Tribunal

(From left to right: Ching Tutua and Pouroto Ngaroto, Ngati Awa; John Turei, Tribunal member; Riparata Tawa, Ngati Awa; and Chief Judge Edward Durie, Tribunal Chair).

5

Biculturalism

> The other side of Maori culture is all around us... far from uniqueness, harmony, and wholeness it immediately and somewhat threateningly reflects New Zealand history and society: the downcast uncomprehending eyes in response to spoken Maori... black wool singlets, gum boots... two street maintenance workers leaning on shovels and watching a third dig around a watermain; young unemployed eyes gazing expressionlessly from under a baggy stocking cap. (Webster 1993:228)

> New Zealand Maori people have trod down many paths in their attempts to come to terms with the Pakeha world. Independence, partnership, armed resistance, withdrawal, messianic movements, litigation, tribal unity, ethnicity, sovereignty, biculturalism: all seemed to promise more than they ultimately delivered. (Levine and Henare 1994:207)

Jews and Maori in New Zealand share a concern with continuity. Leaders of both groups worry about an alarming rate of acculturation and assimilation. While individual Jews can solve their identity problems by migrating to Jewish communities in other countries, Maori have no such option. To ensure continuity and improve their marginal position in New Zealand society they must reinvigorate social groups, and reverse the loss of language, culture and identity at home. To realise these goals Maori articulated a variety of demands since the 1970s for self-determination and the creation of a bicultural state. This chapter focuses on the development, efflorescence, and increasingly apparent limits of biculturalist ideology. The main sources of data for this chapter come from cases heard before the Waitangi Tribunal and other forums that serve as sites for the public elaboration of Maori collective identity. Academics take an active part in producing ideological statements about biculturalism and their analyses, speculations and fantasies also enter into the discussion.

The indigenous people of New Zealand arrived from eastern Polynesia approximately one thousand years ago. The kinship-oriented pre-contact societies that they developed superficially resemble the Papua New Guinean groups discussed in Chapter 3. However, three important differences stand out. Firstly, Polynesian societies are more centralised than those of Melanesia and Maori *iwi* (tribes) and *hapu* (sub-tribes) had a more hierarchical structure than most New Guinean groups. Secondly, the autochthonous inhabitants of New Zealand spoke a common language and shared many cultural traits. Finally, and most importantly for this analysis, the Maori experience of colonisation differed greatly from that of Papua New Guineans.

Papua New Guinea's transition to self-government and preparations for imminent independence occurred during my fieldwork in the early 1970s. Some close informants came from areas that began to experience regular contact with colonial authorities in the 1950s, only twenty years before. The Maori, on the other hand, constitute a "fourth world" segment of New Zealand's population. Like Australian Aborigines and Native Americans of the United States and Canada, their land and other resources passed into the hands of settler governments. They form a minority of their nation's population[22], overrepresented on all measures of social distress: imprisonment, disease, unemployment, lack of educational qualifications, etc.

Colonial History

Calls for a bicultural New Zealand develop and elaborate a particular view of New Zealand history. The Historical Database, developed by Ihi Communications and used in their bicultural training course, provides a comprehensive picture of the marginalisation of Maori people and their continuing attempts to achieve self-determination. It divides Maori history after the arrival of Europeans in New Zealand into five periods: The Age of Experimentation (1769 to 1840), The Age of Domination (1845-1892), The Era of Reconstruction (1890-1945), the Age of Dislocation (1940s to 1970s) and the present Reassertion of Rangatiratanga.

Although Abel Tasman landed in Golden Bay in 1642, Captain Cook's visits in 1769 began the period of continuing Maori contact with Europeans. A motley collection of whalers, sealers, traders, escaped convicts and missionaries established themselves in the country. They introduced potatoes, pigs, European diseases, the musket, Christianity and literacy by the 1830s.

---

[22] The 434,000 Maori represent 7.5% of the entire New Zealand population (New Zealand Official Yearbook 1994:132 Statistics Department Wellington), proportionally a much larger minority than Australian Aborigines or Native Americans.

Europeans were also important in initiating two changes within the Maaori tribes. The first was the recognition that there were other people in the world outside New Zealand with different forms of organisation and a vastly different standard of living. From this came the second change, the realisation that there was a common background between the existing tribes. The word Maaori, to describe themselves began to be used in the 1820s, indicating a significant shift in consciousness. (Ihi Communications n.d.:6)

Despite great changes experienced during this early contact period, Maori remained the dominant population. In 1835 the British Resident, Busby, encouraged chiefs in the North Island to establish the Independent Tribes of New Zealand. Fifty chiefs signed a Declaration of Independence by 1839 that received some international recognition (Levine and Henare 1994:194). About this time the balance of power between the tribes and resident Europeans began to change drastically. The deadly inter-tribal musket wars of the 1820s, together with disease, had decimated the indigenous population. Control of the increasingly disruptive European element, and the Maori who moved beyond their own tribal boundaries, became more difficult. The missionaries called on the British Colonial Office to protect natives from a situation they represented as a developing Sodom in the South Seas. When the New Zealand Company began to purchase vast tracts of land for agricultural settlers the British Crown, initially reluctant to extend the Empire any further, decided to act (McClintock 1958:18). They sought Maori consent to Crown sovereignty in the form of a treaty, translated and vigorously promoted by the missionaries in 1840.

Te Tiriti O Waitangi (The Treaty of Waitangi) consists of a preamble and three articles. The preamble states that the British want to assume sovereignty to prevent anarchy and secure the rights and property of the chiefs. The first article states that the chiefs, whether members of the Confederation or not, give the Queen consent to govern. The second article recognises chiefly control of resources and obligates chiefs to sell land they wish to dispose of to the Crown. Article Three gives Maori the rights and duties of English citizenship.

Forty-six chiefs signed the Treaty on February 6, 1840 at Waitangi and up to 500 others did so in other parts of New Zealand. McKenzie (1985) notes that only 72 personal signatures appear on the document. Government officials wrote a number of others and some signatures consisted of crosses, tattoo patterns and "meaningless marks". The chiefs heard Te Tiriti read out to them in "missionary Maori", and left virtually no record of the occasion "to complement the Pakeha one".

The untidy process of translating and purveying the Treaty, officially recognised as the legal cornerstone of the New Zealand state, leads to conflict and debate about its meaning today. Most signatories marked the Maori document, but its text was not faithfully rendered in the English drafts Hobson sent to Sydney and London. The difference that figured most prominently in Waitangi Tribunal deliberations in the 1980s (legislation requires the Tribunal to take both versions into account) concerns the first article. In the English Treaty the Maori cede "sovereignty absolutely and without reservation" but in Te Tiriti they give *kawanatanga*. This "missionary Maori" term appears in a translation of the New Testament where it refers to the office of Pontius Pilate. Commentators such as the historian Ross (1972) and the anthropologist Kawharu – whose translation was recognised by the Court of Appeal in an important case dealing with State Owned Enterprises (Ihi Communication n.d.:26-29) – gloss kawanatanga as government. The word *mana* provides a much closer Maori translation of sovereignty than does kawanatanga. Article two appears to guarantee this to the chiefs as it expressly states that they shall have *rangatiratanga*, "unqualified exercise of their chieftainship over their lands, villages and all their treasures." Notably, this quote from Te Tiriti also makes no specific mention of forests and fisheries, while the English version does.

The inconsistencies of the Treaty process, so important to ethnic politics in the 1980s and 1990s, were recognised as early as 1850 when the Colonial Office told the Attorney General of New Zealand that "it was for the Queen to interpret her own pledges" (Adams 1977:240). This statement shows that interpreting the Treaty involves exercising power as well as intellect.

British authorities initially seemed willing to work with the chiefs as formal partners in running New Zealand. When George Grey became Governor in 1845 he set out to diminish their place in the administrative structure, weaken the influence of pro-treaty missionaries and assimilate Maori by undermining native custom. The New Zealand Constitution of 1852 did not include provisions for a specific Maori input into government.

Maori numbers continued to decrease and the pace of colonisation and the power of the settlers grew. By the late 1850s the European population surpassed the Maori. Land problems provoked skirmishes and war broke out in Taranaki in 1860. The government confiscated large blocks of territory suitable for settlement and set up a Native Land Court to individualise title to all Maori land. Legally freed from tribal control, more land passed out of indigenous hands than was lost from the wars. A system of Resident Magistrates, Maori schools, and the provision of four parliamentary seats rounded out the government's design for Maori assimilation to European ways.

Between 1896 and 1945 the Maori population doubled and became proletarianised as a result of the loss of their economic base. People worked at seasonal jobs in rural areas, on the roads and railroads, shearing sheep, digging kauri gum, cutting scrub and clearing land. Those with access to Maori holdings tried commercial farming – unsuccessfully because they could not raise loans or prevent other tribespeople taking the proceeds of their endeavours. During the next twenty years, with their population doubling again, Maori began to move from the countryside to towns in ever-increasing numbers. The government supported urban migration to relieve rural poverty and promoted a policy of "integration". The influential Hunn report of 1960 stated that:

> Integration... implies some continuation of Maori culture. Much of it, though, has already departed and only the fittest elements (worthiest of preservation) have survived the onset of civilisation. Language, arts and crafts and the institutions of the marae are the chief relics. Only the Maori themselves can decide whether these features of their ancient life are in fact to be kept alive; and, in the final analysis, it is entirely a matter of individual choice. (Ihi Communications n.d.:9-13,145)

By 1971, 70% of the Maori population resided in towns. An economic recession that started in the late 1960s frustrated hopes of material betterment. Disappointment over their marginal position in New Zealand society prompted public protests on Waitangi Day in 1971, a large Maori Land March in 1975 and land occupations, most prominently of Bastion Point in 1977. In 1975 Matiu Rata, the member of Parliament from Northern Maori, introduced the act that established the Waitangi Tribunal. Any Maori individual or group that felt a current action or policy of the Crown violated the principles of the Treaty could take a claim before the Tribunal. As originally constituted it could only inquire and make recommendations about claims arising from present circumstances. (Because most land confiscations occurred in the 19th century, the first claims involved aquatic resources.) Academics and other observers of Maori affairs seemed elated by the possibilities. Metge, for example, ended her influential second edition of *The Maoris of New Zealand* (1976:331) saying:

> The ideal set out in the Treaty of two races united in friendship and equality as one people is a great national myth... it does not apply only to Maoris and Pakehas but also provides a model for relations between all New Zealand's varied cultural groups, a sound foundation on which to build a truly multicultural society.

Metge's emphasis on multiculturalism comes after an historical discussion of various conceptualisations of the place of the Maori in New Zealand society. She notes the increasing Maori scepticism about the Hunn report's policy of integration and also mentions the fashionable term of the 1980s and 1990s "biculturalism". Introduced by Schwimmer in 1968, it failed to catch on at the time. Metge (1976:309) attributes this to the fact that Schwimmer did not:

> ...clarify the different values of the word when it occurs in the compounds "bicultural individual", "bicultural society" and "bicultural institution" or show how these are related to each other. More importantly the concept has proved unnecessarily restrictive because of its stress on two main groups...the word that has gained most ground in popular usage in New Zealand is "multi-cultural".

Metge's view of multiculturalism in New Zealand involved recognition and provisions for a wide variety of cultural groups to express themselves publicly and influence the administration of the state. Such policies would maximise inclusiveness, participation, and the social integration of minority groups in the polity. An alternative form of multicultural society that accommodates cultural pluralism in private domains and equality of opportunity in the public sector can arise without any explicit recognition of minority cultural rights.

> (I)f our concern in a multicultural society is to preserve cultural pluralism, this is best done by institutions that protect individual rights and freedoms rather than [group] interests. (Kukathas 1993:29)

Kukathas prefers this second variety of multiculturalism. He feels that a people's hold on their culture is diminished by projecting that culture into public arenas. His views about relying on individual freedoms to accomplish group goals also accord well with the current climate of the deregulated market economy and corporatised public sector in New Zealand.

Brownlie's (1992) comments on the legal pitfalls of relying on a Treaty-based strategy provide another argument for Maori to keep their cultural concerns to themselves and rely on existing provisions for individual rights to accomplish their aims. He focuses on the problem of reconciling the chiefly authority of the Treaty with democracy and fundamental human rights. As citizens of New Zealand, Maori (and pakeha) individuals have rights that cannot be contravened by any arrangements that recognise iwi structures of authority. He maintains that the guarantees of the Treaty are incompatible with other laws and conventions that legally bind the government. Brownlie feels that equity issues should be pursued by recourse to international conventions on human rights that accept controlled forms of affirmative action.

Biculturalism

> There are no substantial attractions in invoking the legal concept of indigenous people in the New Zealand context. The concept of indigenous peoples would introduce a disharmony since it does not claim equality but a qualitatively separate status. (1992:94)

Although Brownlie might not feel that the doctrine of indigenous rights holds "substantial attractions," Maori in a position to publicly articulate grievances apparently disagreed. They came to view the equality of recognition that multiculturalism gives to minority groups (either implicitly or explicitly) a disadvantage precisely because multiculturalism accords so well with the values of a liberal democracy. Maori want more than a simple minority group status under the tyranny of an alien majority in their own homeland.

> Against the suggestions of what the bureaucracy came to call 'social equity' they had to assert the strict claims of biculturalism in a way that would overcome the universalism of discourse on equality and of multiculturalism. (Sharp 1990:229)

The ideology of ethnic politics began to focus biculturalism in the 1980s as that concept became elaborated in the reports of the Waitangi Tribunal claims.

The Waitangi Tribunal

Set up in 1977, the Waitangi Tribunal accomplished little initially. Then Edward Durie, Chief Judge of the Maori Land Court, took over as Chairman of the Tribunal in 1981; he promptly acted on a submission from Aila Taylor, on behalf of Te Atiawa, that the Waitara town's sewerage system polluted shellfish collecting grounds used by the tribe. The submission also covered the Motonui synthetic fuels plant, the first "Think Big" project of the Muldoon government, that had gained a right of discharge into the same area. The complainants phrased their claim in terms of material deprivation. They estimated the price of food lost to the tribe because of the pollution and maintained that the Treaty guaranteed the traditional fishery to Te Atiawa.

The tribe's initial position merely recapitulated an historical pattern that had brought no redress to Maori people in the past. Durie's accomplishments in reconceptualising that case, essentially reversing the position Maori culture and concerns take in presenting grievances, can best be appreciated by comparing previous legal procedure (epitomised by the Wanganui River litigation described below) with the protocol developed by the Tribunal in the Motonui (Waitara) case, covered in the following section.

The epic and continuing struggles of the Wanganui tribes chronicled by Haughey (1966) provide an apt paradigm for the pre-Tribunal difficulties orthodox legal practice posed for Maori. Dispute over the river and adjacent territory, a focus for militant protest today, reached the courts in 1938. The tribes living along the Wanganui River depended upon its fish and eels for subsistence and trade. Steamboat companies built groins along the river banks that deflected the currents from the large weirs built by local Maori to trap eels. Also, government and local authorities took river gravel for road building, further undermining the ability of people living along the banks to feed themselves. The claimants sought compensation for these resources and the resulting abandonment of their villages. The State maintained that Maori custom did not recognise ownership of river banks separate from river beds and that the Crown had sovereignty over navigable rivers.

The Maori Land Court first addressed the question of whether the bed of the river constituted land held under Maori custom. They found in favour of the claimants. The Crown appealed, but lost in the Maori Appellate Court. The Government later went to the Supreme Court with an argument that the other courts exceeded their jurisdictions. Crown lawyers maintained that because the local Maori sold land along the banks, the river passed from their control by the convention that owners of land abutting inland waterways own the lake or river to a line midway out and parallel to the bank. The court did not rule on this matter because the Coal Mines Act of 1903 gave the government control of inland waterways. The claimants maintained that the Act amounted to confiscation. A Royal Commission, special legislation and more court cases followed. In the end, the validity of the claim hinged on a question of custom first raised in 1938. Did Maori society in 1840 recognise title to rivers separate from land?

The transcripts of the Aotea District Maori Land Court show how the courts initially handled the question. Council for the applicant produced an expert witness who gave his people's history and said the spirits of the river differed from those of the land. This supported the idea that Maori concepts were not equivalent to those enshrined in English law. The Maori recognition of separate spirits showed that title to the river was not automatically attached to the land or its banks. The Crown cross-examined the witness and produced a Maori expert of its own who maintained that the people living along the river owned the waterways adjacent to their lands. Although the Maori won in the initial case, they lost on the same point in 1962, 24 years after they first began. The entire conduct of the case seems not only futile but demeaning[23]. A state court made pronouncements on (and judgements about) Maori culture,

---

[23] Even the most favourable opinion of the Royal Commission in 1950 sounds callous today. The judge, advocating Crown payment for gravel, said "The abandonment of the villages, the consequential excursus of the Maoris, are, I think, only consistent with the breaking in and progress of the district. The Maoris change to economic labour in place of uneconomic labour was to the benefit of the race" (AJHR 1950:15).

subordinating elders to its own procedures and translating their testimony into the language of a judicial system that justified their loss. Metge notes that Maori often feel *whakamaa* (a term that she characterises as a combination of shyness, embarrassment and shame) "In the presence of civil servants and other officials". Some of her informants specifically mentioned that they "cringe" or "shake" at court (1986).

In contrast to the procedure followed by the Maori Land Court, the Waitangi Tribunal initially held its hearings on the *marae* (the grounds, including the meeting house) of the group bringing the complaint. The etiquette of the complainants was followed and no cross-examination took place. The officials and lawyers came to the home of the complainants to hear them respectfully in an environment that the legal specialists found alien and uncomfortable. The entire process struck one lawyer as a farce where "a decision that was not a decision" was made by "a tribunal that is not a tribunal" (it has no adjudicative power) "about a treaty that is not a treaty" (O'keefe 1983:136). The Tribunal's lack of power also created scepticism among Maori that anything useful would eventuate from the hearings. The weaknesses of the Tribunal as an adjudicative body, although serious liabilities for specific claimants, became sources of strength as the Tribunal developed into a forum for the articulation of new interpretations of custom and history that found their way into domestic law.

Motonui

The Motonui case commenced at Manukohiri Marae in July 1982 and took three separate one-week sessions to hear, finishing in November. Justice Durie opened proceedings suggesting, "perhaps we should seek out... the spirit, the life force of the Treaty" (Waitangi Tribunal Files n.d.). He asked Te Atiawa if they had any suggestions on how to accomplish this. Sir Graham Latimer, a prominent Maori leader and member of the Tribunal, said "I am conscious as I stand here that I stand in the stead of people that have gone on and that have continuously, hui after hui, raised the Treaty of Waitangi." He said that he felt the presence of the ancestors watching the hearing.

These immediate references to important Maori symbols set the tone of subsequent events. The lawyers, experts from the Waitara Council, Taranaki Catchment Commission, Synthetic Fuels Corporation, government departments, etc., gave highly technical evidence relating to the chemistry of the waste products, health and biological impacts, engineering and other issues. The weight given to the Maori cultural evidence overwhelmed these technical submissions. Local people furnished long accounts of customary ways of dealing with waste products and their strictures against mixing products of the realm of the land with those of the sea. Prohibitions on bathing near the reefs, replacing overturned rocks, returning the first food item taken from the sea to ensure calm waters, and the continued use of pre-Treaty territorial boundaries by Maori gatherers, all gave the strong message that shellfish collecting had great cultural significance.

The most important of the tribunal's innovations occurred when the Chief Judge linked cultural values to the language of Te Tiriti. The Maori text does not mention fisheries per se. It specifies lands, villages and *"taonga katoa"*, which Kawharu glosses as "all their treasures". Durie directly asked one witness if:

> "...the ancestors when they signed it understood from the Maori text that fisheries were protected by the use of the word *taonga*.. Is that how you see it?"
> "Well, this is what I see. Yes. The *taonga*, the fisheries of land, *he taonga*.."
> (Waitangi Tribunal Files n.d.:133)

The idea that "taonga" applied to fisheries became part of the findings of the case when the Tribunal found that the Treaty should protect the "use and control of their fishing grounds in accordance with their own traditional culture and customs, and any modern extensions of them" (Waitangi Tribunal Reports 1983:63).

When the reefs became construed as cultural objects, questions of ownership diminished and the scope of things protected by the Treaty expanded. In courtrooms Maori custom became translated into legal concepts, but on the marae the opposite occurred. The apparent weakness of a Tribunal that could not make monetary awards turned into a rhetorical strength for the further elaboration of biculturalism. If the Tribunal had to follow strict legal protocol many points made by the claimants would be subject to cross-examination and rebuttal. Without such challenge they were now free to elaborate and consolidate their grievances.

The value of this rhetorical elaboration was symbolic and accrued to Maori who felt that their culture and status should be reintegrated into the state in a way that accorded them more mana. The claimants received a favourable (but not binding) "recommendation", some renown, and the bills – the Tribunal had a budget of only $30,000 for its hearings (Kelsey 1991:115). Travel to Waitara and accommodation for three members left little to defray the expenses incurred by Te Atiawa as hosts to the hundreds of people moving through their Waitara marae. Later, as the Tribunal expanded and became more legalistic, the financial drain became more serious. Claimants wondered whether rhetorical gains (public goods of the first order) justified their expenditure on lawyers and the investment of their time and effort that took many person-years away from possibly more productive endeavours. Outside observers overlooked these problems and tended to concentrate on the new possibilities the findings seemed to open for Maoridom collectively.

Kaituna and Manukau

Both the Kaituna and Manukau cases involved issues similar to the situation at Waitara. In the first, the town of Rotorua proposed to discharge sewerage from the town's waste water treatment plant into the Kaituna river. The Ngati Pikiao, a Te Arawa sub-group, objected that the effluent would spoil the area around the river mouth. Their lawyer said he "would not rely on scientific evidence but rather that the applicants would prove that the proposed pipeline is offensive to Maori cultural and spiritual values." Citing the Motonui finding that taonga included fishing grounds, he submitted that:

> the assault on the spiritual and cultural values without proven tangible damage is itself sufficient for this Tribunal as such assault is contrary to the spirit of the Treaty. (Hingston 1984:1)

Tribal elders declared that if the scheme went ahead they would declare the river *tapu*. This would prevent local Maori from gathering seafood or material for flax kits and feather cloaks.

> This loss is not to be calculated solely in economic terms. It would be a grave loss of Tribal *mana* for the river and the estuary to be denied them. (Waitangi Tribunal Reports 1984:12)

The case proceeded in much the same way as at Waitara. At one point the Tribunal enquired why Lake Rotorua was not declared tapu. After all, the sewerage went there currently and members of local tribes continued fishing. The Ngati Pikiao replied that their territory did not include the lake and they would not comment on the status of another group's territory. The tribe presented a previously unrecorded genealogy of their people during the hearings. Published as an appendix to the report of the case, it indicated the mana the proceedings held for the Ngati Pikiao.

The Tribunal found that the tribe owned the river and recommended that the pipeline proposal be abandoned. Effluent in their taonga offended Maori cultural and spiritual values. Legislation should take these values into account. The report of this case emphasised that the act that established the Tribunal transformed the Treaty from a "simple nullity" to "a document of importance approaching the status of a constitutional instrument so far as Maori are concerned". Any policy or act of the Crown that adversely affects a Maori person or group could become the basis for a claim (Waitangi Tribunal Reports 1984:26).

The Manukau Harbour case, heard at Makaurau Marae, Ihumatao, Manukau in July, August and November 1984, continued to extend the Tribunal's reach and also contributed to elaborations of the ideology of biculturalism. Despite the fact that the act that set up the Tribunal specified that grievances should relate to current actions of the Crown, the judges took an interest in the history of land seizures around the harbour and recommended that local authorities settle outstanding issues that dated from the 1860s. Such recommendations did not figure in the Waitara case even though the land wars of the 19th century resulted in devastating land loss there.

The cultural agenda in Manukau also included something new. In each of these three cases Maori objections to pollution and unfettered state power gained a good deal of support from a variety of environmental and other interest groups. But the claimants aired a uniquely Maori objection to New Zealand Steel's proposed slurry pipeline. Water from the Waikato River would mix with water from the harbour and they have separate *mauri*, life forces, that should not co-mingle. The judges, who had often commented on how Maori views on wastes and water paralleled those of other cultures, said something quite different about this objection:

> In our multicultural society the values of minorities must sometimes give way to those of the predominant culture, but in New Zealand, the Treaty of Waitangi gives Maori values an equal place with British values and a priority when the Maori interest in their *taonga* is adversely affected. (Waitangi Tribunal Reports 1985:78)

This conceptualisation of the Maori as something more than a minority group but less than fully autonomous forms the basic tenet of biculturalism. Like other "fourth world" people, members of indigenous populations in states established by European settler colonists, the Maori seek "citizen plus" status as *tangata whenua* (people of the land), and special entitlements in keeping with such recognition (Fleras and Elliot 1992). The Tribunal constitutes a government-sanctioned arena where such demands can be articulated. The cultural strategy the Tribunal adopted would, if taken up effectively, incorporate Maori culture into the public domain and give its interpreters considerable power (as "partners" in the bicultural state) to frame governmental policy.

Consolidating Biculturalism

The interpretative work of the Tribunal paralleled and reinforced other developments in Maoridom and government. Led by Sir Graham Latimer

Biculturalism

(one of the Tribunal judges), the New Zealand Maori Council's 1983 declaration on Maori land proposed that all legislation "on Maori matters" should acknowledge the Treaty and that the Maori people alone could define the rangatiratanga (sovereignty) guaranteed by the Treaty. In September 1984, pieces of Maori art from all over the country were assembled for shipment to the Metropolitan Museum in New York City. Controversy about the exhibition prompted the organisers to recognise that Maori had cultural stewardship of taonga owned by the museums and send 46 elders to the United States to ceremonially remove tapu from the pieces. In 1985 Parliament amended the Treaty of Waitangi Act to expand the membership of the Tribunal and allow it to hear cases arising from acts of the Crown that occurred before 1975.

Perhaps the most consequential legal event of this period occurred when Fisheries officers arrested a North Island Maori living on the South Island for taking undersized paua (*haliotis iris*, a species of abalone). He appealed his conviction in the High Court in Christchurch arguing that he asked South Island elders for permission to take the shellfish and his Treaty rights overrode conservation regulations. The court ruled that the Treaty did indeed take precedence over management regulations and effectively began a process of introducing Tribunal perspectives and the Treaty into domestic law after a 150-year absence.

Various government departments also began to adopt a bicultural approach during the mid-1980s. The Department of Social Welfare, Justice Department and Department of Maori Affairs combined in 1981 to develop a programme placing institutionalised children in their own Maori groups. Anticipating a later development of iwi-based (tribal) resourcing, they set up a Tribal Delivery System in 1986 to funnel funds to Maori groups to help prevent difficulties with children. The Maori Language Act established Maori as an official language of New Zealand in 1987, two years after the Tribunal declared it taonga.

At the same time that the Labour government set up the Tribunal and vowed to "honour the Treaty," it simultaneously pushed ahead with a comprehensive programme to dismantle New Zealand's welfare state (Kelsey 1990). Although the progressive economic privatisation of New Zealand has links to the reconceptualisation of ethnicity, culture, and the state, the precise nature of these links remain uncertain. Kelsey (1991) argues that New Zealand faced two crises in the mid-1980s. Maori protest effectively undermined the constitutional legitimacy of the state and the economy could no longer support the current level of welfare expenditure. The government sought to make concessions that would appear substantial to Maori while effectively denying them the power of self-determination. Although Kelsey's argument that the government concerned itself about legitimacy because of Maori protest is not entirely convincing, the Crown did need to defuse Maori opposition in order to achieve privatisation because many of the resources they wanted to sell were burdened by Maori claims.

The need to reconfigure the economy stemmed from an event that also stimulated a reconceptualisation of pakeha identity. When Britain became part of the European Economic Community New Zealand lost its assured outlet for the country's entire production. The profound recession and growing unemployment that followed led to the revolutionary (and continuing) economic restructuring and also promoted the nativist sentiment that had already surfaced among the growing proportion of the population born in New Zealand (Pearson 1991: 208). Many of the most powerful symbols of a uniquely New Zealand identity derive from Maori sources, and the state's reconceptualisation of itself involved appropriating these symbols into a newly imagined multicultural country.

> This revision has arisen partly from consistent attempts by majority group elites to use the state to "manage" minorities in their midst; whilst minorities, in turn, have utilised the "space" allocated to them by state reformism to assert their own interests. (Pearson 1991: 211)

The biculturalism that Maori asserted in their "space" began to develop in unanticipated ways that had the potential to undermine the power of the government to continue privatising the economy. The Treaty and the Tribunal made Maori the only group in New Zealand with any statutory basis to challenge these policies in the courts (Vowles 1991:68-80). This unique position, in a country so dominated by Cabinet in a unicameral political system, gave biculturalism widespread appeal to liberal nativist New Zealanders who opposed the ever-increasing penetration of market mechanisms in health, education and other areas of social welfare. Intent on dividing up fisheries resources and selling rights to them on the open market in 1986, the new National Party administration felt the full impact of this opposition.

Muriwhenua and the Reassertion of Material Claims

Now that the Tribunal could make reference to historical events, its hearings delved into more fundamental questions about the causes of Maori marginality. Simultaneous changes in fishing legislation raised new issues about indigenous fishing rights. Because New Zealand's inshore waters became less productive in the 1970s due to overfishing, The Ministry of Agriculture and Fisheries sought to reduce fishing pressure by declining the issue of new licenses. This approach to fishing management had a serious flaw in that there was no stopping already-licensed fishers from increasing their activity as others retired or left the industry for other reasons. To plug this loophole, during the 1980s New Zealand progressively introduced the world's most comprehensive quota management system. It promised to conserve the resource in a manner compatible with the National government's rigorously market-oriented approach to managing natural resources. Fisheries scientists calculated a total allowable catch consistent with a maximum sustainable yield for each species. The Ministry allocated a proportion of the allowable catch to each fisher based on their fishing returns over the previous five years. Individuals could use, sell or rent these rights.

The government compulsorily bought out small operators with little quota, while others voluntarily sold out to larger operators and fishing companies. Thus the entire regime favoured wealthy fishermen and companies. Maori fishers figured prominently among those who lacked the capital to remain in the industry under these circumstances and an estimated 8000 left fishing (Ihi Communications n.d.). Previous management policies recognised a Maori interest in fishing but treated it as non-commercial in nature. The Muriwhenua tribes, angered by the new regime, took a claim to the Tribunal that the Treaty recognised their complete ownership of the fishing grounds off their coast, in the far north of the North Island.

The Tribunal supported the Muriwhenua view that Maori had always done more than simply consume the fish they caught. Relying on the work of Raymond Firth (1929), but resisting his calls for Maori to become assimilated into the Western economy, the Tribunal report of the case drew a picture of continuity between traditional and Western practices. The Maori themselves had made a rapid transition to commercial fishers and dominated trade in seafood by the 1870s. The monocultural nature of the industry discouraged indigenous participation in its subsequent development. The Tribunal found that the Treaty guaranteed Maori inclusion in the "business and activity in fishing" (Waitangi Tribunal Reports 1988).

Muriwhenua people articulated a wide range of grievances before the Tribunal. They said trawlers from the south entered their area, despoiled the fishery and dumped untargeted species. The management procedures completely ignored local knowledge about fish and reduced local people to the status of beggars when they asked for permission to take food for tribal gatherings. Maori had often suffered such indignities in the past. By altering access to the resource base, the Individual Transferable Quota system provided the Tribunal and Maori Council with the opportunity to gain a substantial share of the inshore fishery.

Fishing provides a textbook example of the problems of managing a common property resource. Overfishing occurs primarily because fish are unowned until they are caught. Fishers therefore compete by building bigger boats and using more sophisticated gear to maintain their share of the catch. Even if profits fall one must match the efforts of competitors. Although the Treaty and various Fisheries acts recognised the Maori right to fish, under a common property regime such rights were never specified or quantified. Section 88 of the 1975 Fisheries Act merely states that, "Nothing in this Act shall affect Maori fishing rights". Crown sovereignty had apparently extinguished specific tribal ownership of the foreshore and inland waters, so – as New Zealand citizens – Maori could go out and fish like everyone else.

Quota management changed this situation by creating property rights in fishing. When these rights were sold, whatever Maori entitlements remained, no matter how vague, became extinguished. An unintended consequence of changing access to fishing was a greatly strengthened Maori claim under the Treaty.

> If Maori fisheries covered the whole of the inshore seas, as past records suggest, the policy was effectively guaranteeing to non-Maori the full exclusive and undisturbed possession of the property right in fishing that the Crown had already guaranteed to Maori. (Waitangi Tribunal Reports 1988:149)

While the Muriwhenua Tribunal case proceeded, the Maori Council asked the High Court to stop issuing fishing quotas in northern areas. On September 30, 1987, the Tribunal sent a memorandum to the Ministry of Fisheries stating that the quotas in Muriwhenua violated the Treaty. The High Court issued a local restraining order later that day. They soon extended this, stopping the entire quota system, and instructed the government to define Maori fishing rights by June 30, 1988. The Crown appointed a working party with Maori members from the Council and Trust Boards of Ngai Tahu, Tainui and Muriwhenua (tribes with prominent fishing claims), but did not establish direct links with iwi (Walker 1994:15).

The Tribunal released its findings on the Muriwhenua claim on the 13th of June, 1988. Their decision that the tribes owned the resources off the coast provoked an immediate backlash. Wellington's morning paper, *The Dominion*, called the findings "legalised apartheid". It quoted members of Parliament from the area who predicted racial violence over fishing rights. Representatives of various commercial fishing organisations anticipated economic doom: investors, unsure of their rights, would withdraw money from the industry causing export markets to collapse, undermining the entire economy. The president of the Federation of Commercial Fishermen put advertisements in the major papers calling for a referendum on the Waitangi Tribunal and "its separatist policies." He later announced that he found a new, third version of the Treaty that made no mention of fisheries and threatened to go to court. Parliament held a special debate two days after the release of the findings. The leader of the National Party (which was the opposition party at the time, but is now part of a coalition government) demanded that the Tribunal cease hearing cases. The Prime Minister replied that the official response to the recommendations would not adversely affect any individual's activities.

Although the Muriwhenua case seemed finally to result in a significant Maori victory in the courts, this came at some cost. The legal view of the Treaty that emerged from the Court of Appeal provides an illustration of Kukathas' point that groups projecting cultural symbols in public arenas can lose control of the power to define these symbols. The court took over the role of interpreting the Treaty by emphasising that it would adhere to Treaty "principles" and not engage in hermeneutic exercises involving the two texts. These principles boiled down to an obligation on the part of the Crown to work in partnership with Maori. The Crown's obligation to consult did not mean Maori deserved a half share of resources or could determine policy. All citizens have to obey the laws of the land, including regulations about corporatisation, and Maori could expect recompense proportional to their numbers (Kelsey 1991, Sharp 1991).

The court also made it clear that their findings bound the Tribunal, not the other way around. The Muriwhenua report may have provided strong evidence of historical events, but the Tribunal's findings lacked legal force and could be challenged in a court. The Tribunal itself seemed weakened by this time. Its recommendations held little concrete benefit for any claimants. New members took a more conservative approach to claims. Procedures became increasingly legalistic as the courts and Parliament reinterpreted them, and the Tribunal appeared more willing to concede the sovereignty issue in the government's favour as time went on (Kelsey 1991, Sharp 1991).

The Court of Appeal's presumption of authority to define the principles of the Treaty threatened to give the judiciary the power, similar to that exercised by American courts, to interpret the constitutionality of laws. The Labour government reacted to this development in 1989 by declaring five principles of its own. "Kawanatanga" gave the government the right to make laws subject to an "appropriate priority" of Maori interests. "Rangatiratanga" meant tribal self-management. Crown action on the Treaty would also proceed with reference to equality, cooperation and redress. "Equality" referred to the fact that both parties to the Treaty were now citizens under the legal regime the partners to the Treaty "selected". "Cooperation" meant consultation on major issues of mutual importance. "Redress" referred to the government's expectation that resolution of grievances would result in reconciliation. Subsequent legislation dealing with town planning and Maori affairs stressed that Maori interests were to be accorded a priority balanced by other concerns. The government solved its crisis of legitimacy by reasserting its sovereignty and continued its economic policies unhindered by Maori opposition (Kelsey 1991: 126-127, Sharp 1991).

In the meanwhile, despite the pressure for a solution for Maori fishing claims, the working party failed to reach a consensus by the court's deadline. The Maori members rejected an offer of 27% of the quota and three seats of seven on the Board of the Fisheries Corporation, and countered by offering the Crown 50% of the fishery. The failure of the working party negotiations led the government to approach the Maori members directly with a proposal for legislation. Although the Muriwhenua negotiators dissented, a Maori Fishery Bill introduced to the House in September granted Maori 2.5% of quota annually for twenty years in return for suspension of Maori fishing claims before the Tribunal and the courts. This latter clause provoked 38 tribes to register objections with the High Court against the bill. Further legislation, aimed at countering these objections and getting the quota system back in operation, established a Maori Fisheries Commission. The Commission was to receive 10% of the quota and $10 million dollars for the next four years while the remaining issues came before the courts and Tribunal.

In order to transfer quota to the Commission, some would have to become available on the open market. When Fletchers, a large New Zealand company, decided to sell its fishing interests in 1992, the Government offered the Maori Fisheries Commission a $300 million settlement – again meaning to dispose of the entire Maori fishing question. The Crown proposed to buy a half share of Fletchers' subsidiary Sealords, 20% of the quota on all new species, and transfer this to Maori in return for cessation of commercial claims under the Treaty. The Maori Fisheries Commission was to hold these resources in trust for distribution to Maori and use the 10% of quota previously promised to establish a self-funding fishing business. The Commission, later renamed the Treaty of Waitangi Fisheries Commission, sought consent from Maori at a national *hui* (meeting) and 23 meetings at marae across the country. They felt these meetings gave them the basis for going ahead with the settlement. Members of 17 different iwi and 32 plaintiffs involved in various court actions signed a deed accepting the offer. More court cases and a Tribunal hearing followed on the question of the acceptability of government abrogating Treaty rights as part of the agreement. The government ignored the Tribunal's subsequent recommendation that claims be allowed to proceed after 25 years and the courts dismissed the cases then being heard.

The focus of dispute now shifted to allocation of the quota. Dividing up resources created new conflicts among Maori groups.

The New Tribalism

Despite the limits to Treaty grievance that emerged in the late 1980s, Maori still entertained hopes for the realisation of the bicultural ideals of partnership and respect for rangatiratanga through the empowerment of iwi. The Labour government agreed to devolve responsibilities and resources to tribes and passed the Runanga Iwi Act in 1990 that allowed iwi to incorporate for the purpose of delivering government services to Maori. Restructuring of the Department of Maori Affairs emphasised that its role should change from implementing programmes to advising departments on policy matters to promote iwi development (Ihi Communications n.d.). New initiatives in education, health, social welfare and justice proceeded on this basis. The authority to deliver social services for the government fell far short of realising the ideal of full partnership between Treaty partners.

> In a nutshell, for the Labour Government, devolution was synonymous with delegation and decentralisation; for the tangata whenua, it encompassed a dialogue about power sharing. Tangata whenua discourse was around parallel development and separate institutions; central authorities talked about tinkering with the existing system by way of Maori add-ons. One was about biculturalism; the other was akin to institutional assimilation. (Fleras 1991:187)

The new National government repealed the Runanga Iwi Act. They seemed intent on carrying further the rigorous reforms put in place by Labour. National privatised more resources, continued to decrease government spending and clearly signalled to Maori that they would not countenance challenges to Crown sovereignty. The Treaty Negotiations Minister announced in 1994 a new policy to settle all outstanding Maori grievances within a fiscal envelope of $1 billion. This cap on spending potentially divides iwi by putting pressure on them to get a share of the money before it runs out. Maori have largely condemned the idea of a fixed pool of funding specified in advance of claims. Tainui leaders signed the one extant tribal settlement, but only 40% of the people on the tribal rolls participated in the vote to approve the deal. Since a third of these voters expressed disapproval, only 27% of eligible Tainui cast an approving ballot – hardly an impressive vote of confidence in the agreement.

Despite persistent opposition, the National government seemed determined to make its fiscal policies on Maori claims work. If anything, the envelope backfired badly and led to increasing tension. Protests and occupations, with some violence and radical rhetoric reminiscent of the 1970s, occurred in several parts of the North Island. Even mainstream Maori spokespersons, disillusioned with the lack of meaningful progress in settling claims, were speaking more in terms of separate development than partnership. In September 1995, a hui of Maori leaders refused to nominate four people to help the government analyse claims under the fiscal envelope. The host, Ngati Tuwharatoa Chief, Sir Hepi Te Heu Heu, used the occasion to call for constitutional change to implement *tino rangatiratanga*, now glossed as self-government or sovereignty. The Prime Minister responded:

> "There will be a single parliament in New Zealand. There will be a single body of law. If you talk about sovereignty as the elected parliament of New Zealand, there are no negotiating positions. We cannot negotiate the division of sovereignty between various groups of New Zealanders." (*The Dominion* 16 October 1995:1)

Although the tribal fundamentalism stimulated by recent developments left the government unable to gain pan-Maori cooperation with its policies, the fisheries settlement provided a good example of how the government could by-pass iwi and save money by appointing its own chiefs. Recent evidence gathered by action under the Official Secrets Act by Roberts (1994) suggests the government probably saved $150-$200 million hammering out the agreement with a group of hand-picked Maori elites thus "avoiding an adverse court outcome". Nevertheless, these Maori negotiators did speak with iwi leaders during hui and marae meetings, which they maintained constituted ratification of the fisheries agreement. Iwi seemed natural groups for quota distribution. However, when the negotiators became members of the Treaty of Waitangi Fisheries Commission they found that allocating Maori-owned resources to iwi was even more complicated and controversial than giving iwi funds to carry out government welfare policies.

The Commission initially advocated that allocation should follow the Maori *tikanga* (custom) that tribes possess the sea off their coasts. Coastal iwi would obviously benefit the most by this, which came to be known as the *mana moana* method. Ngai Tahu who claimed 20,000 members (although only 10,000 people indicated this tribal affiliation in the census) would get at least $50 million from the huge areas off the South Island coast that they controlled prior to 1840. One commentator sceptically observed that Ngai Tahu "is a collection of predominantly European individuals almost as much as it is a Maori iwi. That adds to the irony of the fisheries settlement" (Harrington 1994). Sir Tipene O'Regan, head of the Ngai Tahu Trust Board and Chairman of The Treaty of Waitangi Fisheries Commission, argues that an alternative to mana moana, dividing the resource according to population (that would net his tribe $3.5 million) is illegal, racist and driven by misplaced welfare concerns.

> "My interest as an individual in Ngai Tahu's assets is there by whakapapa because I belong to a group of people who were the owners and who were deprived of the ownership of their property. That is a property ownership issue. I'm not there because I belong to an ethnic group. To chuck it in a great pot and stir it up in a soup is really to revert solely to some big generic group based solely on race."

The Tribunal, and Maori claimants who sought injunctions against the imposition of mana moana, questioned arguments that mana moana accords with tikanga or the Treaty. The Tribunal, in its 1992 inquiry into the settlement (Waitangi Tribunal Reports 1992), opined "it is arguable that traditionally the mana, or authority, did not extend far from the shoreline, and the central feature of this scheme is the value given to the distant fisheries of modern times." Noting the advantages that would accrue to Ngai Tahu, and other groups that had commission members, the Tribunal also drew attention to procedural problems:

> As it turned out the commission's annual general meeting had not approved that option but, according to the resolutions as filed, had directed further inquiry. Nonetheless the commission chairman was of the view that an allocation based on tikanga Maori, by which he meant the off-shore equation, had been approved... and the commission's September 1992 bulletin continues to describe the fishery as "a continuation of lines projecting into the sea from the land boundaries".

Expert opinion of elders also made it clear that iwi never owned fishing resources. *Whanau* (extended family groups) and *hapu* (sub-tribes) constituted the operative traditional units and prior Tribunal reports recognised this. Consent to any allocation should, then, depend on a firm definition of what constitutes an iwi and whether the iwi achieved a consensus of relevant sub-units. These matters fall outside the Treaty because they involve negotiations among Maori, not between Maori and the Crown.

The Commission announced in its August 1995 newsletter that it had made two important advances. It completed a project on iwi identification and also made a step towards settling its allocation method problems. The criterion for iwi recognition "was that an Iwi must be able to show that it had the following characteristics: Shared descent from tipuna [ancestors], hapu, marae, [it] belonged historically to a takiwa [district], [and had] an existence traditionally acknowledged by other Iwi. Particular importance was placed on the final characteristic" (Te Reo O Te Tini a Tangaroa, August 1995). This gave the Commission control of the problem of iwi proliferation. New groups threatened the allocation plan by claiming iwi status in order to achieve quota shares, and the Commission now informed them that they did not qualify as iwi "in matters relating to fisheries" and "that their interests lie within rohe [boundaries] of existing Iwi".

Proponents of mana moana formed a pressure group called The Treaty Tribes, while their opponents, the Area One Consortium, advocated population allocation. Both groups agreed to withdraw court action and work towards a compromise allocation method that would incorporate both approaches. This development held the promise that the Commission could finally begin to distribute its assets (now 38% of all national fishing quota) to the iwi that it identified as legitimate recipients.

The Commission noted that five criteria would guide it in assessing any allocation system. Firstly, the process eventually adopted must conform to tikanga. It also needs to be technically feasible, transparent, accurate and robust. In addition, "Both groups [Treaty Tribes and Consortium] are adamant that allocation must be to Iwi and not to pan-Maori or urban Maori groups." Their Memorandum of Understanding emphasised that Article Two of the Treaty grants fisheries to hapu and iwi. These groups must make sure that the benefits they receive flow on to their members regardless of where they live. "Urban Maori authorities fulfil Article 3 functions and have no rights of Rangatiratanga o Nga Taonga." Article Three of the Treaty makes Maori New Zealand citizens, so the Commission's remarks imply that non-tribal Maori groups exercise welfare functions that have nothing to do with chieftainship or tradition. Some urban Maori disagree and, like hapu and iwi before them, have taken cases before the courts and the Tribunal. Until these cases are cleared, the Commission remains unable to distribute quota.

The Manukau Urban Maori Authority alleged that the Commission "Failed to take account of and address the manifold changes in Maori society since 1840 and particularly the phenomenon of detribalisation." It accused them of promoting "a backward looking 'traditional' based approach." Many of the Maori who live in cities either cannot identify their tribe, do not want to identify their tribe or prefer to associate with a Maori group where they currently live. De-tribalised Maori identify with the Maori people, feel distinct from other New Zealanders, descend from people who engaged in fishing in 1840 and expect protection of their rights as Maori under the Treaty (Fisheries Allocation Claim 1995).

Furthermore, the Treaty itself makes no declaration that people must be connected to tribes to get benefits or that tribes should disburse resources to individuals. The assumed traditional coincidence between iwi and tribes is itself a recent phenomenon. The breakdown of Maori tribal structure came, at least partially, from breaches of the Treaty. The Commission's stance that all quota should go to tribal organisations would prevent the Crown from giving benefits to the people most fundamentally wronged by acts that infringed the rights of Maori people. Urban Maori groups claim that they should receive 25% of the fishing quota because 140,000 people identified themselves as Maori without noting an iwi affiliation in the last census (ibid.).

Inventing Traditions?

The pronouncements of the various parties involved in producing biculturalism and iwi fundamentalism often make reference to Maori tradition. In 1989, an article in the American Anthropologist (Hanson 1989) appeared that combined the literature on "cultural invention" developed by historians (Hobsbaum and Ranger 1983) and anthropologists (Keesing and Tonkinson 1982) with the ideas of certain postmodernist thinkers and applied them to biculturalism.

The main point of the "invention" literature is that rhetoric about tradition validates contemporary interests by invoking images of continuity with a inviolable past. Linnekin provides the frivolous example of t-shirts worn by young males in Hawaii. The shirts show men with "sword and sorcery bows and arrows", Mister Universe physiques, and even pit bull terriers, wearing native dress that includes a tasselled gourd helmet drawn by the artist that accompanied Captain Cooke. Miniaturised helmets hang from the rear view mirrors of cars and pick-up trucks, symbols of Hawaiian warriors. Linnekin says that warriors in fact wore feathered helmets and cloaks and that, "If a student asks me to confirm that this [tasselled gourd] was part of the ancient Hawaiian warrior's garb, I cannot comply, just as I cannot honestly concur with a vision of the ancient society as a counter cultural egalitarian Eden along the lines of a ca. 1968 commune" (1992:259). The bulging biceps, pit bulls etc. also get the thumbs down.

Although Linnekin does not say whether students reacted to her revelations with an outraged dignity or a shrug, the potential to take offence is clear. One wonders, she says, how Scottish nationalists reacted to Trevor-Roper's paper, in the Hobsbaum and Ranger volume, that characterised the entire "Highland tradition" ensemble – kilt, bagpipes and all – as "fabrications". The term "fabrication" like "invention" obviously suggests that the customs lack authenticity and, perhaps more galling, this position sets the observer up as an arbiter of the veracity of someone else's past. The uncovering of inventions thus raises a number of issues about the nature of culture, identity, objectivity and research ethics. Hanson seeks to reconcile these problems in discussing

Maori culture by concocting a New-Age, postmodernist version of cultural invention and biculturalism. However, considering the issues that Hanson's article raises helps us to understand both general manifestations of politicised ethnicity and their particular representations in New Zealand.

In the days when official policy envisaged assimilation or amalgamation, portrayals of Maori culture stressed similarities with British New Zealanders. Accounts of traditional religion, for example, recast elements of belief systems, e.g. the Io cult, to resemble Christian monotheism. The notion that the country was originally settled by the coordinated efforts of a Great Fleet of canoes purportedly showed that the Maori also derived from a group of settlers who crossed the ocean to live in a new and distant land.

Today, biculturalism promotes the idea that Maori culture contrasts with that of the pakeha, especially such negative pakeha traits as coldness, rationality, individualism, lack of feeling for the land, and pollution. Maoriness constitutes a counterbalance these, and promotes feeling, sharing and communing with the environment.

Current anthropological work supports biculturalism in a variety of ways. Some authors seem to be muting or reversing their policy of questioning the authenticity of invented traditions from the "assimilationist" past if Maori appear to accept them. For example, Hanson mentions how Metge's account of the Io cult changed between the two editions of her book "The Maoris of New Zealand". In the 1967 edition she defines Io with apparent skepticism as a "Supreme Being whose existence and cult are claimed to have been revealed to initiates," whereas in 1976 she says, "The existence of a supreme god, Io-matua-kore was revealed to those who reached the upper grades of the school of learning". Other scholars, from a variety of disciplines, seek "to expand social institutions and modes of thinking in New Zealand to the point where they become truly bicultural" (Hanson 1989:895-6).

Hanson feels that Maori believe these ideas about their culture and origins and that when they and some pakeha "open themselves to the emotional and mystical impact of charisma and the non-rational... these and other elements of the current invention of Maori culture become objectively incorporated into that culture by the very fact of people talking about them and practicing them."

The Maori case is interesting for anthropologists because it shows that anthropology itself invents culture. Hanson backs away from a critical evaluation of these developments by emphasising that all culture is invented anyway. Real traditions, transmitted faithfully from the past just don't exist.

He quotes a statement from Derrida to the effect that we need a decentred view where everything becomes discourse and no particular discourse gets privileged treatment as truth. The Maori of the 1760s played the same discursive games their descendants and anthropological associates play now. "It follows from this that the analytic task is not to strip away the invented portions of culture as inauthentic, but to understand the process by which they acquire authenticity" (Hanson 1989 897-8).

Understanding how certain points of view acquire authenticity certainly constitutes an important analytical task. In situations where people justify present positions by advocating their faithfulness to, or departure from, "tradition" they strive to convince others as well as themselves of the historic righteousness of their identity and cause. But Hanson's approach utterly fails to help us comprehend the dynamics of biculturalism (Levine 1991b).

The major problem with his essay is the simplistic perspective it adopts on the production and sedimentation of cultural forms. This particular postmodernistic emphasis on de-centring misses a crucial point. To advance an understanding of ethnic politics in New Zealand we need to maintain the distinction between ideology and culture, not conflate them. Cultural phenomena consist of symbolic forms "produced or enacted, circulated, received, perceived by other individuals in particular socio-historical circumstances drawing on certain resources in order to make sense" of them (Thompson 1990:135). While one may philosophically accept Derrida's point that no particular interpretation of the numerous explications available (or yet to be formulated) deserves privileged treatment as the ultimate truth, some individuals, because of their opportunities and resources, make obviously privileged interpretations.

The production of the symbolic corpus of biculturalism and Treaty claims takes place in centres with particular powers granted by the state, like the Waitangi Tribunal, New Zealand Maori Council, Fisheries Commission, the courts and Parliament. Maori unaffiliated to tribes, and others interested in pan-Maori causes, have suddenly found the authenticity of their identity and concerns defined away by the fisheries settlement. They have taken their challenges to the view of the Treaty of Waitangi Fisheries Commission back to these centres of symbolic production.

The concept "invented tradition" refers to the symbolisation of culture itself as an externalised thing people can claim they value or reject, an ideology. It refers only obliquely, if at all, to lived experiences or culture as a way of life (cf. Keesing 1982). In the realm of text-only discourse this distinction might not matter, and anthropologists could invent culture as easily as anyone else.

But the people we write about actually live multidimensional lives. Anthropologists and other commentators can certainly produce ideology through their writing and discussion. Io, the Great Fleet, and openness to mysticism, charisma and the non-rational certainly make for interesting reading and conversation, but they constitute too impoverished an inventory for describing (let alone experiencing) culture, in the sense of a people's overall way of life.

When individuals talk about biculturalism and its themes they take an ideological position about transforming the state. As mentioned above, adopting Maori perspectives appealed to pakeha liberals because the Treaty provided the only viable challenge to the stranglehold New-Right social and economic policy gained in the New Zealand parliamentary system. For example, we saw that the concept of taonga got reworked by the Tribunal into a claim for cultural control of the reefs off Waitara and that this tactic advanced both Maori causes and wider opposition to New Zealand's first "think big" petrochemical project.

Hanson, too, talks about taonga but focuses his analysis solely on the Te Maori tour. The art exhibition made such an impact because the dawn tapu lifting ceremonies showed Americans "that the Maori people have access to primal sources of power long since lost by more rational cultures." Seeing the American reaction convinced New Zealanders that they, too, should value the spirituality of Maori culture. Hanson may be right in agreeing with the exhibition organiser that:

> The concept of cultural ownership of art objects, which had not been enunciated prior to "Te Maori", has enriched the significance of tribal membership for Maori people and represents an important step toward(s)... bringing the Maori heritage under Maori control. (Hanson 1989:896)

However, translating taonga into a concept of cultural ownership itself had more material origins and purposes, serving as an ideological device to gain power and influence over the structures that determine the place of Maori in New Zealand society. Even Te Maori became translated into a more worldly sphere, when the plans for a new $350 million National Museum, Te Marae Taonga o Aotearoa, included provision for Te Whare Taonga Tangata Whenua, a building devoted to Maori and Pacific art with a functioning marae (Levine 1987:441).

Perhaps the ultimate irony of Hanson's position can best be appreciated by the reception it received in the local press. The story about his article preceded the arrival of the journal *American Anthropologist* in University libraries. The headline "U.S. Expert Says Maori Culture Invented" that appeared in the

Dominion in Wellington on February 24, 1990, appeared to support the view that Maori positions lack authenticity and legitimacy. This may be unfair to Hanson, but if we take seriously the view that discourse equals culture, he invented something as well, a backlash against Maori aspirations.

Returning to the more productive possibilities inherent in a focus on how and where particular views of tradition gain authenticity, we can see a number of interesting developments in the material presented above. The initial strategy of claiming that taonga meant cultural value fit the Tribunal context perfectly. Invoking the Treaty could not help plaintiffs gain material recompense in 1980, and the Tribunal could not investigate historic land claims. Unable to make findings that bound the Crown to a course of action, the Tribunal found itself free to use non-adversarial techniques and marae protocol to investigate complaints about common property aquatic resources. The successful "cultural ownership" strategy reinserted the Treaty into common law, establishing the basis for challenging quota management. When the government dismantled common property in fishing, cultural claims became material and the focus of rhetoric about tradition moved from the realm of constructing pan-Maori cultural symbols in the Tribunal to iwi getting a share of the resources.

For Treaty of Waitangi Fisheries Commission members who identified with iwi owning long coastlines, the Treaty guarantees of rangatiratanga justified following tikanga, and mana moana provided the model that most closely adhered to tradition. However, the anthropological literature and Maori elders themselves hardly support the view that Maori social organisation was much affected by iwi leadership. In a recent review of the literature van Meijl says that, "As corporate groups iwi are even likely to be a post-colonial development" (1995:308). The musket wars of the 1820s to 1840s created the conditions that caused iwi organisation and leaders (*ariki*) to gain prominence. Whanau and hapu, led by *kaumatua* (elders) and *rangatira* (chiefs) respectively, constituted the groups that used and controlled resources.

Representatives of urban and other pan-tribal Maori groups also questioned the authenticity of iwi fundamentalism. They emphasised the changes that have taken place since 1840. Regardless of whether the chiefly authority and traditional forms of social organisation the Treaty recognised referred to iwi, colonial governors soon intentionally undermined the foundation of kin group leadership. "With their land base gone the chiefs were disempowered. Although the Maori leaders today are still referred to as rangatira, the fundamental bases that underpinned the institution of chieftainship changed towards recognition of leaders by achievement as much as ascription." The government constructed the negotiations of the fisheries claim as a meeting of chiefs with chiefs and then by-passed existing post-colonial iwi structures. According to Walker the Maori negotiators were manoeuvred into a subaltern role and "surrendered a portion of their treaty rights, thereby setting a precedent for the global settlement of tribal land claims by the same strategy, and the ultimate negation of the treaty itself" (Walker 1994: 6).

The government set up institutions for Maori development and the negotiation of Treaty issues, carefully establishing limits to their power. When its privatisation programme had the unintended consequence of letting the genie of biculturalism out of its bottle, the courts took upon themselves the right to define the principles of the Treaty. With its sovereignty attacked on two fronts, the government redeclared parliament the only sovereign entity and proceeded to define principles of its own. Ministers appointed chiefs (subsequently knighted) to reach an agreement to ultimately extinguish Treaty claims, an act that set off more protest and mounting calls for self-determination. Sharp's critique of the Waitangi Tribunal and its "anachronistic interpretations" of taonga and fishing apply to the discourse of the courts and Parliament on Treaty issues as well.

> What might appear to be a process of strict interpretation – the search for clear rules of action in the text of the Treaty – is in fact not that at all... It is to construct entitlements by dishonest retrospection rather than by considering the rights people now ought to have. (Sharp 1991:140-141)

In other words everyone involved invents unauthentic treaty discourse. Or, perhaps, everyone's discourse is authentic, at least to themselves and at most to some other small constituency. What seems to count most in the entire process is the institutional context of the discourse makers.

Among academics, discussions of the Treaty have an uncanny tendency to adopt a lyrically postmodernistic cultural flavour. Even Sharp, the rational, sceptical critic, seems unable to avoid this:

> So the best we might do, I think, is to go on both appealing to the Treaty and denying its worth. But we should accept that the appeals and the denials derive their force from considerations extrinsic to the Treaty. Then the Treaty and its history will truly become a symbol: of both unity and disunity, of a past both profound and shameful, for the various futures of the kind we want. It will then be seen for what it is: something that not only means, but ought to mean many different things to different people. (Ibid.:145)

This is all well and good as far as it goes, but the discourse of the courts and Parliament is far more constrained by legal precedent and has powerful and direct consequences. Any point of view can acquire authenticity within a specific arena, but the authenticity that can reach furthest is the authenticity that emanates from individuals and structures put in place by the state. The interests of the state are circumscribed by precedence, practicality and politics, and this sets definite and predictable bounds to the arguments about sovereignty, justice and compensation. Academics looking at these issues, especially anthropologists, remained free of such mundane fetters when they considered the ramifications of Treaty discourse for the conceptualisation of identity and have let their imaginations positively soar. Their flights have allowed other academics to clip their wings, bringing a certain steely-eyed scepticism to bear on their romantic postmodernistic fancies.

Bicultural Identity, and Counter Identity

Certainly Hanson missed the social-structural underpinnings of the ideology of ethnic politics when he naively represented biculturalism as a romantic, warm and fuzzy way of life. However, he did capture some of the flavour of the bicultural portrayal of personal identity. The idea that Maori spirituality counterbalances cold pakeha rationality contains a number of messages. It asserts in a "culture as symbol" way that a pakeha culture exists. Biculturalism in fact requires pakeha cultural self-recognition to make any sense at all. Proceeding from this recognition, at least some commentators (whom Hanson echoes) feel that non-Maori can improve themselves and their culture by incorporating Maori perspectives into their identities. Shroeder, for example, says:

> To be Pakeha... means being prepared to acknowledge that the colonising values, procedures, priorities and structures were, and in many respects still are, unashamedly monocultural. To be Pakeha... means to begin taking seriously the possibility of sharing power and inevitably giving up power, and looking to a future which must involve a more equitable use of power. (Cited in Spoonley 1991:158)

Perhaps more to the point, such bicultural individuals can help establish bicultural organisations to work and communicate effectively with Maori to advance their development.

Metge (1976, 1986) provides the epitome of this latter point of view. She presents a rationale for her writing that accords with the bicultural view of Maori culture. Metge says her books translate this culture for pakeha.

> I do not pretend to present a Maori view of Maori culture... I know from experience what most Pakehas do not know and need to have explained, what misconceptions and misunderstandings need to be corrected, what problems

overcome, before they can begin to see things from a Maori point of view. (1986: xiv)

Despite the fact that official policy in New Zealand no longer demands that Maori assimilate, the country's public institutions still evoke feelings of whakamaa. Metge glosses this concept as a state of shyness, embarrassment and shame, feeling at a disadvantage. "There is a general consensus among Maori that the whakamaa experienced in relation to Pakeha and especially in Pakeha-dominated settings such as schools and courtrooms is particularly deep and damaging. Several contributors suggested that such whakamaa is different in kind from that felt in Maori settings." Children in school, people in court, feel helpless and freeze. "In the land of their ancestors, many Maori feel that they are powerless and have lost their mana as a people" (1986:35-36, 140). Pakeha should accept responsibility, along with Maori, to redress this imbalance in mana for reasons of fairness, to prevent violence and so Maori can better realise their potential and take part in improving society. Pakeha need to work in partnership with Maori people. Although individuals can do a great deal, only public policy carried out by well-resourced, motivated public servants can make a real difference.

Metge calls for people, policy and institutions to implement five principles. Firstly, to recognise the Maori as *te tangata whenua* "the original settlers of Aotearoa and thus hosts to all who followed and one of the two parties to the Treaty of Waitangi." Secondly, recognise Maori sovereignty; that is, provide avenues for Maori to use their own cultural methods to address issues important to them so that they can re-establish their mana. Thirdly, pakeha need cultural training, to come in contact with Maori on marae where they can experience whakamaa and better understand Maori problems, aspirations and ways of doing things. In order to foster group pride the media should pay more attention to Maori achievements to balance the negative image that reinforces feelings of shame. In her final principle Metge proposes that the state adopt official practices that accommodate Maori culture and develop "a distinctly New Zealand way."

Although he does not refer to her directly, Sharp (1995) makes some interesting comments about the logical relations that pertain between the various levels of biculturalism that Metge invokes. He argues that the concept of culture gets two different treatments in bicultural discourse. On the one hand, summary representations of Maori and pakeha cultures represent them as incommensurable, holistic ways of life. The bicultural training manual from Ihi Communications, cited previously, provides a good example of this approach and seems to constitute an implementation of Metge's third principle. It contains a section "Tikanga Maaori" that discusses six topics, *whanaungatanga* (descent as a principle of social organisation), *wairuatanga* (spirituality), *te ao tuuroa* (the natural environment), *te marae* (marae protocol), and *waiata* (performance). Each topic contains discussions of more specific concepts that give a picture of a way of life that contrasts greatly with that of pakeha trainees.

Such a conceptualisation of Maori and Pakeha culture has certain implications for policy. To advance biculturalism requires some separate institutions, e.g. a Maori justice system. Existing government departments can take account of Maori cultural differences by establishing units with special perspectives and cultural expertise. Employees must learn how to communicate with Maori non-verbally as well as verbally and have some familiarity with the Maori language.

This conceptualisation of cultures defining integrated wholes recalls the more relativistic anthropological treatment of exotic peoples as inhabitants of different worlds. Sharp feels that people interested in making broad comparisons between Maori and pakeha will inevitably adopt this way of framing culture. However, when we discuss any specific person's way of life, we must adopt quite a different perspective and acknowledge both Maori and pakeha lives are composed of an idiosyncratic mix of behaviours and traits from many sources. One cannot become a bicultural person, for example, without doing this.

To increase legitimacy the state does need to provide bicultural public procedures in the Tribunal, courts and bureaucracy. Such procedures should promote intercultural communication and provide people with opportunities to develop bicultural identities. However, at this point Sharp parts company with advocates like Metge rather dramatically. The government cannot force anyone, Maori or pakeha to adopt a private bicultural identity, to believe what Maori say about their spiritual connection with the land, taonga, etc. This leads him to portray Maori claims for a special status in a bicultural New Zealand as an imposition on non-believers. Sharp, therefore, rejects these claims for special rights and expresses a preference for a multicultural society (1995:128).

Leaving the issue of multiculturalism aside for a moment, these presentations of biculturalism in policy, practice and identity seem to accept uncritically a pakeha-ness reciprocal to Maori-ness. Although Maori can claim that they lead bicultural lives because, like everyone in New Zealand society, they live in a country with an individualistic western culture, social structure and economy, for non-Maori this is not an issue. Although we may describe a pakeha culture, in the sense of a summary of a way of life, the people called pakeha generally lack the consciousness, values, myths, sense of solidarity etc. of an ethnic group or community. Defined as non-Maori with certain stereotyped characteristics, pakeha connote a category (Pearson 1989). In order to become actual bicultural selves, they need a self-conscious Pakeha identity (with a capital "P") to start with, that includes a subjective belief in their commonality, parallel to Maori.

At present, would-be Pakeha have little alternative but to adopt the Maori critique of pakeha identity. One academic has tried to explicate a positive way of inventing bicultural Pakeha selves. Spoonley suggests constructing a cultural identity "fundamentally different from the class-based and work-focused politics of industrial society." By defining oneself as a Pakeha a person commits a political act that creates an "imagined community" of values, lifestyles and progressive orientations:

> ...a contemporary identity that has been formed by interaction with iwi and a sympathy for their aspirations. It is an identity informed by an understanding of both iwi histories and a self-aware and self-critical appreciation of the ethnic history of Pakeha. [This "fictive ethnicity"] affirms the centrality of biculturalism and the ambition of *tino rangatiratanga* for *iwi*. It reflects a post-colonial position that privileges equity in terms of biculturalism (1995:104-105)

Spoonley realises that the position he articulates hardly describes a movement with mass appeal and participation. Bicultural Pakeha of the type he describes exist in those religious, secular, educational and governmental organisations that have adopted bicultural policies. He says that they are mainly middle-class, middle-aged males who see that the gains made by iwi under the mantle of the Treaty have been negated by the destruction of the welfare state. Working-class pakeha and the architects and foot soldiers of the corporatisation and privatisation of government services remain unmoved or heap scorn on the "sickly white liberals" who wear bone carvings around their necks.

These individuals reject the idea of partnership, stress the invented nature of the bicultural view of Maori culture and question the authenticity of Maori in more fundamental ways. Gould's previously cited comments about the Ngai Tahu, for example, ranks the Maoriness of 16 tribes, apparently by looking at the percentage of people who declared themselves as purely Maori in the last census. He finds the Ngai Tahu the least Maori group, and maintains that "a large proportion of the [fisheries] settlement is likely to go to the iwi which is not only undoubtedly the richest in the country but which is the least Maori in the country."

A small, isolated group of sceptical pakeha has also emerged among the architects of tradition, complete with their own anthropological translocuter, in one of New Zealand's most isolated regions, the South Island high country. High country run-holders graze sheep on properties spread over thousands of hectares. Their stations include large blocks of land leased from the Crown, typically for generations. The Crown lease of this land, which includes some of the most dramatic scenery in New Zealand, has generated conflict between the farmers, conservationists, recreational groups and the Ngai Tahu (Dominy 1993, 1995).

Part of the government's policy of privatisation in the 1980s led it to turn several departments into enterprise units and transfer assets, forests, mines, land etc. to these units. Since some of these assets were subject to Waitangi Tribunal claims, an impasse developed similar to that pertaining in fisheries management. If a state-owned enterprise wanted to sell holdings, the new owner might find them subject to claims, demonstrations and possibly occupation by Maori protesters. In order to remove this impediment to privatisation, the government passed a bill in 1988 allowing the Tribunal (which could now hear claims going back to 1840) to prevent the transfer to a state-owned enterprise of assets subject to a Maori claim. The high country farmers soon found the Ngai Tahu arguing in the Tribunal that the Crown should transfer ownership of the leased land back to them.

Ngai Tahu representatives alleged that the government failed to establish reserves promised when they purchased land from the tribe, and also dispossessed them of their food-gathering territory. They also maintained that a large block of land, the Kemp purchase, did not include 20 million acres of high country land eventually sold to settlers. Since the tribe could not bring a Tribunal claim for private property, the high country Crown land provided an ideal solution. "Ngai Tahu land claims include 2.6 million hectares of South Island high country (one tenth of the nation's land area), currently held under Crown pastoral lease tenure by 360 sheep farming families of European descent" (Dominy 1995:362).

Representatives of the farmers went to give evidence before the Tribunal to prevent the government from using the leased land to settle the claim. They presented a number of legal arguments, but also wanted to convince the Tribunal that they too had a spiritual connection to the land. Some farmers asked Dominy to testify on their behalf. She did so and presents an interesting rationale for her actions that paints a picture of discursive invention of identity similar to Hanson's. Where Hanson merely asserted that Europeans invented Maori culture, Dominy, who gave evidence before the Tribunal, makes it clear that she helped high country people construct their identity.

Dominy (1990) stresses that she does not want to undermine the Ngai Tahu position. She aims to show that the "post-colonial" inhabitants claim authenticity by articulating a spiritual and cultural connection to the landscape as well as the "post-indigenous". "The statements of high country farmers before the tribunal suggest that their evidence, although culturally located, is not only a self-conscious politicised referential expression of belonging, but part of a larger process of claiming and sustaining powerful connections to the land through a new, more explicit, discourse of authenticity" that establishes their resistance to being labelled imperialistic white settlers (1995 370-371). She resists the idea that the run-holders appropriated Maori symbols by saying that they did not seek to invalidate the Ngai Tahu claim.

This last position is disingenuous. The farmers may not usurp (one meaning of the verb "appropriate") the rhetoric of the Maori claimants, but they certainly adopt (another meaning of the word) some core Maori symbols. Station owners alleged in their testimony that they constitute the indigenous people of the high country because no one ever lived there before them. The Ngai Tahu crossed over the land on the way to west coast greenstone grounds but never inhabited the area.

Indeed, Dominy herself noted in her earlier article that the poetic and narrative images of place that the farmers use:

> ...can be examined anthropologically as an indigenous high country trope or discursive practice which contributes to a particular understanding and construction of identity at a time in New Zealand when high country people are defining themselves actively as the *tangata whenua* or "people of the land". (1993: 568)

The term tangata whenua means more than just indigenous. It connotes a status inside Maori culture that asserts the special connections with the land mentioned above, and particular ceremonial rights on marae vis-à-vis guests and other outsiders (Metge 1967:107-9). The demand by Maori that they be recognised as te tangata whenua of New Zealand constitutes the cornerstone of the bicultural agenda (Metge's first principle) of according Maori "citizen plus" rights. Claiming tangata whenua status for high country run-holders clearly constitutes symbolic appropriation. Nothing could more clearly signal the farmers' intent to resist the demands biculturalism laid at their door than their use of its metaphors to describe themselves. Authenticity seems somewhat besides the point in this context. After all, constructing a genuine cultural identity of high country farmers could only become possible when Ngai Tahu ceased to have dominion over the land the farmers now use.

The high country saga seems to have brought us full circle on the question of identity. Hanson maintains that anthropologists invent Maori culture. Maori invent pakeha in the course of articulating their ideological position. Some non-Maori respond by inventing a Pakeha "fictive ethnicity" to help Maori attain their goals. Other pakeha resist by heaping scorn on the whole enterprise, maintaining that the Maori position lacks authenticity and question whether the people claiming Maori identity are Maori at all. Farmers appropriate Maori rhetoric and enlist anthropological assistance to indigenise themselves. I will let a postmodernist have the last word for the moment:

> Under these circumstances, the foremost paradox of the frantic search for communal grounds of consensus is that it results in more dissipation and fragmentation, more heterogeneity. The drive to synthesis is the major factor of endless bifurcations. Each attempt at convergence and synthesis leads to new splits and divisions... The search for community turns into a major obstacle to its formation. (Bauman 1991:251)

6

Reconstructing Ethnicity

The case studies in this book cover a good deal of territory, theoretically as well as geographically. We have some elements of primordialism, situationalism, postmodernism and cognitive psychological explanation applied to new migrants, in new towns, in a new country; to representatives of the world's oldest ethnic community; and to the rhetoric of a fourth world people intent on redefining their relationship with the state that envelops them.

In this chapter we will use this body of case data and conceptual approaches in two ways: firstly, to re-examine the minimalist approach to ethnicity. Does the notion of classification based on descent hold up as a concept that describes a type of sociocultural phenomena? What can such a minimalistic definition contribute to an understanding of the extremely varied identities examined in the cases? The expressions of ethnicity range from the solid and down to earth, closely linked to issues of economic and social inequality, to others which apparently reflect whimsical flights of fancy.

The second goal of this chapter is to explore themes from the cases comparatively. I want to draw out dimensions of similarity and contrast to better understand how fragments of different realities and political agendas accrete to ethnic classification and produce instantiations of collective identity that overlap as much as they differ.

The Fundamentals of Ethnicity and Ethnic Identity

According to Thompson (1989:16-17) theoretical accounts of ethnicity need to explain ethnic classifications (the extent to which they are social or biological), ethnic sentiments, and ethnic social organisation. The idea that ethnicity boils down to subjective ideas about descent seems most relevant to ethnic classifications and sentiments. Ethnic social organisation may build upon classifications and sentiments, but categories clearly require something more than empathy to become established social facts.

The Papua New Guinean case provides the clearest examples of how categorisation, sentiments and organisation can come together. People used administrative locality names to denote ethnic categories. Place names like this, imposed on the map by a colonial bureaucracy, have no link with the descent concepts of indigenous social and cultural groups. How do these names become ethnic identities? We should perhaps label Gorokans, Papuans, Hageners etc. locality groups?

Detailed ethnographic examination of how people actually used the administrative labels in talk and action made their ethnic nature readily apparent. In the incidents that occurred between Kofena in Port Moresby (e.g. Balau's beating) they used their own subgroup terms, Ongobayufa, Kombiangwe and their various divisions. Kofena recognised that few other people in the town knew about their groups, their names and components. Others just called them "Goroka" or "highlander". They, in turn, accepted that in the wider arena the general categories served as proxies for their own descent groups. This willingness to accept and internalise the labels of others seemed the most striking peculiarity of urban ethnicity in Papua New Guinea. Matiabe Yuwe, for example, the Southern Highlander at the Papua Besena rally, said "Europeans put us in Papua so we are Papuans."

Cognitive psychologists note that the very existence of categories generates competition and a view of opposing categories as containing groupings of undifferentiated people. Ethnicity constitutes an example of "strong" social categorisation. Ethnic labels continue to get applied, even when it is known they are not strictly accurate, as when plantation workers in Rabaul got called highlanders though some came from the Sepik. The willingness of Papua New Guineans to apply these categories to themselves, to put them in their own heads, stems from their realisation that urban diversity makes the social group concepts of their own cultures irrelevant to urban social life. As events occur in the town that result in a member of a person's clan being wronged by a stranger, notions of commonality get mapped onto the wider categories. A simple matter like calling yourself a "Gorokan" when talking to a "Hagener" in Port Moresby or some other town sets these cognitive effects in motion. When the labels also prove useful to denote eclectic urban groupings of people from the same general area that form opportunistically – in settlements, at work, during social occasions, etc. – such tendencies get further reinforced.

This combination of pre-existing labels, cognitive effects and interaction in specific social contexts, causes sentiments and classifications to blend with each other. To address Thompson's query about the social or biological nature of ethnic sentiments, they clearly do not bubble up from the depths of the human psyche. The emotional commitments derive from the fact that ethnic labels connect identity to social categories. Identification, the act of applying a category to oneself, has cognitive and psychological dimensions that attach to socially meaningful labels. The plasticity and force of identification is evident when people like Tobeas or Matiabe Yuwe acknowledge the meaningfulness of the urban ethnic categories. Then the ethnic construction of urban social reality becomes instantiated in their actions.

Maori and Jewish identities also rest on a base provided by descent categories. Commentators like Neusner deplore the ethnicisation of Jewishness because they feel it leads to secularisation and communal disintegration. The Jewish religion itself, however, emphasises that the Jewish people descend from Abraham, Isaac and Jacob. Converts become sons or daughters of Abraham. Whether Jews opt for religious or non-religious identification, their peoplehood rests on a belief in common descent from the ancient Israelites.

The term "Maori" means normal, ordinary, or usual, in the Maori language (Williams 1994). Like "Goroka" or "Hagener", "Maori" has no intrinsic ethnic meaning and co-exists with a variety of indigenous descent-based social and cultural collectivities. When pakeha arrived in Aotearoa, the people from the various hapu and iwi used the term "Maori" (from the 1820s) to designate themselves. What happened in this early period of contact in New Zealand probably closely resembled the sequence of ethnic categorisation that occurred in urban Papua New Guinea. When people applied the label "Maori" to themselves it came to designate a pan-tribal ethnic category. New Zealand's development into a settler colony and state, where Maori people continued to confront pakeha domination, led to the formation of the type of political organisation and solidarity that turned an ethnic category into an ethnic community. Similar events may have occurred long ago to unify the tribes of Israel. Although Jewish ethnogenesis may be lost in the mists of time, we can see that the invisibility of contemporary New Zealand Jews – essentially a lack of public application of an ethnic category – coincides with the diminished salience of Jewishness in all its dimensions.

The descent perspective probably also applies to the origin of the category pakeha. The bulk of New Zealand's early settlers were white and British, and must have seemed to constitute a unitary ethnic group, the counter-group, to the tribespeople labelling themselves "Maori". The continued salience of the term, and its extension to refer (much like the Jewish concept "goyim") to any people "not Maori", despite the historical transformations of New Zealand, surely provides testimony to the power of basic categories of origin to serve as channels to interpret new social realities.[25]

Although white New Zealanders may in their turn call themselves pakeha, they do so without developing notions of common origin. If Pakeha-ness (with the capital "P") means to renounce monoculturalism, and welcome the sharing of power with Maori, as Spoonley says, this describes a type of New Zealand, liberal identification based on political philosophy. White biculturalists may develop solidarity and form political associations but, if they did, their groupings would constitute communities of assent rather than descent. Morris, talking about religious doctrine (particularly Christian claims to replace Jews as God's chosen people), makes an interesting point about the differences between communities of assent and descent.

> Communities of assent are based on strategies of successful rhetorical persuasion designed to lead to assent to a body of shared truths, or values... normally missionary, reflecting their potential universality. Identity is dependent on assent to the foundational truths and/or doctrines... The community of assent necessarily requires a progressive narrative of its own temporal supersession and replacement of the community of descent. (n.d.:26)

Pakeha identity, in the sense used by Spoonley, clearly constitutes an attempt to produce such a community. Biculturalism provides the body of shared truths, complete with a version of original sin. The children of rapacious, capitalistic settlers renounce their origins (Britain as home) and adopt a set of progressive values to define a new community. In other words, they deconstruct what remains of their ethnicity (appropriate since Britain abandoned New Zealand to join the Common Market), and attempt to construct a more contemporary collective identity from its ashes.

Rhetorical persuasion and missionary-like zeal pervades the ideology of other cultural groups. The proliferation of cultural identities, the culturalisation of ethnicity and the ethnicisation of culture derive much of their appeal from the ability of "spokespersons" to freely define their nature and content. Ideologues can invent Pakeha and high-country farmer cultural identities (and deaf or gay identity) more easily than Jewish or Maori identity because, without having to use any specific principle, they can characterise group solidarity in any way convenient to the circumstances. By conflating culture and ethnicity the cultural movements bolster their claims to "own" the issues.

---

[25] Metge (1995:20) gives the term Pakeha two meanings. It can refer to immigrants from Europe and their descendants, or simply non-Maori. She says that the particular meaning "is usually clear from the context". The hypothesis advanced here is that the concept developed from an ethnic label used by Maori to a more general category adopted, or at least understood, by all New Zealanders.

Ethnicity, in the minimal sense of subjective beliefs in common descent, has no specific cultural content. We can see, especially in the Papua New Guinean case, that ethnicity constitutes one method among many of classifying other humans, that anthropologists and sociologists can observe people using in specific contexts[26].

The cases in this book, and the wider literature show that ethnic identities, groups and communities wax and wane. Iwi were temporarily submerged in the 1980s and early 1990s versions of biculturalism as Maori identity strengthened. Now that some tangible gains have begun to flow in their direction, new hapu and iwi emerge to fight for their share of resources. Jewishness, once an unalterable fact of life, now constitutes a part-time private interest or symbolic identity in New Zealand. The literature is full of other cases of such efflorescence and withering. In order to understand this aspect of the phenomenon of ethnicity, we need to consider the place of collective identities in the wider context of social and cultural organisation. Regardless of the important contribution other factors make to specific manifestations of identity, for ethnicity and its imitators, these organisational elements stimulate secondary elaborations of categories of origin.

Ethnicity in Context – Comparisons of the Cases

Since ethnic labels connect identity with meaningful social categories, and categorisation itself generates opposition, ethnicity readily becomes an effective basis for the political mobilisation of groups. Ross (1980:15) defines an ethnic group as a "politically mobilised collectivity... a group option for pressuring for public goods to be allocated to the members of the self-differentiating collectivity." Ethnicity certainly helps to organise oppositions on a group level but the oppositions themselves come into existence as ethnic categories form, consequences of the cognitive sequelae of categorisation itself.

When contrasting categories become mapped onto inequalities in the distribution of public goods, oppositions deepen and become reinforced. This was especially clear in the Papua New Guinean and Maori cases. The initial "push" of categorisation came from classifying newly encountered people. Grievances – to an academic observer, matters of class-based, developmental and even randomly generated conflicts (e.g. the car crash in Mt. Hagen) – adhered to the classifications, which became idioms of protest and foci of

---

[26] Of course, if we take Hirschfeld's (1994) point seriously, that racial and ethnic categorisation reflects the working of a specific cognitive domain, this way of classifying people should be more salient and ubiquitous than many other forms of social categorisation.

cultural elaboration. The potential of diverse categories to serve as foundations of group mobilisation clearly differs from situation to situation. These divergent potentials cannot be explained by "the basics" of ethnicity alone. The various expressions of identity discussed in this monograph show that in order to account for the fate of the entities for which categories provide the substrate, whether they endure and grow or stagnate and dissolve, analysis must take account of the particular economic, social organisational and political circumstances of the categorisations.

Jews, Maori and urban Papua New Guineans all experienced a similar kind of transformation of their relationship with the state. Formerly peripheral peoples, who lived as members of distinctive small communities at the margins of modernity, they have become incorporated at different times, different places, and to different extents, into societies that continue to undermine the autonomy of their groups. Looking at particular experiences and responses to this incorporation provides a way to elucidate the major similarities and differences between the various expressions of ethnicity and identity contained in the specific case studies.

In an article comparing Israeli and Haitian immigrants to the United States, Mittleberg and Watters (1992) found that both faced identity demands from the host society that conflicted with their own self-definitions. American Jews want Israelis to identify as Jews and de-emphasise their national origins because of the general Jewish disapproval of emigration from Israel. The Israelis resist assimilation to the Jewish community because they feel alienated from the Jewish religion and stigmatised by the fact that they left the promised land. Haitians find that Americans categorise them as blacks, but in Haiti, where everyone is descended from Africans, blackness is too taken-for-granted to become a politicised identity. Haitians want Americans to recognise them as immigrants. The Israelis can ignore such external pressures more easily than Haitians because they can hide their origins in a way that black immigrants cannot.

Mittleberg and Watters suggest that a spectrum of types of ethnicity exists in the United States diffused along a continuum defined by the relative freedom that members of different groups have to define themselves unconstrained by external labelling.

Spectrum of Types of Ethnicity in the United States

Individual Choice <—————————————> Societal Constraint

Unhyphenated Whites	Symbolic Ethnics	Ethnics	Language Minorities	Racial Minorities

(Mittleberg and Watters 1992:417)

Mittleberg and Watters say that the existence of an organisational component demarcates the line between ethnics and symbolic ethnics. Italian and Irish Americans provide examples of symbolic ethnicity. Jews who belong to congregations or other organisations remain ethnics. The fact that increasing numbers of Jews disaffiliate indicates their continuing shift from the right to the left of this spectrum. The diagram nicely illustrates the changing face of Jewish ethnicity in the diaspora.

Members of highly visible minorities just a few generations ago, most Jews were under mutually reinforcing internal and external restraints to remain Jewish. As time went on they began to acculturate and assimilate to their respective diaspora societies. Mobility and success undermined the structural supports of ethnic mobilisation. Jewish distinctiveness – in neighbourhoods, occupational specialisations, etc. – diminished generationally and no pool of underclass Jewish immigrants arrived to refill the residential areas, jobs, and intergroup conflicts left behind. These now-undesirable niches became the territory of other ethnic groups – existing language and racial minorities – in American society. A shrinking core of observant Jews resist the pull of assimilation by exercising their individual choice to encapsulate themselves in Jewish social and institutional networks while most of their fellows join the mainstream of postmodern selves who use ethnicity as an ingredient in their continual reconstructions of personal identity.

Gross (1993:8) argues that ethnic affiliation should be viewed as a matter "of rational choice and strategic judgement based on an individual's evaluation of the most effective means available to achieve political goals within a competitive environment." He believes that many Jewish groups achieved their major goals to promote the civil rights and the social welfare of Jewish immigrants, but now pursue policies that emphasise segregative and parochial forms of ethnic programming. Gross argues that these new initiatives conflict with American pluralism.

The culture of the democratic system does not disparage segregated groups if they strive to promote integration, but liberal democracy remains adverse to their persistence. The fact that Jews currently tend to disaffiliate from synagogues and voluntary organisations indicates that the accomplishments of these groups have caused them to run out of incentives for most individuals to remain active members, except for the significant minority who now embrace a segregative religious focus. According to what Gross calls the "organizational perspective" on ethnicity, Jews who have adapted to democratic diaspora societies should be expected to assimilate. If he is correct, Jewish symbolic ethnicity and their "spectrum of choices" may constitute an illusion. The incorporation of Jews into American society pushes them along paths that undermine domestic ethnic political organisation.

Jews in New Zealand, and other diaspora countries also face these pushes and respond to them in a variety of ways. French Jews, for example, have developed three modes of conceptualising their relationship to the French state (Schnapper 1994). The first view is that citizenship does not in any way clash with attachment to Judaism. Expressions of the former take place in public while Judaism operates in private contexts. "The second group criticized not the principle of citizenship, but the particular form that it took in France. In their view, the political tradition, which they consider excessively centralised and culturally unified has led to the demise of many collective forms of Jewish life". They want to develop a Jewish community concept in France, similar to the situation pertaining in Britain or the United States.

The final group (that Schnapper identifies as predominantly recent Sefardi immigrants from North Africa, who have not fully internalised French ideas of citizenship) calls for something that sounds very similar to Maori demands in New Zealand. "They want recognition for the Jewish community as such, in the public and political domain – not only the cultural and social domains, as both a religious and a secular entity. They voice a fundamental criticism of the place accorded to Jewish citizens, in that their specific characteristics have never been given recognition." This diversity of opinion signals that Jewishness in France is changing. Jews there now call themselves *juifs,* the term of abuse used in Vichy times. The expression *israelites* coined by more assimilated Jews has taken on negative connotations.

The transition from "Negroes" to "blacks", also a former term of abuse for Americans with African ancestry, constituted a potent symbol of blacks' redefinition of their place in America. Members of this group also articulate ideological visions of their relationship with the state. Ellison argued in his essay "What America Would Be Like Without Blacks" that, constitutive of Americanness rather than candidates for it, blacks are the moral centre of America's hybrid culture. They push democratic culture towards fruition, with the most obvious test being "the inclusion – not assimilation – of the black man." America "could not survive being deprived of their presence because, by the irony implicit in the dynamics of American democracy, they symbolise both its most stringent testing and the possibility of its greatest human freedom" (Boynton 1995:67-68).

Blacks in America, Maori in New Zealand and other "fourth world" people, Jews in France, the United States and Australia, have all articulated ideologies to reject assimilation and promote the recognition of their integrity and demands to define for themselves how their identity is represented in the public sphere. Elites elaborate these ideologies, while individuals act in accordance with their own needs and desires, spreading themselves into the niches available to their ethnic category along the spectrum of types of identification. These ideological positions bear no necessarily direct relationship to the hard-and-fast realities of individual life, ethnicity, or the contexts of ethnic collectivities in the state. They provide examples of politically driven culturalised myths, attempts to create particular expressions of the nature and plight of one's people to advance mobilisation and specific political agendas.

Schnapper, for example, feels that the Jews who demand a kind of biculturalism in France express utopian views. She notes that nothing like this position has ever existed for Jews anywhere in the diaspora. Ellison's ideas about blackness in America and the strong versions of biculturalism Maori and Pakeha invent in New Zealand seem equally utopian. These ideologies constitute myths very similar to those discussed by Smith and cited in the introduction. Smith says that such myths function to give ethnicity potency as a basis for collective action. They mediate and direct "the economic, cultural and political conditions, endowing otherwise random events and chaotic processes with a peculiarly 'historicist' form and 'ethnic' content." Ethnic myths promote and define the basis for solidarity, and provide a blueprint for future political action to realise the groups' goals and ultimate destiny.

Modern bureaucratic interventionist governments stimulate ethnic nationalism in their attempts to create loyal citizens. Groups that perceive the state as an alien "colonialist" institution often develop counter national agendas of their own. (Smith 1984:299-302). Smith notes elsewhere (1981:15-17) that strategies other than national self-determination are open to ethnic communities seeking political expression in poly-ethnic states. They can become isolated, accommodate to the host society, demand greater control of specifically communal matters, call for autonomy in various degrees from specific cultural rights to full-blown self-rule, or try to unite with fellow ethnics in different countries to form an irredentist state.

The Jewish community in New Zealand obviously accommodates. Jews participate fully in New Zealand society without articulating ideological expressions of New Zealand Jewishness. Virtually all individuals acculturate and many assimilate. Their dispersal in the secular social and economic structures of the country reinforces a privatisation of Jewish identity. This privatisation lowers participation in Jewish cultural and social life and reinforces assimilative trends. The most committed members of the community leave for Australia and Israel rather than challenge communal invisibility. Nevertheless, Neusner's gloomy prognosis of New Zealand as the site of the first voluntary extinction of a Jewish community seems overstated. Symbolic ethnicity constitutes a form of ethnic identification that "the wider society fosters and legitimates" (Smith 1981). It combines a sense of individuality with connotations of community (Watters 1990). The wide appeal of these two values in western democratic states may well encourage the persistence of a symbolic attachment to Jewishness.

A casual observer might expect Jewish ethnicity to provide a complete counterpoint to the rather minimalist ethnicity that exists among urban Papua New Guineans. The product of over 3,000 years in the making, Jewishness should surely come more elaborately polished than the tentative, sometimes confused-sounding statements of my Melanesian informants about the social categories in towns they lived in sporadically for only a few years. And of course on an abstract level Jewishness contains infinitely more content than urban Papua New Guinean identities. Jewish culture, its contribution to world history, great works of literature, art and philosophy constitutes a civilisation, nothing less. Most of my New Zealand Jewish informants, heirs to this great tradition, know little of its content and can hardly relate its main themes to their lives.

Both urban Papua New Guineans and New Zealand Jews have tangible reasons for lacking certainty about the cultural elaborations of their ethnicities. Papua New Guineans worked them out on the fly as events proceeded in their newly developing towns and state. With little input from a professional intelligentsia that could elaborate ethnic myths for collective mobilisation, and unstable competition between mutually antagonistic identities, the categories – Hageners, Wabags, highlanders in Port Moresby, etc. – could only mobilise sporadic acts of antagonism. They did not become foci of sustained action against marginality in this emerging state.

Less fragmented, New Zealand Jewish identity nevertheless becomes irrelevant in the wider context which is characterised by biculturalism, disaffiliation, migration, intermarriage and other threats to continuity. Moving in opposite directions, and crossing near the inchoate end of a continuum of solidarity, urban Papua New Guineans and New Zealand Jews provide us with examples of tentative identities, one a result of new ethnic construction, the other a product of dissolution.

Statements about Maori ethnicity examined in this book appear more certain than those of Jews or urban Papua New Guineans, especially in regard to goals and programmes for change. Professional elites in special forums work to polish a rhetoric of grievance and reconciliation that develops considerable weight as a representation of New Zealand's history and race relations. The fact that Maori have such sites and ideologues, and New Zealand Jews and urban Papua New Guineans generally lack them at least indicates that Maori ethnicity, percolating into the heart of New Zealand's discourse about itself, has become "hot" in a way that the others have not.

Maori obviously occupy a fundamentally different position in New Zealand society than do Jews. New Zealand's political system recognises the legitimacy of their grievances, but the government seeks to limit the costs of settlements and to promote Maori participation in the current political system. The developments traced in the Waitangi Tribunal cases show that the Crown vigorously resists claims that undermine its sovereignty. This has become more apparent as Maori gained resources as a result of early tribunal claims.

However, biculturalism, in the soft sense of attaching Maori names and logos to New Zealand's public institutions with the cooperation and advice of *te tangata whenua,* and settling some especially glaring injustices, gives New Zealand a Maori patina that helps indigenise somewhat the secular, rationally bureaucratic state. The ethnicisation of the Maori cultural category "Pakeha", with some breast beating, enables white New Zealand liberals to adopt aspects of Maori culture without appearing to appropriate them in an imperialistic manner. If Maori use their quota and other gains from settlements wisely, the government will benefit by defusing opposition to its privatisation policies and achieving a decrease in negative Maori welfare spending.

This "soft" vision of biculturalism appears to be fading like a mirage. Treaty grievance generates the dissipation and fragmentation Bauman sees as symptomatic of our times when the Crown and the tribes argue over sovereignty. Initial pan-Maori successes have stimulated new forms of tribal fundamentalism and corporatism that threatens Maori unity and drives away pakeha supporters appalled at the potential exploitation of nature reserves. A stronger version of biculturalism, one that gives Maori full autonomy and powers that conflict with majoritarian democracy, appears unlikely in the contemporary context of a more legalistic Waitangi Tribunal whose powers have been continually limited by the courts. The recent intensification of Maori protest may signal the end of biculturalism and the start of a new phase in Maori relations with the state.

During the heyday of the Tribunal, biculturalism seemed set to deliver what Metge called "a distinctively New Zealand way". Recall that her five principles of partnership included a request for the recognition of Maori sovereignty. Metge defined sovereignty as providing avenues for Maori to use cultural methods to address important issues and re-establish mana. Although one can point out that prior to the new age of biculturalism the word "sovereignty" meant ultimate power, and Metge was expressing a demand for community control or limited autonomy, at least she defined her construction of sovereignty clearly.

An interesting tendency found specifically in bicultural rhetoric, and in cases of invented tradition generally, is the blurring of the meanings of terms or use polysemic words as symbols, so they signify whatever members of the audience want them to.[27] Keesing (1982:297) notes that appeals to custom in Melanesia "illustrate in particularly striking ways the nature of political ideologies and the role of abstract symbols in them: the extent to which deep contradictions can be disguised and denied: the diverse uses to which such abstract symbols can be put, to defend old ways or change them radically, to assert national or supra-national unity or promote regional separatism and so on." Buddy Mikaere, the departing director of the Waitangi Tribunal, himself noted how confusing he found the sovereignty debate.

> "Many claims to the tribunal talk about Crown actions impinging on tino rangatiratanga without defining what is meant. From my reading of the treaty it means Maori control over things Maori. That can span quite a range of things. But this suggestion that it should mean Maori control over anything that affects Maori life – I don't think that's how it was meant originally." (quoted in Barlow 1995)

Mikaere seems to saying that the Treaty does not support calls for autonomy expressed in separate parliamentary, justice and educational structures as some activists maintain.

Civil Judaism, with its emphasis on Israel, the Holocaust and the fight against anti-Semitism, also contains elements of symbolic obfuscation. In this case the polysemic symbols hide the contradictions between fully participating in American life and surviving as a distinctive community. Although logic dictates the impossibility of doing both simultaneously, civil Judaism denies the tension. It provides "a complex ideological mechanism for dealing with ambivalence by integrating it into an understanding of contemporary American Jewish life and validating it as appropriate and necessary". (Woocher 1986:97).

---

[27] Durie (n.d.:27-29) presents a continuum of five bicultural goals and five bicultural structural arrangements. The goals ("attaining cultural skills and knowledge, better awareness of the Maori position, a clearer focus on Maori...best outcomes for Maori...[and] agreed joint ventures") and structures ("unmodified mainstream institution, a Maori perspective, active Maori involvement, parallel Maori institution, independent Maori institutions") can be combined in a bicultural matrix that contains 25 logically possible definitions of organisational biculturalism.

For example, concentrating on both Israel and the Holocaust allows American Jewish organisations and their constituents to avoid some of the conflicts between supporting Jewish causes and American pluralism. These symbols conveniently allow people to mobilise around events that do not refer to domestic issues. Jews can "support Israel" without specifying what they support, beyond the country's right to exist. They can condemn the Holocaust as a crime against humanity relevant to other cases of mass murder and also stress its unique aspects and continuity with other historical outrages against the Jewish people. New Zealand Jews use these same symbols, but in private contexts in keeping with their accommodation to the wider society.

Conclusion

This analysis of the basics and elaborations of ethnicity generally concurs with Smith's explication of "The Ethnic Revival in the Modern World" (1981). His blend of elements of primordialism, situationalism and invention, as well as the emphasis on the role of myths (illustrated here in civil Judaism and biculturalism) transforming opposition into sustained political mobilisation remains convincing. Smith's distinction between ethnic categories, groups and communities, mentioned in the introduction, is also clear and sensible. But for all his valuable insights Smith, like other sociologists and anthropologists, does not incorporate a cognitive dimension into the study of ethnicity and this imposes some important limitations on our understanding of this phenomenon itself, and the connections between ethnic and cultural identities. In a discussion about the difference between regionalism and ethnicity Smith says that:

> ...whereas a "region" refers to a category rather than a community, with an ethnic group it is the other way round... For the most part, an "ethnic group" is a type of community, with a specific sense of solidarity and honour, and a set of shared symbols and values... Now the important point about an ethnic, as opposed to other kinds of social grouping, is the rationale that sustains the sense of group belonging and group uniqueness, and which links successive generations of its members. That rationale is to be found in the specific history of the group, and, above all, in its myths of group origins and group liberation. The more striking and well-known these myths of group formation and group deliverance, the greater the chances for the ethnic group to survive and endure. (1981:65)

The "city men", the economic elite of London discussed by Abner Cohen (1974), gays, the "deaf community" (Dolnic 1993), in fact any collection of people categorisable as an entity can develop such myths of formation and deliverance to enhance solidarity. In some ways, all these "communities" seem ethnic. A recent magazine article about dwarfs flirtation with identity politics

(Berreby 1996) makes a case for Little People ethnicity that provides a particularly striking instance of the reification of the concept and its linkage with a simplistic notion of culture in what Gerd Baumann (1996) calls a "dominant discourse" of "community".

Some dwarfs oppose, as an assault on their identity, the limb lengthening operations that can give affected children normal height. Little People spokespersons note that except for the prejudice of others they can function normally without the invasive medical interventions that would turn them into something else. After all, Attila the Hun was a dwarf who managed to create the largest empire the world has known. "Once stereotyped as little more than freaks, dwarfs are now on the edge of the dilemma of science and identity. How their culture finally determines the question could have ramifications beyond their small world" (Berreby 1996:18).

Note how easily Berreby's comment glides from the obvious observation that being different, dwarfs suffer inequalities in society, to the notion that difference constitutes identity. People with a common identity naturally form a group or community. To complete the narrative the author gives dwarfs a culture, one with a primary capacity of intelligent entities, the ability to act rationally. Many anthropologists have deplored the increasingly pervasive tendency to turn culture, a key concept of a discipline that studies the ongoing creation of meaning, into an object, the property of each naturally occurring and therefore unique group. Ethnic minorities seem extremely plausible targets for such an ideological exercise, especially when ethnicity is conceived of in primordialistic terms. Gays, the deaf, dwarfs and other "identity groups" can obviously play the same game when they call for equality and resist interventions aimed at changes in sexual orientation, hearing and height.

Identity politics has become pervasive as a myriad of groups demand, not just inclusion and civil rights, but more fundamental changes in cultural categories and socioeconomic organisation. Often their ideologues will invoke rhetorical representations of "communities" that have little or no substantiation in networks of personal relations (Calhoun 1995:220). As the postmodernists insist, "The distinction between reality and representation threatens to become meaningless" (Szaz 1995:211). If these groups are ethnic – after all, they do many of the things that ethnic groups do, indeed, they even fit Smith's criteria for ethnic groups (and those of other scholars who stress mixtures of cultural traits and solidarity) – the concept has indeed become too nebulous to have any analytical use.

All people have many potentially manipulable identities, but a careful consideration of them leads to the conclusion that "City men", gay, dwarf and deaf identities are not ethnic. Undoubtedly lifestyles, orientations or "disabilities" can generate solidarity, ideology and reified notions of culture no less meaningful than those elaborated in biculturalism, or among Jews and urban Papua New Guineans. Certainly the truth value of elaborations of ethnicity seem no less problematic than any other claims of identity politics. Why, then, stress the distinction between subjective descent categories and those built from other foundations when all representations of identity now seem as real as bricks and mortar?

Ethnics – Jews, Maori and urban Papua New Guineans – create their categories of identity and organisation in corresponding ways. Like everyone else they have an infinite variety of potential markers and possible identities. Yet ethnicity seems to provide what looks to informants like a natural basis of solidarity. It involves a realm of cognition (perhaps a domain and certainly cognitive effects) not entirely reducible to any aspect of culture or cultural transmission.

As observers and analysts of society and culture, anthropologists, properly wary of imposing our notions on informants, nevertheless need precise concepts to account for the creation of specific social and cultural realities. When we encounter people so ubiquitously using subjective notions of descent to operate in and discuss certain aspects of social life we must conclude that these descent-based notions have a genuine reality. Our most important task is to investigate how they engage social structure to produce cultural representations (cultural in the unreified sense of shared, constructed meanings). Anthropologists should not hesitate to label the specific, readily discernible aspects of discourse and social action highlighted in this book as ethnicity.

Aside from the fact that such a concept of ethnicity can help us to describe and distinguish between the types of identity people construct in various times and places, ethnic categories, at least when they stay to the right of symbolic ethnicity in Mittleburg and Watter's continuum, have different consequences for social situations than the lifestyle categories that seem so compatible with New Zealand Jewishness and bicultural visions of identity. By providing the categorical basis for groups that can reproduce themselves and demand territory, autonomy or sovereignty, ethnicity often becomes an ingredient that shapes some of the most violent and intractable disputes in human history.

This monograph stresses a particular kind of social categorisation, not myth, culture, lifestyle or disability, as the "switch" that turns ethnicity on. The Maori and Papua New Guinean cases show that once categories form that make sense to participants as markers of identification in a wider social field, even if they describe entities that have no objectified cultural symbols, they quickly accrete meaning through both the cognitive processes of categorical opposition and the "dominant discourse" of community and cultural reification that exploits apprehensions of difference. Particular categories form in specific contexts and these contexts determine how far processes will go towards the formation of enduring identities. Smith may be correct that ideology helps to establish stable groups and communities, but such stability only develops when the categories and oppositions are not undercut by competing ones. The symbolic ethnicity of New Zealand Jews demonstrates (to paraphrase Johnson) that the extraordinary endurance and particular strength of the all-consuming ideal which made the Jews different, their striking and well-known myths, do not automatically provide the basis for a type of identity that is more immutable in the face of social and cultural forces than any other.

References

Adams, P. 1977. *Fatal Necessity*. Auckland University Press, Auckland.
Alba, R. 1990. *Ethnic Identity: The Transformation of White America*. Yale University Press, New Haven.
Ardener, E. 1989. Language, Ethnicity and Population. Pp. 65-71 in M. Chapman (ed.) *The Voice of Prophecy and Other Essays*. Blackwell, Oxford.
Banks, M. 1996. *Ethnicity: Anthropological Constructions*. Routledge, London.
Barlow, H. 1995. Waitangi Wayfarer. *The Dominion* newspaper, October 16:7.
Barnes, J. 1962. African Models in the New Guinea Highlands. *Man* 62: 5-9.
Barsalou, L. 1992. *Cognitive Psychology*. LEA, New Jersey.
Barth, F. 1969. *Ethnic Groups and Boundaries*. Allen and Unwin, London.
Bauman, Z. 1992. *Intimations of Postmodernity*. Routledge, London.
Baumann, Gerd. 1995. *Contesting Culture: Discourses of Identity in Multi-Ethnic London*. Cambridge University Press, Cambridge.
Beaglehole, A. 1990. *Facing the Past*. PhD Dissertation, Victoria University of Wellington.
Beaglehole, A. 1988. *A Small Price to Pay*. Allen and Unwin, Wellington.
Beaglehole, A., Levine, H. 1995. *Far From The Promised Land? : Being Jewish In New Zealand*. Pacific Press, Wellington.
Bell, D. 1976. *The Cultural Contradictions of Capitalism*. Basic Books, New York.
Bellah, R., Hammond, C. 1980. *Varieties of Civil Religion*. Harper and Row, San Francisco.
Belshaw, C. 1957. *The Great Village*. Routledge, London.
Bendix, R., Lipset, S. 1967. Karl Marx's Theory of Social Class. Pp. 6-11 in R. Bendix and S. Lipset eds.*Class, Status and Power*. The Free Press, New York.
Berreby, D. 1996. Up with People: Dwarves Meet Identity Politics. *The New Republic* 214:18 14-18.
Biksup, P., Jinks B., Nelson, H. 1968. *A Short History of New Guinea*. Angus and Robertson, Sydney.
Bowers, N. 1968. *The Ascending Grasslands*. PhD Dissertation, Columbia University.
Boyer, P. 1994. Cognitive Constraints on Cultural Representations: Natural Ontologies and Religious Ideas. Pp. 396-415 in L. A. Hirschfeld and S. A. Gelman (eds.) *Mapping the Mind Domain Specificity in Cognition and Culture*. Cambridge University Press.
Boynton, R. 1995. The New Intellectuals. *Atlantic Monthly* March: 53-70
Brown, P. 1962. Non-agnates Among the Patrilineal Chimbu. *Journal of the Polynesian Society* 71:57-69.
Brownlie, I. 1992. *Treaties and Indigenous Peoples*. Clarendon Press, Oxford.
Bureau of Immigration and Population Research. 1994. Census New Zealand Born. In *Community Profiles*. Australian Government, Canberra.
Calhoun, C. 1995. *Critical Social Theory*. Blackwell, Oxford.
Cohen, Abner. 1969. Introduction. Pp. ix-xxiii in A. Cohen (ed.) *Urban Ethnicity*. Tavistock, London.

Cohen, Anthony P. (1994) *Self Consciousness: An Alternative Anthropology of Identity.* Routledge, London.
Cohen, R. 1978. Ethnicity: Problem and Focus in Anthropology. *Annual Review of Anthropology* 7: 379-403.
Cohen, S. 1988. *American Assimilation or Jewish Survival?* Indiana University Press, Bloomington.
Colebatch, H. et al. 1971. Free Elections in a Guided Democracy. Pp.218-274 in A.L. Epstein (ed.) *The Politics of Dependence, Papua New Guinea 1968.* Australia National University Press, Canberra.
Connor, Walker. 1993. The Ethnonational Bond. *Ethnic and Racial Studies* 16:3 373-390.
Crystal, D. 1987. *The Cambridge Encyclopedia of Language.* Cambridge University Press, Cambridge.
D'Andrade, R. 1995 *The Development of Cognitive Anthropology.* Cambridge University Press, Cambridge.
Darnovsky, M., Epstein, B., Flacks, R. (eds.) 1993. *Cultural Politics and Social Movements.* Temple University Press, Philadelpia.
Dominion newspaper. 1995. October 16:7.
Dominy, M. 1990. New Zealand's Waitangi Tribunal. *Anthropology Today* 6(2): 11-15.
Dominy, M. 1993. Lives Were Always Here. *Anthropological Forum* 6: 567-585.
Dominy, M. 1995. White Settler Assertions of Native Status. *American Ethnologist* 22 (2): 358-374.
Durie, M. n.d. Maori and the State: Professional and Ethical Implications for the Public Service.
Edwards, D. 1991. Categories are for Talking. *Theory and Psychology* 1: 515-542.
Epstein, A.L. 1958. *Politics in an Urban African Community.* Manchester University Press, Manchester.
Epstein, A.L. 1969. *Matupit: Land, Politics and Change Among the Tolai of New Britain.* University of California Press, Berkeley.
Firth, R. 1929. *Economics of the New Zealand Maori.* Government Printer, Wellington.
Fisheries Allocation Claim. 1995. *Record of Proceedings Wai 447 #1.2(a).* Waitangi Tribunal, Wellington.
Fiske, S.T., Taylor, S.E. 1991. *Social Cognition,* 2ed. McGraw-Hill, N.Y.
Fleras, A., Elliot, J. 1992. *The Nations Within.* Oxford University Press, Toronto.
Fleras, A. 1991. Tuku Ranga. Pp 153-194 in P. Spoonley (ed.) *Nga Take.* Dunmore Press, Palmerston North.
Gans, H. 1979. Symbolic Ethnicity. *Ethnic and Racial Studies* 2: 1-20.
Giddens, A. 1991. *Modernity and Self Identity.* Polity Press, Oxford.
Glazer, N. 1989. *American Judaism.* University of California Press, Los Angeles.
Gluckman, A. 1990. *Identity and Involvement.* Dunmore Press, Palmerston North.
Gluckman, M. 1958. *Analysis of a Social Situation in Modern Zululand.* Rhodes-Livingstone Institute, Manchester University Press.
Goldschieder, C., Zukerman, A. 1984. *The Transformation of the Jews.* University of Chicago Press, Chicago.
Gross, M. 1993. Paradigms of Jewish Ethnicity. *Jewish Journal of Sociology* 35,1: 5-34.
Hanson, A. 1989. The Making of the Maori. *American Anthropologist* 91: 890-902.
Harrington, W. 1994. The White Tribe of Ngai Tahu. *Dominion* newspaper, August 16 : 6.
Haughey, E. 1966. Maori Claims to Lakes, River Beds and the Foreshore. *N.Z. Universities Law Review* 2: 29-42.
Hingston, P. 1984. *Submissions of Council for Ngati Pikiao.* Tribunals Division Wellington.

References

Hirschfeld, L.A. 1994. Is the Acquisition of Social Categories Based on Domain Specific Competence or Knowledge Transfer? Pp. 201-233 in L.A. Hirschfeld and S.A. Gelman (eds.) *Mapping the Mind: Domain Specificity in Cognition and Culture.* Cambridge University Press.

Hirschfeld, L.A., Gelman, S.A. (eds.) 1994. *Mapping the Mind: Domain Specificity in Cognition and Culture.* Cambridge University Press.

Hobsbaum, E., Ranger, T. (eds.) 1983. *The Invention of Tradition.* Cambridge University Press, Cambridge.

Hogg, M.A., Abrams, D. 1988. *Social Identifications.* Routledge, London.

Holland, D., Quinn, N. 1987. *Cultural Models in Language and Thought.* Cambridge University Press, Cambridge.

Horowitz, B. 1994. Findings From the 1991 New York Jewish Population Study. *Contemporary Jewry* 15: 4-25.

Hunter, A. 1995. Rethinking Revolution in Light of New Social Movements. Pp. 320-343 in M. Darnovsky, B. Epstein and R. Flacks (eds.) *Cultural Politics and Social Movements.* Temple University Press, Philadelpia.

Ihi Communications n.d. Historical Database. In *Bicultural Training.* Ihi Communications and Consultancy.

Jaffe, R. 1990. The Ebb and Flow of Post-War Jewish Identity in Auckland. Pp. 33-41 in A. Gluckman (ed.) *Identity and Involvement.* Dunmore Press, Palmerston North.

Johnson, P. 1987. *A History Of The Jews.* Harper & Row, New York.

Kaplan, M. 1981. *Judaism as a Civilization.* Jewish Publication Society of America.

Keesing, R. 1982. Kastom in Melanesia: An Overview. *Mankind* 13: 297-301.

Keesing, R., Tonkinson, R. (eds.) 1982. Reinventing Traditional Culture. *Mankind* 13(4).

Kelsey, J. 1990. *A Question of Honour.* Allen and Unwin, Wellington.

Kelsey, J. 1991. Treaty Justice in the 1980s . Pp. 108-130 in P. Spoonley (ed.) *Nga Take.* Dumore Press, Palmerston North.

Kukathas, C. 1993. The Idea of a Multicultural Society. In C. Kukathas (ed.) *Multicultural Citizens.* Centre for Independent Studies, Auckland.

Lakoff, G. 1987. *Women Fire and Dangerous Things.* University of Chicago Press, Chicago.

Lane, H. 1992. *The Mask of Benevolence.* Knopf, New York.

Levine, H. 1976. *The Formation of Ethnic Units in Urban Papua New Guinea.* PhD Dissertation, SUNY Stony Brook.

Levine, H. 1987. The Cultural Politics of Maori Fishing. *Journal of the Polynesian Society* 96: 421-444.

Levine, H. 1991a. Participation in the Modern Sector and Width of Ethnic Interaction. Pp. 585-589 in A. Pawley (ed.) *Man and a Half: Essays in Honour of Ralph Bulmer.* The Polynesian Society, Auckland.

Levine, H. 1991b. Comment on Hanson's "The Making of the Maori". *American Anthropologist* 93: 444-446.

Levine, H., Henare, M. 1994. Maori Self-Determination. *Pacific Viewpoint* 35: 195-210.

Levine, H., Levine, M. 1979. *Urbanization in Papua New Guinea.* Cambridge University Press.

Lewkowicz, B. 1994. Greece is My Home But. *Journal of Mediterranean Studies* 4: 225-240.

Lieberman, C. 1985. *A Certain People.* Summit Books, New York.

Linnekin, J. 1992. On the Theory and Politics of Cultural Construction in the Pacific. *Oceania* 62: 249-263.

Maori Fisheries Commission. 1995. *Te Reo O Te Tini a Tangaroa.* August.

McKenzie, D. 1985. *Oral Culture: Literacy and Print in Early New Zealand.* Victoria University Press, Wellington.
McLintock, A. 1958. *Crown Colony and Government in New Zealand.* Government Printer, Wellington.
Medding, P. 1968. *From Assimilation to Group Survival.* Cheshire, Melbourne.
Metge, J. 1967. *The Maoris of New Zealand.* Routledge, London.
Metge, J. 1976. *The Maoris of New Zealand Rautahi.* Routledge, London.
Metge, J. 1986. *In and Out of Touch.* Victoria University Press, Wellington.
Mihalic, F. 1971. *The Jacaranda Dictionary and Grammar of Melanesian Pidgin.* Jacaranda Press, Melbourne.
Miles, J., Spoonley, P. 1985. The Political Economy of Labour Migration. *Australia New Zealand Journal of Sociology* 21: 103-126.
Mitchell, J.C. 1956. *The Kalela Dance.* The Rhodes-Livingstone Papers no. 27. Manchester University Press, Manchester.
Mitchell, J.C. 1974. Perceptions of Ethnicity and Ethnic Behaviour. Pp. 1-36 in A. Cohen (ed.) *Urban Ethnicity.* Tavistock, London.
Mitchell, J.C. 1983. Case and Situation Analysis. *Sociological Review* 31: 187-211.
Mittleberg, D., Watters, M. 1992. The Process of Ethnogenesis Among Israeli and Haitian Immigrants in the United States. *Ethnic and Racial Studies* 15: 412-435.
Morris, P. n.d. Community Beyond Tradition. Unpublished Paper.
Nagel, J. 1994. Constructing Ethnicity. *Social Problems* 41: 152-176.
Nash, R. 1990. Society and Culture in New Zealand: An Outburst for 1990. *New Zealand Society* 5: 99-124.
Newman, P. 1965. *Knowing the Gururumba.* Holt, New York.
Ngata, J. 1981. In Defense of Ethnic Boundaries. Pp. 87-97 in C. Keyes (ed.) *Ethnic Change.* University of Washington Press, Seattle.
Norden, E. 1991. Counting the Jews. *Commentary* 92:4: 36-43.
O'keefe, J. 1983. Waitangi Tribunal "Decision". *New Zealand Law Review* : 136-7.
Okamura, J.C. 1981. Situational Ethnicity. *Ethnic and Racial Studies* 4: 452-465.
Olzak, S. 1992. *The Dynamics of Ethnic Competition and Conflict.* Stanford University Press, Stanford.
Patton, M. 1990. *Qualitative Evaluation and Research Methods.* Sage, New York.
Pearson, D. 1989. Pakeha Ethnicity Concept or Conundrum? *Sites* 18: 61-72.
Pearson, D. 1990. *A Dream Deferred.* Allen and Unwin, Sydney.
Pearson, D. 1991. Biculturalism and Multiculturalism in Comparative Perspective. Pp. 194-214 in P. Spoonley (ed.) *Nga Take.* Dunmore Press, Palmerston North.
Roberts, T. 1994. *Fishing for Solutions.* Research Paper, VUW Geography Department, Wellington.
Richards, T., Richards, L. 1990. *Manual for Mainframe Nudist.* Replee, Eltham, Australia.
Ross, R. 1972. Te Tirity O Waitangi Texts and Translations. *New Zealand Journal of History* 6:2: 129-157.
Ross, J. 1980. The Mobilization of Collective Identity, an Analyical Overview. In J. Ross and A. Cottrell (eds.) *The Mobilisation of Collective Identity.* University Press of the Americas.
Rubinstein, W. 1991. *The Jews in Australia.* Heinemann, Sydney.
Salinger, J. et al. 1983. *Wellington Jewry.* B'nai B'rith, Wellington.
Sandberg, N. 1986. *Jewish Life in Los Angeles.* University Press of America, Washington.
Schnapper, D. 1983. *Jewish Identities in France.* University of Chicago Press.

References

Schnapper, D. 1994. New Jewish Identities in France. Pp. 171-178 in J. Webber (ed.) *Jewish Identities in the New Europe*. Littman Library of Jewish Civilization.
Schwimmer, E. 1968. *The Maori People in the 1960s*. Blackwood and Paul, Auckland.
Sharp, A. 1995. Why be Bicultural? Pp. 116-133 in M. Wilson and A. Yeatman (eds.) *Justice and Identity: Antipodean Practices*. Bridget Williams, Wellington.
Sharp, A. 1990. *Justice and the Maori*. Oxford University Press, Auckland.
Silberman, Charles E. 1985. *A Certain People : American Jews And Their Lives Today*. Summit Books, New York.
Sissons, G. What did the Shark say to the Kawhai? *New Zealand Sociology* 7: 20-35.
Smart, B. 1993. *Postmodernity*. Routledge London.
Smith, A. 1984. Ethnic Myths and Revivals. *European Journal of Sociology* 25: 283-305.
Smith, A. 1981. *The Ethnic Revival in the Modern World*. Cambridge University Press, Cambridge.
Smith, A. 1989. The Origins of Nations. *Ethnic and Racial Studies* 12: 340-367.
Sollars, W. 1989. *The Invention of Ethnicity*. Oxford University Press, New York.
Sowell, T. 1994. *Race and Culture*. Basic Books, New York
Spoonley, P. 1987. *The Politics of Nostalgia*. Dunmore Press, Palmerston North.
Spoonley, P. 1995. Constructing Ourselves The Post-colonial Politics of Pakeha. Pp. 104-122 in M. Wilson and A.Yeatman (eds.) *Justice and Identity Antipodean Practices*. Bridget Williams, Wellington.
Spoonley, P. 1991. Pakeha Ethnicity: A Response to Maori Sovereignty. Pp. 154-170 in P. Spoonley (ed.) *Nga Take*. Dunmore Press, Palmerston North.
Statistics Department. 1994. *New Zealand Official Yearbook*. Statistics New Zealand, Wellington.
Stein, H.F., Hill, R.F. 1977. *The Ethnic Imperative*. Pennsylvania State University Press.
Szaz, A. 1993. The Iconography of Harzardous Waste. Pp. 197-222 in M. Darnovsky, B. Epstein and R. Flacks (eds.) *Cultural Politics and Social Movements*. Temple University Press, Philadelpia.
Thompson, J. 1990. *Ideology and Modern Culture*. Polity Press, Cambridge.
Thompson, R.H. 1989. *Theories of Ethnicity*. Greenwood Press, New York.
Vowles, J. 1991. How do we Treat the Treaty?. *Political Science* 43(1):68-80.
Waitangi Tribunal. n.d. *Files of Evidence*, ed. 133. Waitangi Tribunal Wellington.
Waitangi Tribunal Reports. 1983. *Report...in Relation to Fishing Grounds in the Waitara District*. Tribunals Division, Wellington .
Waitangi Tribunal Reports. 1984. *Finding...on the Kaituna Claim*. Tribunals Division, Wellington.
Waitangi Tribunal Reports. 1985. *Finding...on the Manukau Claim*. Tribunals Division, Wellington.
Waitangi Tribunal Reports. 1988. *Muriwhenua Fishing Report*. Tribunals Division, Wellington.
Waitangi Tribunal Reports. 1992. *The Fisheries Settlement Report*. Tribunals Division. Government Printer, Wellington.
Walker, R. 1994. Maori Leadership. Paper Presented to Hui Whakapumau, Maori Development Conference. Massey University, Palmerston North.
Watters, M. 1990. *Ethnic Options: Choosing Identities in America*. University of Chicago Press.
Weber, M. 1968. *From Max Weber : Essays In Sociology*. Translated, edited by H.H. Gerth and C. Wright Mills. Routledge, London.

Webster, S. 1993. Postmodernist Theory and the Sublimation of Maori Culture. *Oceania* : 222-239.
Wetherell, M., Potter, J. 1992. *Mapping the Language of Racism*. Harvester, N.Y.
Whiteman, J. 1973. *Chimbu Family Relationships in Port Moresby*. New Guinea Research Unit Bulletin 52. Australia National University Press, Canberra.
Williams, A. 1994. *A Dictionary of the Maori Language*. G.P. Publications Wellington.
Woocher, J. 1986. *Sacred Survival: The Civil Religion of American Jews*. Indiana University Press.
van Meijl, T. 1995. Maori Socio-Political Organization in Pre- and Proto-History. *Oceania* 65: 304-321.
Yancey, W., Ericksen, E., Juliani, R. 1976. Emergent Ethnicity: A Review and Reformulation. *American Sociological Review* 41:3 391-403.

Index

Abaijah, J. 62
acculturation 119
Alape 51
Alba, R. 74
American Jews 86
anti-Semitism 78, 93-95, 166
Anton 41-43, 59, 68
Asaro-Watabung 43, 50
assimilation 74-78, 83, 119, 142, 162
assimilationism 65
assimilationists 75, 85
Australia 163
Australian 56
authenticity 143-146, 150, 152
B'nai B'rith 89
Balau 51-55, 156
Barsalou, L. 68
Barth, F. 18
Bauman, Z. 22
Beaglehole, A. 88, 90
Bell, D. 28
Bellah, R. 77
bicultural 20, 120-124
biculturalism 125-132, 141-152, 158-167
Bougainville 36, 62
Boyer, P. 18, 23, 26, 65
Brownlie, I. 124
categorical ethnicity 17
categorical labels 47
categories 65, 69, 156, 170
categorisation 22
category 73
Chimbu 46, 61-62
civil Judaism 166-167
civil religion 77
class 62, 70
coastals. 48
cognition 22, 34, 69
cognitive 167
cognitive psychology 32
Cohen, Abner 18, 24, 46, 64
conventional Jews 98
convert 99, 101

Crystal, D. 33
cultural reification 20
cultural symbols 20
culturalisation of ethnicity 158
culturalised identity 21
culture 19
defining ethnicity 14
Della-Pergola, S. 78
Derrida, J. 143
discourse 34
Dominy, M. 151, 152
Dunedin 84, 96
Durie, E. 125, 128
Edwards, D. 24, 68
Emendai 51
Enga 57, 59, 66
Epstein, A. 18, 46
ethnic categories 16, 20, 47, 69, 155-159
ethnic community 157
ethnic constructions 32
ethnic elites 29
ethnic identification 15
ethnic labels 15
ethnic myths 29, 169
ethnic sentiments 155
ethnic social organisation 155
ethnicisation of culture 158
fiscal envelope 137
Fiske, S. 24
Fleras, A. 130, 137
fourth world 120, 130, 155, 162
France 162-163
fundamentals of ethnicity 155
Gans, H. 74, 80
gentile friends 88
gentiles 15, 76
Glazer, N. 76, 86
Gluckman, M. 64
Goldscheider, C. 76
Goroka 56
Gould, B. 150
grievance 70
group invisibility 97

Hagener 68, 156
Haitians 160
Hakai 59, 68
halachic tradition 82-84
Hammond, R. 77
Hanson, A. 141-143, 147-153
hapu 120, 139-140, 145
Hebrew school 87
Henare, M. 119, 121
high country 151, 152
highlander 25, 37, 48, 156
Hirschfeld, L. 23
Hobsbaum, E. and Ranger, T. 141
Hogg, M. and Abrams, D. 67
Holocaust 78, 88- 92, 166
Hunn report 123, 124
identity politicisation 31
ignorance 95
independence 56
inter-marriage 78
interviews 26
invented tradition 143
Israel 78, 90-97, 102, 163, 166
Israelis 160
iwi 120, 124, 137-140, 145, 150
iwi identification 139
Jaffe, R. 91
James 44, 45
Jewish Chronicle 88, 94
Jewish friends 87, 88
Jewishness 75
Jews 15, 160-170
Johnson, P. 73
Judaism 75-77, 96, 162
Kaituna 129
Kapopa 50, 56
kawanatanga. 122, 135
Keesing, R. 141-143, 166
Kelsey, J. 128, 131, 135
Kepaka 59, 66
Kepaka Clan 41, 56
Kindeng 57
Kofena 50-52, 56, 156
Koita 39
Kokopo 61
Kombiangwe 50, 51, 156
kosher 82-83
Kukathas, C. 124, 135
Lakoff, G. 68
Lane, H. 21

Lapopa 50, 52, 56
Latimer, G. 127, 130
Lenu 51, 54
Levine, H. 119, 121, 143
Levy family 98
Lidima 50
Linnekin, J. 141
Lulu 51
mana 122
Manukau 129, 130
Manukau Urban Maori Authority 140
Maori 15, 20, 157
Maori Council 133, 143
Maori Fisheries Commission 136
Marx , K.70
Matthew 42, 43, 45
McClintock, A. 121
Medding, P. 90
Melbourne 90-91, 101
Melpa 39-43, 59, 66-68
mental models 18
Metge, J. 123, 127, 142, 147-152, 165
method 25, 80
missionaries 121
Mitchell, J. 17, 26, 46, 64
Mittleberg, D. 160
Mondo 43, 50
Morris, P. 158
Motonui 127-129
Motu 39
Mount Hagen 37, 42-44, 56-66, 159
multiculturalism 124, 125, 149
Muriwhenua 132-136
musket wars 121
myths 163
Nagel, J. 65
Nash, R. 20
nationalism 29
Ndika 56
Neusner, J. 73, 157, 164
New Guinea 35
New Guinea Islander 37
New Zealand Company 121
New Zealand Jews 73-79, 164-167
New Zealand Maori Council 131
Ngai Tahu 134, 138, 150-152
Ngati Pikiao 129
O'Regan, T. 138
Okamura, J. 18
Olzak, S. 60

Index

Ongobayufa 50, 51, 54, 55, 156
orthodox 82-83, 97, 103
pakeha 20, 132, 147-153, 157
Papua 35
Papua Besena 62, 63, 64, 156
Papua New Guinea 17
Papua New Guinea, colonial history 35
Papua New Guinea, rural societies 34
Papuan 37, 40, 47-48, 156
Papuan Separatism 62
partnership 135, 148, 150
Patton, M. 27
Pearson, D. 20, 132, 150
pluralism 65
Port Moresby 25, 37, 42-66, 156
postmodern 19, 22, 142, 143, 153
Potter, J. 24, 68, 70
primordial 18, 73, 167
primordial approach 17
primordial sentiments 69
Progressive Jews 82-84
psychological theories 18
qualitative analyses 25 80
quota management 133-134
Rabaul 37, 39, 61, 62, 156
rangatiratanga 131-138, 145, 150, 166
Rata, M. 123
representativeness 26
Richards, T. and Richards, L. 81
Ross, J. 122
rural identity 56
rural-urban continuity 57
Sandberg, N. 86
Schnapper, D. 73, 162-163
Schwimmer, E. 124
self-determination 119
Sharp, A. 125, 135, 146-149
Shils, E. 16
Siane 50
Silberman, C. 75
situational 17-18, 167
Smith, A. 29, 163, 164, 167, 170
social Networks 40, 43
South African Jews 96
sovereignty 122, 138, 146, 165-166
Sperber, D. 9
Spoonley, P. 20, 93, 147, 158
statistical analysis 49
stereotypes 45
survey data 49, 80

symbol 146
symbolic ethnicity 74-75, 80, 86
symbolic 103, 143
symbolic groups 74
symbols 77-78, 127, 132, 135, 152, 166, 170
synagogues 82
Tainui 134, 137
Tambul 41-43, 56-59, 66
Tamoka 60
tangata whenua 130, 148, 152, 165
taonga 128, 129, 130-149
Taylor, S. 24, 125
Te Atiawa 125, 127
Te Tiriti O Waitangi (The Treaty of Waitangi) 121-150, 166
Temoka 68, 69
Thompson, J. 16, 143, 155-157
tikanga 138-145
Tobeas 43-55, 157
Tolai 39, 61-62
Tonkinson, R. 141
traditionalists 75
transformationalists 75-78, 85
Treaty of Waitangi Fisheries Commission 138
Treaty of Waitangi) 121-150, 166
tribal fighting 56, 59
Two Mile 44, 50-54, 66
urbanisation 33, 40
Wabag 57, 69
Waitangi Tribunal 27, 119,-127, 165
Waitara 125-129
Walker, R. 146
Wanganui 125
wantok 45-49
Watters, M. 160, 164
Weber, M. 13, 22, 67
Webster, S. 119
Wellington 80
Wellington Jewish Survey 87
Wetherell, A. 24, 68, 70
whakamaa. 148
Whiteman, J. 46
Woocher, J. 77, 166
Yamka 56
Yuwe 156, 157
Zionism 73, 92, 97
Zionist 88
Zukerman, A. 76

Franz Pöggeler (Ed.)

National Identity and Adult Education

Challenge and Risk

Frankfurt/M., Berlin, Bern, New York, Paris, Wien, 1995.
305 pp., 4 fig., 3 tab.
Studien zur Pädagogik, Andragogik und Gerontagogik.
Edited by Franz Pöggeler. Vol. 25
ISBN 3-631-48353-8 · pb. DM 89.–*

As well by streams of migration as by nationalistic conflicts (even in countries with a good tradition of adult education) national identity has come into a new vivid discussion. Experts of several countries and continents try to analyse this problem referring to historical and actual political and educational trends in their countries. Some contributions of the book offer criteria for comparing the reactions of adult education and show the importance of national elements in culture and adult education.

Frankfurt/M · Berlin · Bern · New York · Paris · Wien
Distribution: Verlag Peter Lang AG
Jupiterstr. 15, CH-3000 Bern 15
Tel. (004131) 9402131
*includes value added tax
Our prices are subject to change without notice